Books in the Contemporary World Issues series address vital issues in today's society such as genetic engineering, pollution, and biodiversity. Written by professional writers, scholars, and nonacademic experts, these books are authoritative, clearly written, up-to-date, and objective. They provide a good starting point for research by high school and college students, scholars, and general readers as well as by legislators, businesspeople, activists, and others.

Each book, carefully organized and easy to use, contains an overview of the subject, a detailed chronology, biographical sketches, facts and data and/or documents and other primary-source material, a directory of organizations and agencies, annotated lists of print and nonprint resources, and an index.

Readers of books in the Contemporary World Issues series will find the information they need in order to have a better understanding of the social, political, environmental, and economic issues facing the world today.

RICH AND POOR IN AMERICA

A Reference Handbook

**CONTEMPORARY
WORLD ISSUES**

A B C   C L I O

Santa Barbara, California
Denver, Colorado
Oxford, England

Cataloging-in-Publication data is on file with the Library of Congress

11   10   09   08   07   06   1   2   3   4   5   6   7   8   9   10

ABC-CLIO, Inc.
130 Cremona Drive, P.O. Box 1911
Santa Barbara, California 93116-1911
This book is also available on the World Wide Web as an ebook. Visit
http://www.abc-clio.com for details.
This book is printed on acid-free paper. ∞

Manufactured in the United States of America

To Mundy, *for richer, for poorer*

Contents

Preface

The growing income gap between the richest Americans and the poorest, once barely noticed, is now widely known and debated. Front-page articles in *The Wall Street Journal, The New York Times,* and many other mainstream news outlets have driven home the unsettling truth that the United States is growing more unequal, at least in economic terms. Some suggest that we are in a new Gilded Age, pointing to concentrations of wealth and income at the very top not seen since the 1920s or earlier. The public tends to focus less on the statistics and more on the glitz: private jets, mega-yachts, and palatial residences. Magazines and television programs are devoted to voyeuristic explorations of the lifestyles enjoyed by billionaires. And while the lifestyles of those at the opposite end of the income distribution sell very few magazines, there are indications that poverty—and the lengthening distance between society's haves and have-nots—may be reentering the realm of political and policy debate, just in time for a presidential election.

This handbook is a primer on the dimensions, the trend lines, the causes, and the consequences of the widening gap between America's rich and poor. It also considers some of the policy options for slowing or halting the current trend. There are strong differences of opinion about how seriously to take the "stretching out" of the income distribution, with liberals more likely and conservatives less likely to see it as problematic. Valid arguments can be made on both sides, and this book does not prejudge the question of whether the present degree of inequality exceeds what is acceptable or desirable. The real purpose of the book is merely to offer a handy, single-volume guide to an issue that is becoming more prominent with each passing year.

For those who are not familiar with the general topic of income and wealth disparity, the best starting point will be chapter 1. It provides background information on inequality trends, defines key terms, and identifies some social issues to which economic inequality has been linked, for example, the health status of rich and poor, the educational opportunities afforded the well-off and those less privileged, and racial-ethnic disparities of wealth and income. It also explores the question of whether it has become more difficult to lift oneself from a lower to a higher income level (or to fall from higher to lower) in the course of a generation. There are indications that growing income inequality coincides with falling income *mobility* in the United States.

To engage immediately with some of the critical issues and controversies related to the rise of economic inequality, one should go straight to chapter 2. That chapter lays out all of the major explanations for the widening *wage gap* we have seen in U.S. labor markets: skill-biased technological change, increased trade with the rest of the world, immigration, the long decline of labor unions, and the shrinking value of the minimum wage. It looks at a range of policy changes that might address these developments in the labor market, from pre-school interventions to helping low-income kids build their human capital, to passage of so-called living wage ordinances. The chapter also explores various tax and asset-building policies that have been put forward as ways to modify current inequality trends.

Chapter 3 offers a global perspective on what has been happening in the United States. It answers questions one may have about whether the widening rich-poor gap is unique to the United States or is seen in other rich, developed nations; whether corporate chieftains in other developed countries are rewarded on the same scale as American CEOs; how the United States ranks among industrialized nations on the issue of income mobility; and whether the gap between the *world's* rich and poor, as in the United States, is getting wider. The chapter also asks whether a wealth tax, such as several European nations impose, might make sense in the United States.

A time line of significant laws, publications, speeches, and events involving the gap between America's rich and poor is presented in chapter 4. A selective listing, as any such chronology must be, it nevertheless can help build a historical context for understanding how we view economic inequality today. Chapter 5 offers biographical sketches of a number of significant individuals, be they scholars, advocates, or persons whose own financial achievements have put a human face on American wealth. Again, the list can only be selective. Chapter 6 presents data and documents related to the rich-poor divide. The data, culled mainly from government statistics, cover such parameters as the Gini coefficient for the United States and all other countries; U.S. wealth distribution; the minimum wage; probability of achieving a bachelor's degree contingent on family economic status; and poverty rates dating back to 1973. The documents chosen for inclusion express a range of opinion about poverty, wealth, and how the gulf between them might be kept from further widening.

Chapter 7 gives a selective listing of organizations that take a direct interest in some aspect of the rich-poor divide. Think tanks of the left and the right are included, as are some more advocacy-oriented organizations. Several academic institutions also make the list. Full contact information is provided for each organization. The final chapter gives annotated lists of print and nonprint resources that can extend one's knowledge of (and interest in) any topic covered in the book. All the books listed are in print, and all the videos are fairly recent and available. Nineteen Web sites of special relevance to the rich-poor gap are identified; all are presently supported and likely to be in the future.

I am pleased to acknowledge the support of Hobart and William Smith Colleges, the splendid small institution where I have taught for many years, in advancing this project. A term's sabbatical leave and some funding through the Lloyd Wright Professorship were most helpful. The editorial and production teams at ABC-CLIO have impressed me greatly with their friendly, efficient support not only on this project but two previous ones. Dayle Dermatis and Holly Heinzer have kept me on track with the current volume. Special thanks go to Mim Vasan for proposing the idea (and title) of this handbook years ago and for her warm words of encouragement as it gradually took shape.

1

Background and History

Life is good for America's rich. Their consumption possibilities exceed what the majority of their fellow citizens can even imagine. At a bar in Chicago, they can order a special cocktail featuring premium vodka, Dom Pérignon champagne, a few other ingredients, and a stirrer topped with a one-carat ruby—at a cost of $950. At home they can keep their food and drink nicely cooled in a Sub-Zero PRO 48 refrigerator costing $12,000. If they carry the ultimate American Express Black credit card, issued by invitation only to people who customarily charge at least $250,000 a year, they can receive a luxury magazine so exclusive that its cover bears no name. If they wish to spend a million dollars on an automobile, they have that option as of late 2005 in the Bugatti Veyron, built by Volkswagen. (Industry analysts expect most buyers to treat the car as a "piece of art" rather than a means of transportation.) For vacation travel to the Caribbean, the Mediterranean, and other luxury destinations, billionaires can now acquire mega-yachts as long as football fields and costing $200 million or more. When it comes to real estate, the sky is the limit: four penthouse apartments atop the Trump World Tower in New York City were on the market as a single unit in early 2006 for $58 million. Occupying three floors, the unit featured 16 bedrooms, 24 bathrooms, 17-foot-high windows, and bird's-eye views of an important neighbor, the United Nations.

For America's poor, consumption possibilities are much more limited. A minimum-wage worker does not earn in a month what the special ruby cocktail costs. She or he does not earn in a year what the Sub-Zero refrigerator costs. A surprising number of America's poor do not have a bank account, much less an

American Express credit card. Vacation travel is not something the poor have to be overly concerned about, whether by yacht, plane, or train. For many, a vacation is an almost unthinkable luxury. As for housing, the conditions under which America's poor are sheltered range downward from "adequate" to crowded, and then to unsafe, unhealthy, and shoddy—hardly what would be expected in the world's richest democracy.

In talking about America's rich and poor, we find ourselves confronting a language problem. The term "rich" is problematic on two counts. First, it has no operational definition. The U.S. government has never issued guidelines on the income level needed to qualify as rich. One could take a cue from the federal income tax tables (2006), which push individuals and married couples into the top marginal tax bracket when their annual incomes reach $336,550. Or one might draw a *wealth line* at some multiple of the *poverty line*, for example, seven or eight times the poverty line, and declare anyone with an income above that level to be rich. Or one might define as rich anyone with an income in the top 2 percent of Americans, or anyone with a net worth of, say, $5 million. The problem with any and all of these definitions is that they are fundamentally arbitrary. They will omit some people we might feel really *are* rich and include others about whom we have serious doubts. A second problem with the term "rich" is the reluctance of those to whom it should apply to accept the designation. Oddly enough, many affluent Americans are uncomfortable with being called what they so clearly are—rich. Perhaps they resist the label believing that it makes them sound pompous, over-privileged, or snooty. And yet the United States has always been a place where wealth receives respect and confers power. Wealth is a part, small or large, of what most Americans mean when they refer to someone's having achieved "success," and it surely figures in the fantasies and daydreams of millions of Americans, given the evidence of billions of dollars in lottery ticket sales every year.

The term "poor" poses neither of the problems just noted. For more than 40 years, the U.S. government has defined poverty thresholds that make it perfectly clear—at least in an official sense—who is poor and who is not. Critics have found fault with the poverty lines for a long time, but that is a separate issue. Any family in the United States can see for itself whether the government categorizes it as poor. There is also none of the ambivalence about the word "poor" that attaches to the word "rich." People neither want to *be* nor be *labeled as* poor. In an unintentional way, that is exactly what the government does when it declares that 36.5 million Americans, or one in eight, fall below its poverty line (in 2006). Of course, people who have no health insurance, who make lengthy commutes on public transportation every day to get to jobs that pay seven or eight dollars an hour, who send their children to dilapidated public schools (from which they drop out at alarming rates), and who face the recurring challenge of stretching their cash and food stamps to the end of the month, do not need government guidelines to inform them that they are poor. They know poverty firsthand. What some may not know is that economists, sociologists, journalists, and policymakers see a growing divide between them and the rich.

A Widening Gap

"The rich get richer and the poor get poorer," according to an old saying. As a description of what has been happening in the United States in recent decades, this is at least half-true. The rich have indeed gotten richer—much richer. America's poor on the whole have not gotten poorer, but their income gains have been minimal at best, causing the gap between rich and poor to grow much wider. A similar widening has occurred between those at the top of the income scale and those in the *middle*. Average Americans have to lift their gaze much higher than a few decades ago to glimpse the heights now occupied by those making top incomes. The highest 1 percent of income recipients in 2006, for example, had incomes that ranged upward from $400,000 into the many millions of dollars (Krugman 2006). With incomes getting stretched farther apart, it comes as no surprise that accumulated wealth is also becoming more concentrated. Wealth disparities in the United States have reached levels not seen since the 1920s, when men like Henry Ford, Andrew Mellon, and John D. Rockefeller were living reminders of the not-so-distant Gilded Age.

The widening gap between haves and have-nots can be brought into sharper focus by looking at what chief executive officers (CEOs) at big U.S. corporations earn in comparison to the ordinary employees below them. In 1965, the average CEO salary in the United States was 24 times that of the average worker; by 1989, the ratio had climbed to 71; by 1995, it was 100; and in 2005, the ratio had reached 262 (Mishel 2006, 203). In other words, the imbalance between the highest-paid and average-paid Americans is now *ten times greater* than it was 40 years ago. Executive compensation has vaulted to such lofty levels that it is prompting concern even in the pages of reliably business-friendly publications like *Fortune* and *The Wall Street Journal.* Elsewhere in the developed world, the gap between chief executive pay and that of ordinary workers does not approach what is found in the United States. This is mainly because corporate chief executives are paid much less in Europe and Japan than in the United States—less than half as much in most places.

While the long-term trend toward inequality is beyond dispute, there is a lively range of opinion about the meaning of the trend, the underlying reasons for it, whether anything can or should be done about it, and what role, if any, the government might play in slowing or reversing it. Much of the balance of this chapter and the next will explore these issues. First, however, it is important to be clear on one point: economic inequality is not, in and of itself, an unacceptably bad thing. It may be disagreeable or morally repugnant to some. It may fuel envy, guilt, stress, and even health problems. It may weaken social cohesion. In the workplace, it may promote shirking and corruption. But on the other side of the equation are several pluses for inequality, and they are substantial. Economic inequality plays a role in motivating personal effort, innovation, investment, and entrepreneurship. Without these manifestations of ordinary individuals trying to "get ahead"—taking risks to achieve more-than-average gains for themselves and their families—it is hard to see how an economy could be kept dynamic and growing. Analyses of inequality that overlook its positive aspects, therefore, give an incomplete picture and cannot be the basis for balanced policy proposals.

Whatever their views on all of this, most Americans have been willing to accept a considerable amount of economic inequality, in part because they believe theirs is a country in which everyone has a fair chance to climb the ladder of economic success. What worries many observers now is the possibility that the trend toward greater inequality may be rendering American society more rigid. Put another way, the growing gap between rich and poor may be contributing to a decline in economic and social *mobility* in the United States. If true, this would be a serious blow to the nation's "land of opportunity" image. A society in which some are able to reserve the upper rungs of the ladder for their children and grandchildren, while others are consigned to the lower rungs with little chance of climbing upward, meets the definition of a caste system rather than a healthy, democratic society. We return to this issue later in the chapter.

Measuring Income Inequality

Statisticians use a number of different tools to quantify how equally or unequally a nation's income is distributed. One of the most widely used is the Gini coefficient, named for its developer, Corrado Gini, a 20th-century Italian statistician. The details of its computation are too complex to go into here. Suffice it to say the Gini coefficient always has a value between zero and 100. A Gini coefficient of zero would indicate a perfectly equal distribution of incomes—the egalitarian's dream. A coefficient of 100 would indicate perfect *in*equality, with all income going to a single individual or family. Obviously, no society in the world is at either of these two extremes. Those with the highest Gini values—in other words, the most inequality—tend to be located either in Latin America or southern Africa. According to the United Nations, Namibia, in sub-Saharan Africa, has the world's highest Gini coefficient, at 71. Brazil, Chile, Colombia, Guatemala, and Paraguay all have Ginis in the high 50s. The countries with low Gini ratios, evidencing the least income inequality, are widely dispersed outside Latin America. Most European nations have Gini coefficients in the range of 30 to 40. Scandinavia and Japan have greater income equality than that, with coefficients under 30 (UNDP 2005, 270–273). The Gini coefficient for the United States in 2006 was 47 (U.S. Census Bureau 2007, 7). It has been on the rise for more than three decades.

Gini coefficients are challenging to compute and difficult to interpret. (What, after all, does a coefficient of 47 really *mean?*) Experts find them useful for tracking changes in income distribution over time and for comparing the distributions of different countries, but other statistical measures give a more intuitive sense of the extent of economic inequality. There are many such measures. Some look at income shares for particular subsets of the population, for example, quintiles. A quintile is a 20 percent, or one-fifth, share of the population. In the United States, each quintile represents about 60 million people. In 2006, the top quintile of American households took home 50.5 percent of total national income. The bottom quintile received only 3.4 percent. It is important to note that the "income" measured by these figures is pre-tax and exclusive of such noncash benefits as food stamps, housing subsidies, and government-paid medical benefits. Many people in the lowest quintile qualify for, and receive, such benefits. This suggests that the 3.4 percent share for the lowest quintile should be considered an underestimate of the true economic status of that group. Even so, the long-term trend toward inequality is apparent from the fact that in 1970 the top quintile of households received about 43 percent of total income, considerably less than its current 51 percent share (U.S. Census Bureau 2007, 38–39).

Other U.S. income shares have been calculated for the top 10 percent, 5 percent, 1 percent, 0.1 percent (the top one-thousandth), even 0.01 percent (the top ten-thousandth), and, at the other end of the distribution, the bottom 10 percent, 20 percent, and 40 percent. At the top end, the most systematic and widely cited research has been done by Thomas Piketty and Emmanuel Saez, economists at the Ecole Normale Superieure (Paris) and the University of California at Berkeley, respectively. Their data series on top incomes, based on income tax returns filed with the Internal Revenue Service, reach as far back as the early 20th century. Piketty and Saez found that the share of income going to the top 10 percent, or decile, of Americans climbed from roughly 32 percent in 1973 to about 43 percent in 2004. The share of income going to the top 1 percent has also jumped in recent decades, from about 8 percent in 1979 to 16 percent in 2004. This trend has been similar for the smaller, more elite "fractiles" within the top percentile (Piketty and Saez 2006).

A final way of measuring income inequality is by forming ratios of income percentiles. Picture every American household being lined up by income level, from the super-richest to the very poorest. If you picked out the household that was exactly one-tenth of the way down from the top income, it would define the 90th percentile. In 2006, the income at the 90th percentile, or P90, was $133,000. One-tenth of the population received more income than that, and nine-tenths received less. At the opposite end of the spectrum, the household at the 10th percentile, or P10, had an income of $12,000 in 2006. Nine-tenths of the population received more income than that, and one-tenth received less. If we form the ratio of P90 divided by P10, we get a useful gauge of income inequality. In 2006, this ratio stood at 11.1 ($133,000 divided by $12,000). As might be expected in an era of growing inequality, the ratio has moved higher in recent decades; in 1967, the P90/P10 ratio was only 9.2. Similar increases are found when looking at other percentile ratios, like P95/P20 and P95/P50 (U.S. Census Bureau 2006, 38–39).

Wealth Inequality

Not only is there a growing *income* gap in the United States, but there is also a growing *wealth* gap. The terms income and wealth are sometimes casually, and mistakenly, substituted for each other. Properly speaking, income consists of annual dollar flows such as wages and salaries, interest, dividends, capital gains, rental income, and transfer payments like Social Security. Personal wealth consists of what people own minus what they owe. On the plus side, they may own bank accounts and certificates of deposit (CDs), stock portfolios (including 401(k) and 403(b) accounts), bonds, mutual fund shares, the surrender value of life insurance policies, homes and rental properties, durables like cars and appliances, and unincorporated business firms. On the minus side, households typically carry some debt, whether mortgage balances, credit card balances, college loans, consumer loans, or simply unpaid bills. When a family's total debts are subtracted from its total assets, the difference is net worth or wealth. Net worth can be negative, of course, as anyone filing for bankruptcy can attest. Whether formally bankrupt or not, millions of the poorest Americans have zero or negative net worth. At the other extreme, wealth can run into the billions of dollars. Consider this: to be listed by *Forbes* magazine in 2006 as one of the 400 richest people in the country, one needed to be worth, at a minimum, $1 billion. Effortlessly qualifying was the man who has headed the *Forbes* list since the 1990s, Bill Gates, with wealth estimated at $53 billion.

One might ask what is gained by broadening the analysis from income distribution to wealth distribution. Do we actually get a fuller understanding of economic inequality at the national level, or make more realistic assessments of people's economic circumstances at the individual level, by looking at both income *and* wealth? The short answer is a resounding yes. At the national level, wealth is often found to be distributed much differently than income. (This is true of the United States, for example.) On an individual level, too, the picture one gets from looking at income alone can vary considerably from the picture one gets when both income and wealth are considered. For individuals and families, one of the key differences between income and wealth lies in year-to-year variations. Income by its nature is volatile. This year it may be high if one is receiving a bonus, collecting on an insurance claim, taking a second job, or receiving an inheritance. Next year it may be low if one's working hours are reduced, wages are cut, one's personal relationship with an income-earner ends, or one loses eligibility for an income transfer program. Wealth, for those who have it, can provide a stabilizing influence on family finances. As one leading expert on U.S. wealth inequality puts it, "In times of economic stress, occasioned by such crises as unemployment, sickness, or family breakup, wealth is an important cushion" (Wolff 2002, 6).

We may now consider two central propositions about wealth in the United States: first, for the country as a whole, and for most individuals above the bottom two income quintiles, wealth is a larger magnitude than annual income; and second, wealth is more unequally distributed than income. The extent of U.S. wealth inequality can come as a great surprise to those un-acquainted with the numbers. One way it can be seen is in the Gini coefficient for wealth. With wealth, as with income, there is a range of possible Gini values. If the wealth Gini were computed to be zero, it would mean that every American family had equal wealth; if it computed to 100, all wealth would be held by a sin-gle family. In 2004, the U.S. Gini coefficient for wealth was 80, *far above* the income Gini of 47 and, some would say, uncomfortably close to the value that would signal maximum possible wealth inequality.

Another way to express wealth inequality is through the size shares of wealth held by various subgroups of Americans, such as the top 20 percent, 10 percent, 5 percent, 1 percent, and bottom 50 percent, 25 percent, or 10 percent. Often cited is the fact that in 2004, the top 5 percent of Americans held more wealth (over 57 percent) than the bottom 95 percent. Generally, however, the most attention is paid to the share of wealth held by the top 1 per-cent of Americans. In 2004, their share was 33.4 percent. That fig-ure is higher than was seen in 1989, just as the 2004 wealth Gini of 80 was somewhat higher than was found in 1989. At the same time, the share of wealth held by the bottom *half* of the popula-tion dropped from a meager 3.0 percent in 1989 to an even more meager 2.5 percent in 2004. The statistical evidence strongly supports the conclusion that between 1989 and 2004, wealth became more concentrated in the United States (Kennickel 2006, 10–11).

Why the wealth gap should be so much wider than the income gap is an intriguing question. One answer is simple, intuitive, and undoubtedly correct to some degree: people with low incomes live from paycheck to paycheck, with no money left over at the end of the pay period. Barely able to make ends meet, such families are not in a position to save, invest, or build up their assets to any significant extent. By contrast, those with high incomes can easily afford a comfortable lifestyle with funds to spare most of the time. Because their incomes exceed their spending, they are able to save. They invest their surplus funds in stocks, bonds, CDs, and other kinds of investments, and their wealth grows almost automatically, like water rising behind a dam. Even without regular infusions of savings, the "water behind the dam" would continue to rise over the long run because bonds and money market funds earn interest, stocks earn dividends and also appreciate in price, rental properties generate rents, and so on. Diversified portfolios tend to grow regardless of the occasional "down" years for certain investments. The rich in this way get richer, and the poor tread water. In chapter 2, we consider some asset-building proposals designed to help low-income Americans break out of this vicious circle.

Long-Term Trends

What has been the long-term trend for income and wealth distribution in the United States? Is there an economic theory that makes some sense of the trend? As a matter of fact, the best-known theory put forward by any economist on this issue predicted a pattern of income changes exactly the opposite of what has occurred in recent decades. Simon Kuznets (1901–1985), a Russian immigrant to the United States in 1922 who won the Nobel Prize in Economic Science a half-century later, argued in the mid-1950s that income inequality was likely, over time, to follow an inverted U-curve pattern. As per capita incomes rose in the early stages of economic growth, Kuznets suggested, income inequality could be expected to increase. Why? Because economic development would entail a massive shift of workers out of agriculture, where incomes tended to be low and relatively equal, into industrial occupations, where they tended to be higher but more unequal. At some point, inequality would reach a peak and then begin to decline, in part, because the special skills that had enabled some workers in the industrial sector to command extra-high incomes would be disseminated more widely across the workforce, thus evening out the highs and lows of earned income (Kuznets 1955). For half a century, social scientists have debated the validity of Kuznets's inverted U-curve. All that can be said today with any confidence is that, however valid the theory may have been with respect to the U.S. income distribution up to the 1950s, it does not describe inequality trends from that time onward.

Considering the 20th century as a whole, experts see a broad U-shaped pattern—not the inverted U-curve described by Kuznets—characterizing top American income and wealth shares. At the end of the 1920s, the top 1 percent and 5 percent of American income recipients engrossed a larger share of national income than they have ever done since, and the same was true of the top 1 percent of wealth holders. The year 1928 was truly the high-water mark for inequality during the 20th century. Things changed abruptly the next year. Stock prices plunged in late 1929, and the economy followed. The Great Depression eroded income and wealth concentrations during the 1930s. Hard times for the wealthy were to be expected with the crash of the stock market and the ongoing liquidation of business equity during the worst economic contraction most Americans had ever seen. The erosion continued and even accelerated during World War II. The startling damage done to top wealth positions during the early 1940s was mainly due to steeply progressive wartime taxes and wage-price controls. The income share of the top 1 percent of Americans fell by a remarkable one-third in only five years, dropping from 15.7 percent in 1940 to 10.5 percent in 1944; other top shares took similar hits (Piketty and Saez 2006).

For a few decades in the middle of the 20th century, from roughly the mid-1940s to the mid-1970s, U.S. income inequality was relatively stable and low. The top decile's share, for example, dropped to 31.6 percent of total income in 1944, and in 1972, it was still at that level, following some minor fluctuations in the intervening years. In the 1970s, the United States entered upon an economic landscape—some have called it the postindustrial economy—that Kuznets did not and could not envision in 1955. Contrary to his expectation, inequality not only failed to keep falling, but it reversed course and began an upward climb that has not yet ended. The Gini coefficient has been trending higher since 1974. The share of total income accounted for by the top decile of earners has been moving upward since about 1972, and the share of the top 1 percent increased sharply during the 1980s and 1990s; meanwhile, some 30 years ago the bottom quintile began its slow, steady shrinkage to today's 3.4 percent share of total income (Piketty and Saez 2006; U.S. Census Bureau 2007, 38). Essentially, the final quarter of the 20th century and the first years of the 21st century have been a period of growing dispersion of wealth and income in the United States.

Rowboats, Yachts, and Rising Tides

Historically, and fortunately for all concerned, the normal condition of the American economy is one of expansion. As the production of goods and services increases, and as the selling of those goods and services generates the incomes paid to workers, farmers, managers, and other contributors to the national output, national *income* rises. Living standards improve over time when people's real (inflation-adjusted) per capita incomes grow, and that happens when the output per worker, or productivity, rises. These simple facts have a strong bearing on the issue of income inequality. Since the end of World War II, the productivity of American labor has indeed risen, along with national output and income, so there has been more gross national product (GNP) to go around. But while the GNP pie has gotten bigger, it has not been sliced in equal-sized shares, especially since the mid-1970s.

To switch metaphors from culinary to nautical, it has been said that "a rising tide lifts all boats." In relation to income distribution, what this means is that when the economy grows, it raises everyone's income, from the corporate chieftain to the short-order cook. As an economic proposition this is more hypothetical—or perhaps aspirational—than factual. It is a statement of what *can* happen, not what *must* happen. Looking at Graph 1.1, we see the second half of the 20th century broken down into two periods, 1947–1973 and 1973–2000. For each period, the growth experience of each of the five income quintiles is shown. Two facts jump off the page: First, income growth was much stronger during the immediate postwar decades than during the final quarter of the century, with *all* groups experiencing at least an 85 percent increase in average real family income. Second, growing national income—the extra pie, so

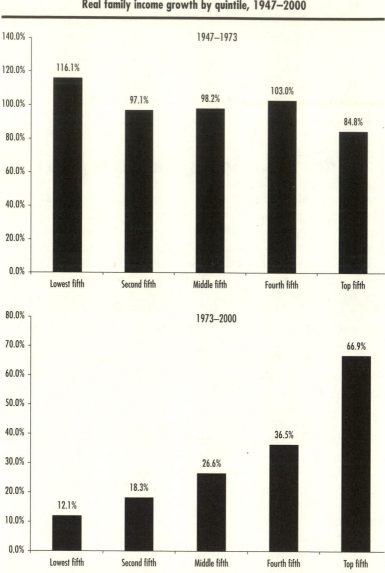

GRAPH 1.1
Real family income growth by quintile, 1947–2000

Source: Mishel, Bernstein, and Alegretto 2005, 71.

to speak—was shared much more evenly across the income spectrum in the earlier period than in the later.

The prosperity of the 1950s and 1960s was truly widespread; the rising tide did lift all boats. In the later period, by contrast, the poorest quintile saw their incomes rise by only 12 percent over a 27-year period—an almost negligible change—while higher quintiles fared better. For the top quintile, there was a 67 percent rise in real income. The rising tide lifted the yachts far higher than the rowboats.

To push the metaphor one step further, what about the ordinary tugboat berthed next to a yacht or a cruise ship? Let the tugboat represent the *median* American household income, that is, the income that is exactly in the middle of the distribution, with half the population above it and half below it. This would be, in some sense, the most ordinary or typical income. In the recent period 1973–2005, the median income, in 2006 dollars, rose from $41,700 to $47,800—a 15 percent gain. Over the same period, the average income of the top 10 percent of households rose from $136,381 to $207,681; the top 1 percent rose from $331,473 to $815,378; and the top 0.1 percent rose from $807,641 to $3,607,046. The percentage gains of these yachts and mega-yachts were, respectively, 52 percent, 146 percent, and 347 percent, far above the tugboat's 15 percent rise. None of these gains are illusory, caused by inflation. All are computed in constant dollars. One cannot escape the conclusion that the tide has been showing tremendous favoritism toward the high-end boats (U.S. Census Bureau 2007, Table A-1; Piketty and Saez 2006).

Race, Ethnicity, and Economic Inequality

An important added perspective on the picture of rich and poor in the United States comes from taking into account racial and ethnic differences. America's diversity by race and ethnicity, with all the circumstances surrounding it, raises a whole range of issues related to economic inequality, some of which lie beyond the scope of this handbook. Our purpose here will be fairly modest—to highlight the basic facts regarding income and wealth inequality as experienced by the two largest minority groups in the country, Hispanics and African Americans, so that a context can be established for later comments, observations, and analyses. It should be noted at the outset that "Hispanic" is an ethnic rather than a racial category; Hispanics can be of any race.

No one disputes that wealth in the United States has always had a lighter-skinned complexion than poverty. This may change in the future, but for now the reality of the color divide is obvious. Starting at the pinnacle of American wealth, we note an almost complete absence of blacks and Hispanics from the *Forbes* list of the 400 richest Americans in 2006. The well-known entertainment figure Oprah Winfrey makes the cut at No. 242, with a net worth of $1.5 billion. Two Hispanic businesspeople are also listed: Jorge Perez, ranked No. 197, with $1.8 billion from real estate, and Arturo Moreno, at No. 354, with $1.1 billion from billboards. Beyond this handful of names, it is unclear what other minority individuals have achieved billionaire status in the United States. Many Hispanic Americans are millionaires, of course, with Cuban Americans particularly well represented in that group, and the ranks of black millionaires extend far beyond the highly publicized sports and entertainment personalities like Tiger Woods, Kobe Bryant, Bill Cosby, and Spike Lee.

At the opposite end of the distribution, African Americans and Hispanics are distressingly well represented among those who fall below the poverty line. As documented by the Census Bureau, the poverty rates for America's largest minorities are routinely higher—much higher—than the rates for non-Hispanic whites. In 2006, the poverty rates for African Americans and Hispanics were 24.3 percent and 20.6 percent, respectively, as compared with 8.2 percent for non-Hispanic whites. One consequence of minorities' lesser command of economic resources in the United States is that they have less access to insured medical care: while 10.8 percent of whites lack health insurance coverage, the comparable figures for blacks and Hispanics are 20.5 percent and 34.1 percent (U.S. Census Bureau 2007, 11, 19).

How substantial are the income and wealth gaps *within* the minority populations, and how divergent from the population as a whole? Government statistics shed some light on these questions. Recent Census Bureau data suggest that there are no large differences among blacks, whites, and Hispanics when it comes to how evenly incomes are distributed within each racial or ethnic group. The income Gini for blacks in 2004 was 48, for non-Hispanic whites, 46, and for Hispanics, 45. (As previously noted, the overall income Gini for the nation is 47.) Wealth distributions are also fairly similar within each racial or ethnic group. Data from the latest Federal Reserve survey put the wealth Gini for black households at 80, for Hispanics at 83, and for all families at 80. Summing up, then, it seems fair to say that income- and wealth-holding patterns among minorities in the United States are so similar to the national, multiracial pattern that they do not significantly skew the national pattern in any one direction (U.S. Census Bureau 2006a; Kennickel 2006, 34).

But what about the actual income and wealth levels of minorities in the United States as compared with whites? The facts are very simple: whites receive more income, typically, than either blacks or Hispanics, and they also have more wealth. In 2006, the median white household income was $52,400, well above the median income for both blacks ($32,000) and Hispanics ($37,800). The measured white income advantage over black incomes has declined somewhat, from 71 percent in 1973 to 64 percent in 2006. Yet it remains the case that the typical African American household receives only three-fifths the income of the typical white household. (Part of the explanation is demographic: more African American households than white households are headed by single adults, making dual-earner support of the household less common in the African American community.) The white income advantage over Hispanic incomes is smaller than over black incomes, but unlike the black-white gap, this one has grown somewhat wider over the decades, with the white-over-Hispanic household income advantage rising from 36 percent in 1973 to 39 percent in 2006 (U.S. Census Bureau 2007, Table A-1).

Wealth comparisons only reinforce the impression of a racial economic gap. On the lower rungs of the wealth ladder, the Federal Reserve consumer survey in 2004 found the net worth for African American households at the 25th percentile to be $1,700. One quarter of all black households had total wealth of less than $1,700. (Many, of course, had no wealth at all.) The comparable figure for Hispanics was $2,800. Across the American population as a whole, wealth at the 25th percentile was $13,300, a figure high enough to suggest that white wealth at the 25th percentile was a large multiple of minority wealth. The same Federal Reserve survey put median African American net worth in 2004 at $20,600, median Hispanic net worth at $18,600, and median net worth for all American households at $93,100, indicating a racial wealth gap of major proportions. One scholar who has studied the racial wealth issue carefully, Thomas M. Shapiro, argues in *The Hidden Cost of Being African American* that family wealth levels are critical to homeownership, which in turn bears on the question of where a family's children will be schooled. Families that are asset-poor, as minority families tend to be, will find themselves shut out of the neighborhoods where the best schools are located, schools with the most qualified teachers, the best equipment, and the strongest academic programs. They will have limited chances to attend the educational institutions that confer real competitive advantages on their students (Kennickel 2006, 9, 34; Shapiro 2004).

Income Inequality and Health

Income inequality can be harmful to people's health in two ways. It is clearly bad for the health of individuals and families at the lower end of the income scale, who almost everywhere have lower life expectancies, worse health habits, higher disease rates, and, in the United States, less access to regular, professional health care than those at the upper end of the scale. Inequality may also be bad for people's health in a much less obvious way. In a society characterized by wide income disparities, there appears to be "more violence, less trust, more hostility, and less involvement in community life" than in more egalitarian settings, and this could well take a toll on the health of people at all socioeconomic levels (Wilkinson 2000, 20).

Evidence on the first point is abundant: more income, in general, translates into better health. The list of health advantages enjoyed by those with incomes above the poverty level is extensive: better nutrition, higher rates of vaccination, higher rates of preventive health care, lower exposure to various pollutants and other toxic substances, fewer occupational hazards, lower rates of obesity, lower use of tobacco, and so on. A sampling of relevant numbers makes the picture clear. Twenty-nine percent of American adults below the poverty line smoked in 2004; less than 21 percent of those above the poverty line smoked (CDC 2005). In 2003, 21 percent of poor respondents to a government survey rated their own health as fair or poor. Among the near-poor—those with incomes between the poverty threshold and double the threshold—the figure was 15.5 percent, and among the nonpoor just 6.2 percent rated their health unfavorably. Even mental health appears to be statistically correlated to income levels: in 2002–2003, serious psychological distress was reported by 8.7 percent of the poor, 5.4 percent of the near-poor, and only 1.8 percent of the nonpoor (NCHS 2005, 242, 248, 250). In a 2002 survey of Americans nearing retirement age, respondents were divided into three income categories, which might be labeled high, middle, and low. The self-reported incidence of diabetes among high-income people was less than half the incidence among the low-income. The same was true for heart attacks. Even more dramatically, the rates of lung disease and stroke for high-income individuals were less than one-third the rates for low-income individuals (Banks, Marmot, Oldfield, and Smith 2006, 2039).

Beyond the linkage between income and disease rates, there is the truly bottom-line issue of income and mortality. Lots of data support the proposition that the poor face a higher risk of death at all ages than those with higher incomes. A study published in the *American Journal of Public Health* in 1996 documented an income-mortality gradient for white men, showing an almost continuous decline in the age-adjusted mortality rate with higher income levels. For example, the death rate per 10,000 person-years was 91.8 for men with annual incomes below $10,000 and ranged downward to a low of 51.4 for those with incomes over $34,000. (Income levels appear low because they were drawn from census data now a quarter-century old.) When a variety of other risk factors—blood pressure, cholesterol, cigarette smoking rates, etc.—were taken into account, the gradient still existed, although less steep, with the death rate remaining more than 50 percent higher for those receiving the lowest incomes by comparison with those receiving the highest incomes (Smith, Neaton, and Wentworth 1996). A similar and even stronger pattern was seen in African Americans, as reported in the second installment of the article. Black men with the lowest incomes faced an age-adjusted death rate 109 percent higher than those with the highest incomes. When both age and other risk factors were taken into account, the poorest men still faced a 92 percent higher mortality risk than those with top incomes (Smith et al. 1996). Even pain itself appears to be measured out according to income level: the pain experienced by people nearing death depends on economic standing, with the least pain reported by those with the most wealth (Silveira 2005).

There can be little doubt that a reduction in the U.S. income gap, if it were achieved by raising the incomes of the poorest Americans, would improve health and mortality rates for the nation as a whole. That is what all the statistics just cited imply. But there could be another way in which reducing the income gap would improve the nation's health, namely, through the indirect, psychological benefits of having a society with fewer class and income divisions. The British epidemiologist Richard Wilkinson has been the foremost proponent of this viewpoint. He argues that societies with wide disparities of income tend to be places of chronic stress, social anxiety, and violence, compared to societies that are more egalitarian. Communities of greater income equality are conducive to better social relationships, which translate to physical benefits, such as lower blood pressure, and behavioral benefits, such as mutual social support and low levels of violence (Wilkinson 2000). Much empirical research has been done on what might be called the "Wilkinson hypothesis," some supporting it and some not. Among the stronger studies in support is one published in 1998 that looked at 282 U.S. metropolitan areas and measured the statistical association between mortality rates and levels of inequality seen in those areas. Mortality was indeed highest in places with low average incomes and a high degree of inequality; it was lowest in places with high incomes and a low degree of inequality. The mortality difference between the two extremes was enormous, "comparable to the combined loss of life from lung cancer, diabetes, motor vehicle crashes, HIV infection, suicide, and homicide in 1995" (Lynch et al. 1998, 1074).

Income Inequality and Education

If the amount and quality of education that individuals receive in the United States were quantifiable in the same way that income is quantifiable, one would find the distribution of education to be far from uniform. Some people receive a great deal of education, others very little. This is important because education and income are strongly interconnected. More education brings higher lifetime income; higher incomes enable parents to live in neighborhoods with excellent public schools or to send their children to private schools; and well-educated children are favorably positioned to repeat the cycle. An inferior education brings a reduced stream of lifetime income, limits housing options, puts the best public schools out of reach, and so on. There are exceptions at both ends, of course—some rich kids drop out of school, and some poor kids make it to the Ivy League—but they *are* exceptions. The United States does not offer anything like a "level playing field" to its children when it comes to education, and this is surely one of the factors behind the gap between rich and poor.

Variations in school quality have much to do with variations in family income. By and large, the best schools are found in localities where housing prices are high enough to exclude families with low incomes. These are the schools with the most up-to-date laboratory equipment, the best-stocked libraries, the most demanding curricular offerings, and, crucially, the best-qualified and highest-paid teachers. (They also tend to have guidance counselors who are on a first-name basis with admissions staff at the better colleges and universities.) Such schools function as virtual conveyor belts to college for the great majority of their students. The schools attended by America's poor can be dismal and dispiriting, as documented by Jonathan Kozol in *Savage Inequalities*. Roofs leak, classes are overcrowded, books are too scarce to go around, teachers are underpaid, students are underserved by counselors, and dropout rates are high.

It would not be inaccurate to describe American schools today as segregated—not by law or design but by economic realities. The segregation is both racial and socioeconomic. This may come as a surprise to those who recall that in 1954 the Supreme Court banned school segregation in the famous case of *Brown v. Board of Education*. That decision forbade state-imposed racial segregation but not the spontaneous segregation that results from the way the housing market works. Since race and poverty are closely linked, since neighborhoods have become ever more stratified by housing price, and, finally, since the courts no longer impose busing for the purpose of achieving desegregation, schools tend to be populated by children of the same race and socioeconomic class. The typical black student attends a school that is only 31 percent white, while the typical white student attends a school that is 80 percent white. (The typical Hispanic student attends a school that is 29 percent white.) Segregation by class or income is equally widespread. Statistically speaking, a student who qualifies for free or reduced-price school meals is counted as poor. Poor students typically attend schools that are 58 percent poor, while nonpoor students go to schools that are only 25 percent poor (Kahlenberg 2005; Phillips and Chin 2004, 473–474).

The problem with having low-income children attend school mainly with other low-income children, from an educational standpoint, is that most of the research singles out peer influences as the main determinant of student academic achievement.

If one's classmates are poor, one will spend a major part of every day with children who entered kindergarten with weaker letter and number recognition, smaller vocabularies, less likelihood of having been read to by an adult, and a greater tendency to be disruptive in class than higher-income children. Time alone does not eliminate the cognitive gaps. Being placed in a school with more balanced enrollments by socioeconomic status can make a difference. Creating schools that have such a balance, however, presents a tough political challenge, despite the clear social and educational benefits they promise. In chapter 2 we explore some of the evidence on this point.

The rich-poor divide in the United States comes into particularly sharp focus when considering the issue of college attendance. The necessity of being a college graduate if one aspires to a life in the middle class has never been clearer, yet college costs have been rising faster than most Americans' incomes. Grade school and high school are publicly financed, that is, essentially free. College costs are subsidized out of the public coffers but not covered completely, and private scholarship aid is limited, leaving a hefty part of the cost to be borne by students and their families. Although most studies of the value of a college education conclude that it is an excellent investment, many high school graduates from poor families either do not appreciate that fact or do not believe that they have access to the financial resources to pay for it. A telling demonstration of the importance of family income in determining college attendance emerged from a study by Mathtech, Inc., in 1998. The researchers grouped a random sample of students from around the country by (1) test scores as they finished high school, and (2) family income. In both categories, there were three ratings: bottom, middle, and top. No matter what their academic promise, as indicated by their test scores, students from the bottom-income group went on to college in much lower numbers than students from top-income families. For high-scoring students, the attendance gap was about 20 percent, for middle-scoring students, about 30 percent, and for low-scoring students, 35 percent. Almost two-thirds of the affluent kids who scored low on the test went on to college anyway; only 29 percent of low-income kids with low scores did so (Schiller 2004, 184).

Attending a highly selective college has been shown to be especially beneficial, in terms of economic payoff, to students from lower socioeconomic backgrounds. Unfortunately, this fact has not produced a significant presence of such students on those well-manicured campuses. A 2003 study found that only 3 percent of the students attending the most selective 146 colleges in the United States came from the bottom quartile (one-fourth) of the population as ranked by their socioeconomic status, and only 10 percent came from the lower half. The same study found that low-income students are even more underrepresented at top colleges than racial minorities, who themselves are underrepresented. Those who could benefit the most from the education available at elite schools are, at present, the least likely to attend them (Draut 2005, 96).

Part of the explanation for why low-income students are scarce at the leading colleges may lie in the trend away from need-based financial aid and toward merit-based aid. To improve their position in various national rankings, colleges nowadays seek to attract more students with high SAT scores by offering them rich financial-aid packages. By putting more of their aid dollars into grants to high-testing students, colleges are essentially "buying academic talent" in the same way many have traditionally bought sports talent with athletic scholarships. The extra "merit" dollars, however, come at the expense of those students whose main claim to aid is that their families lack the financial resources to see them through four years of higher education. Under this new approach, grants and loans are often a kind of bonus to students who do not really require the help. The problem of keeping college affordable for low-income students is exacerbated by the dwindling of federal aid dollars in recent years. We explore the issue of college finances in greater depth in chapter 2.

A Shrinking Middle Class?

Does the growing gap between America's rich and poor mean the ranks of the middle class are thinning out? Worries about a disappearing middle class in the United States have been voiced for decades, and not without cause. Modern democratic societies function most successfully, it is believed, when they rest on broadly middle-class foundations. If those foundations are weakened, the economy may lose its stability and the political system its resiliency. But answering questions about the size of the middle class is a challenge, since the term "middle class" is no more

easily defined than "rich." It refers to a subset of the total population, but should the subset be identified in terms of education,
occupation, social values, income, or some combination of indicators? Even a simple income-based definition can be tricky. Are
we looking at the middle 60 percent of families, sandwiched between an upper-class 20 percent and a lower-class 20 percent?
That sounds reasonable until we notice that it defines away the
question before we have even begun to tackle it, since a middle
class of pre-set size—60 percent or any other number—can never
shrink (or expand).

An alternative approach would set a dollar range within
which a family is considered to be middle class. This would
allow changes in the distribution of income over time actually to
affect the size of the middle class, either upward or downward.
Suppose we arbitrarily set the range for middle-class membership at, say, $25,000–$100,000 of family income, in 2002 dollars.
The data required to count the number of families in this income
range can be found in the 2005 edition of *The State of Working
America*, compiled by the Economic Policy Institute. With the
issue posed in this specific way, we find a clear pattern over time:
the middle class is indeed shrinking, although very gradually. It
accounted for 70 percent of families in 1969, 68 percent in 1979,
64 percent in 1989, and 61 percent in 2002. The downward trend
is unmistakable. Of course, the way in which the shrinkage occurs makes a big difference in the way we feel about it. If most of
the families losing middle-class status were dropping into
poverty, we would probably view it quite differently than if most
were gaining upper-class status. As it happens, the squeeze on
the middle class has produced a "bulge" to the upside, not the
downside. The share of families with incomes above $100,000 in-
creased from 4.3 percent in 1969 to 17.8 percent in 2002; the share
with incomes below $25,000 declined from 25.5 percent to 21.0
percent. Middle-class shrinkage is completely accounted for, in
the raw statistical sense, by an enlargement of the well-off class
at the top (Mishel, Bernstein, and Allegretto 2005, 88).

The image of middle-class American families being
squeezed upward into the comfortable "over $100,000" category
is a reassuring one, but like all statistical artifacts it reveals only
a part of the full picture. Another way to rate the progress of middle-class Americans is to examine what has been happening to
median family income, generally considered the single most
telling measure of how the typical family is doing over time. It is

the income that lies at the precise midpoint of the overall distribution of family incomes. Adjusted for inflation, median income moved upward from $44,400 in 1973 to $54,100 in 2004, a rise of about 22 percent stretched out over three decades. To put it another way, median income grew at a rate of less than two-thirds of 1 percent annually (U.S. Census Bureau 2006b).

Accompanying the snail's-pace improvement in middle-class incomes, there has been a significant erosion of middle-class neighborhoods in American cities and, to some extent, its suburbs. A recent Brookings Institution study, which defined middle income as between 80 percent and 120 percent of median income, found that people in the nation's 100 largest metropolitan areas are increasingly "sorting themselves" in their housing locations by income level. (For the impact of economic segregation on schooling, see the previous section.) Formerly middle-class neighborhoods have tipped either toward wealth or poverty. As a share of all neighborhoods, middle-income ones dwindled from 58 percent to 41 percent between 1970 and 2000 (Booza, Cutsinger, and Galster 2006). The most severe residential segregation by income was found in Los Angeles, where more than two-thirds of residents now live in "neighborhoods that are solidly rich or poor" (Harden 2006). Not a single American city became *more* integrated by income during the past three decades, according to one of the scholars at the Brookings Institution who worked on the study. For people who want to move up the social ladder by buying a house in a decent neighborhood with good schools and low crime rates, this is not encouraging news. A rung of the ladder has been removed (Harden 2006).

From Rich to Poor and Poor to Rich: Mobility

Suppose youngsters with parents in the top one-fifth of the U.S. income distribution had a one-in-five chance of remaining in that quintile as adults and an equally good chance of ending up in one of the lower quintiles, including the lowest. Suppose the same were true for kids born into every other quintile—a one-in-five shot at any of the five quintiles when they grew up. Family background would count for nothing: one's life chances would be essentially unconnected to one's origins. In a world of such maximum generational mobility, it would be hard to find fault with big income differences between the rich and the poor. People would feel as if their adult position on the income ladder was perfectly fair, or at least as fair as any outcome determined by pure luck. The poor could reconcile themselves to their position knowing that their children would have the chance to do better, possibly much better, than they had done, and the rich would understand that their good fortune had a low probability of being repeated in the next generation.

Needless to say, economic mobility in the United States today falls far short of what would be seen in a random-outcome society. Adult economic status depends rather significantly on the status of one's parents, on their income, their race, and various other characteristics they impart to their offspring. This works to the advantage of those at the top, while stacking the deck against those at the bottom. As a familiar quip goes, people benefit greatly from choosing the right parents. One way to quantify the benefit is to compare the statistical odds of becoming rich in the United States if you were already well-off in childhood with the odds if you started out poor. Tom Hertz, an economist at American University, has done interesting research that answers this question. Defining "rich" as being in the top 5 percent of incomes, he finds that those who start in the highest quintile have a 14.2 percent chance of becoming rich. That is well above the 5 percent chance they would have in a random-outcome society, and *way* above the 1.1 percent probability of ending up rich for those who start in the lowest quintile (Hertz 2006, 9).

The model of maximum economic mobility, as we saw, gave every person one-in-five odds of remaining, as an adult, in the same quintile in which he or she began. What Hertz finds for the United States is that those who start in the bottom quintile have about a 42 percent prospect of remaining there. The odds of someone who starts in the top quintile remaining *there* are also, coincidentally, 42 percent (Hertz 2006, 9). This is not the sort of social fluidity most people would associate with the American Dream, an ideal which assures us that anyone can make it to the top. One's real chances of rising to the top turn out to be better the closer one is born to the top. Education is one factor helping account for the stickiness of movement up and down the ladder: higher-income people can afford to invest more in their children, improving their future earning prospects. Race is also a factor. African Americans have much lower mobility than whites. White children born in the bottom one-quarter of the population between 1942 and 1972 had a 32 percent probability of remaining in that quartile as adults; for black children, the probability was almost twice as high at 63 percent. Even health can play a role in limiting mobility: children in low-income families experience more health problems than those in better-off families, and their health tends to remain worse as adults (Hertz 2006, 4).

Intergenerational mobility in the United States is more limited than we used to think it was; it is lower than in a number of other rich democracies, including Canada, France, Germany, and all of the Scandinavian countries; and it appears to be in decline (Mazumder 2005, Hertz 2006, Bernstein 2003). In light of the widening gap between rich and poor in the United States, evidence of fading economic mobility raises awkward questions about the "land of opportunity" and "rags to riches" faith that has been central for so long to Americans' sense of national identity. If the ladder is getting more stretched out, and the middle rungs are getting more slippery—or even disappearing entirely—how valid is the picture of the United States as a dynamic, socially fluid, meritocratic society? And if mobility continues to decline, how will it affect public attitudes toward wealth and income gaps that are now approaching historic levels? For now, the public's sense of the possibilities of upward mobility remains quite strong. A *New York Times* poll in early 2005 asked people, "Is it possible to start out poor, work hard and become rich" in the United States? In 1983, just under 60 percent said yes, while in 2005, fully 80 percent said yes (Scott and Leonhardt 2005).

Rich and Poor: The Political Dimension

Given the polarization that American politics has undergone in recent decades, it stands to reason that the issue of a growing gap between rich and poor would be viewed quite differently by those on the left and those on the right. Liberals, who tend to vote Democratic, decry the gap. It disturbs and worries them because it violates their egalitarian ideals. They usually attribute income inequalities to racial and gender discrimination, exploitation of labor, and the ability of the rich to influence public policy to their own advantage. Liberals support redistributive policies to narrow the income gap while opposing policy changes that would widen it. Conservatives, who tend to vote Republican, say little about the gap—a good indication that it does not particularly concern or offend them. They value free markets, economic growth, and personal responsibility above social solidarity and economic equality. For them, equality of opportunity is far more important than equality of outcome. A distribution of income that is heavily skewed toward the wealthy strikes them as reasonable, even natural, in a free-market society. Income disparities, they believe, create incentives for saving, investment, and risk-taking, and thus promote economic growth. Most conservatives support policies aimed at quickening economic growth even if a side effect would be greater disparities of wealth and income.

Several tax cuts advanced by the George W. Bush administration have provided fuel for heated debate between liberals and conservatives since 2001. Liberals have cited (and written) a number of studies that indicate that the benefits of the Bush tax cuts go overwhelmingly to the wealthiest Americans. The Center on Budget and Policy Priorities, a left-of-center think tank in Washington, D.C., has calculated the probable future impact of the Bush tax cuts if Congress makes them permanent. It finds that in the period 2007–2016, the top 1 percent of taxpayers will reap 29 percent of the benefits of the tax cuts, and the top 20 percent will garner 72 percent of the benefits, while the bottom 40 percent will receive just 5 percent of the benefits (Aron-Dine and Friedman 2006). Most liberals disapproved of the 2003 tax cut on investment income. According to a *New York Times* analysis, that legislation had a noticeably uneven impact on rich and poor, providing an average annual tax benefit of $500,000 for those with incomes of $10 million or more, and a mere $10 average benefit for those earning less than $50,000 (Johnston 2006, C4). Conservatives retort that the highest-income Americans pay the biggest share of the federal tax bill, so it is only right that they should reap disproportionate benefits from tax rate reductions. Conservatives also argue that estimates of tax-cut impacts that fail to note the jobs created by added spending and investing by high-income individuals do not tell the whole story. The term "trickle-down" has gone out of fashion, but conservatives continue to believe that extra infusions of income at the top eventually work their way into the wallets of those at the bottom.

Liberals are especially critical of the Bush-led repeal of the federal estate tax. This tax, on the books since 1916, clearly targets those at the high end of the income distribution. It affects only the wealthiest 1 or 2 percent of Americans. Liberals see it as the ideal progressive tax, one that draws far more revenue from the rich than from anyone else. In their eyes, it is a useful and perhaps essential means of preventing the nation from evolving into a plutocracy, that is, a system of rule by the rich. Conservatives, on the other hand, present the estate tax as a "death tax," highlighting the way in which it deprives sons and daughters of their parents' hard-earned lifetime financial accumulations. They claim the tax has a devastating impact on small business owners and family farms. (Supporting evidence on this point is exceedingly scarce.) Both sides claim the moral high ground, with liberals arguing the fairness of a tax that burdens only the rich, and conservatives arguing the *un*fairness of a tax that denies people the right to leave whatever they have, in its entirety, to the next generation. In 2001, the Republican-controlled Congress voted to phase out the estate tax by 2010. Most Democrats voted against repeal. Because the 2001 legislation provides for full reinstatement of the tax in 2011—politics required this bizarre provision as a way to keep projected revenue losses acceptably low—the issue has not yet reached a permanent resolution (Graetz and Shapiro 2005).

As we will see in the next chapter, experts have identified a number of factors that might explain the widening dispersion of incomes in the United States. One factor in particular excites indignation among liberals: public policy. Liberals view government action as a means to *lessen* economic inequalities—they cite the New Deal programs of Franklin D. Roosevelt and the Great Society programs of Lyndon B. Johnson—and not as a means to *exacerbate* inequalities. Hence they have strongly opposed the tax policies of the Bush administration and denounced it for failing to propose any increase in the federal minimum wage from the level it reached in 1997. (The increased minimum wage enacted by Congress in 2007 resulted from Democratic successes in the election of 2006, not a change of position by the Bush administration.) Liberals believe that public policies in these and many other areas now reflect the economic interests of the wealthiest Americans much more than they do the national interests of all Americans. Howard Rosenthal, a political scientist at New York University, has noted a pattern of increasing partisan polarization and widening income disparity since the 1970s. This has great significance for public policy. It means that policies intended to blunt or reverse the trend toward inequality—the sorts of policies Congress enacted during the Great Society era of the

1960s, for example—stand little chance of being enacted today (Rosenthal 2004). Rosenthal would probably concede, however, that political trend lines, like economic trend lines, eventually change direction.

References

Aron-Dine, Aviva, and Joel Friedman. "The Skewed Benefits of the Tax Cuts, 2007–2016." Washington, DC: Center on Budget and Policy Priorities, 2006. Accessed at http://www.cbpp.org.

Banks, James, Michael Marmot, Zoe Oldfield, and James P. Smith. "Disease and Disadvantage in the United States and in England." *Journal of the American Medical Association* 295 (2006): 2037–2045.

Bernstein, Aaron. "Waking Up from the American Dream." *BusinessWeek* 3860 (December 1, 2003): 54–58.

Booza, Jason C., Jackie Cutsinger, and George Galster. "Where Did They Go? The Decline of Middle-Income Neighborhoods in Metropolitan America." Brookings Institution, Metropolitan Policy Program, *Living Cities Census Series,* June 2006.

Bowles, Samuel, Herbert Gintis, and Melissa Osborne Groves, eds. *Unequal Chances: Family Background and Economic Success.* New York: Russell Sage Foundation, 2005.

Centers for Disease Control and Prevention (CDC). "Cigarette Smoking among Adults—United States, 2004." *MMWR Highlights* 54 (November 11, 2005): 44.

Draut, Tamara. "The Growing College Gap," in Lardner and Smith 2005: 89–101.

"The 400 Richest Americans." *Forbes* (November 21, 2006). Accessed at http://www.forbes.com.

Graetz, Michael J., and Ian Shapiro. *Death by a Thousand Cuts: The Fight over Taxing Inherited Wealth.* Princeton, NJ: Princeton University Press, 2005.

Harden, Blaine. "U.S. Losing Its Middle-Class Neighborhoods." *The Washington Post* (June 22, 2006): A3.

Hertz, Tom. "Understanding Mobility in America." Report prepared for Center for American Progress, Washington, DC, 2006. Accessed at http://www.americanprogress.org.

Johnston, David Cay. "Big Gain for Rich Seen in Tax Cuts for Investments." *The New York Times* (April 5, 2006): A1, C4.

Kahlenberg, Richard D. "The Return of 'Separate but Equal,'" in Lardner and Smith 2005: 54–64.

Kennickel, Arthur B. "Currents and Undercurrents: Changes in the Distribution of Wealth, 1989–2004." FEDS Working Paper No. 2006–13. (2006). Accessed at http://www.federalreserve.gov.

Kozol, Jonathan. *Savage Inequalities: Children in America's Schools*. New York: Crown Publishers, 1991.

Krugman, Paul. "Graduates Versus Oligarchs." *The New York Times* (February 27, 2006): A19.

Kuznets, Simon. "Economic Growth and Income Inequality." *American Economic Review* 45, no. 2 (1955): 1–28.

Lardner, James, and David A. Smith, eds. *Inequality Matters: The Growing Economic Divide in America and Its Poisonous Consequences*. New York: The New Press, 2005.

Lynch, John W., et al. "Income Inequality and Mortality in Metropolitan Areas of the United States." *American Journal of Public Health* 88, no. 7 (1998): 1074–1081.

MathTech, Inc. *Factors Related to College Enrollment*. Washington, DC: U.S. Department of Education, 1998.

Mazumder, Bhashkar. "The Apple Falls Even Closer to the Tree than We Thought," in Bowles, Gintis, and Groves, 2005: 80–99.

Mishel, Lawrence. "CEO-to-Worker Pay Imbalance Grows." Economic Policy Institute, *Economic Snapshots* (June 21, 2006). Accessed at http://www.epinet.org.

Mishel, Lawrence, Jared Bernstein, and Sylvia Allegretto. *The State of Working America 2004/2005*. Ithaca, NY: ILR Press for Economic Policy Institute, 2005.

National Center for Health Statistics (NCHS). *Health, United States, 2005*. Hyattsville, MD: U.S. Department of Health and Human Services, 2005.

Neckerman, Kathryn M., ed. *Social Inequality*. New York: Russell Sage Foundation, 2004.

Phillips, Meredith, and Tiffani Chin. "School Inequality: What Do We Know?" in Neckerman 2004: 467–519.

Piketty, Thomas, and Emmanuel Saez. "Income Inequality in the United States, 1913 to 2002," in A. B. Atkinson and T. Piketty, eds., *Top Incomes over the Twentieth Century: A Contrast between European and English Speaking Countries*. Oxford: Oxford University Press, 2006.

Rosenthal, Howard. 2004. "Politics, Public Policy, and Inequality: A Look Back at the Twentieth Century," in Neckerman 2004: 861–892.

Schiller, Bradley R. *The Economics of Poverty and Discrimination.* 9th ed. Upper Saddle River, NJ: Pearson Prentice Hall, 2004.

Scott, Janny, and David Leonhardt. "Class in America: Shadowy Lines That Still Divide." *The New York Times* (May 15, 2005): A1, 26–29.

Shapiro, Thomas M. *The Hidden Cost of Being African American.* New York: Oxford University Press, 2004.

Silveira, Maria J., et al. "Net Worth Predicts Symptom Burden at the End of Life." *Journal of Palliative Medicine* 8, no. 4 (August 2005): 827–837.

Smith, George Davey, James D. Neaton, and Deborah Wentworth. "Socioeconomic Differentials in Mortality Risk among Men Screened for the Multiple Risk Factor Intervention Trial: I. White Men." *American Journal of Public Health* 86, no. 4 (April 1996): 486–496.

Smith, George Davey, et al. "Socioeconomic Differentials in Mortality Risk among Men Screened for the Multiple Risk Factor Intervention Trial: II. Black Men." *American Journal of Public Health* 86, no. 4 (April 1996): 497–504.

United Nations Development Programme (UNDP). *Human Development Report 2005: International Cooperation at a Crossroads.* New York: Oxford University Press, 2005.

U.S. Census Bureau. "Household Income Tables – Households, Table H-4, Gini Ratios for Households, by Race and Hispanic Origin of Householder: 1967 to 2004." 2006a. Accessed at http://www.census.gov.

U.S. Census Bureau. "Historical Income Tables – Families, Table F-7, Type of Family, All Races by Median and Mean Income: 1953 to 2004." 2006b. Accessed at http://www.census.gov.

U.S. Census Bureau. *Current Population Reports,* P60–233, "Income, Poverty, and Health Insurance Coverage in the United States: 2006." 2007. Accessed at http://www.census.gov.

Wilkinson, Richard. *Mind the Gap: Hierarchies, Health and Human Evolution.* London: Weidenfeld & Nicolson, 2000.

Wolff, Edward N. *Top Heavy: The Increasing Inequality of Wealth in America and What Can Be Done about It.* New York: The New Press, 2002.

2

Problems, Controversies, and Solutions

The income gap between America's rich and poor stretches wider today than at any time in more than half a century, and the gap continues to widen. A growing distance also separates the wealth holdings of those at the top of the ladder from those at the bottom. A deep-seated, ongoing trend toward economic inequality is acknowledged by observers across the political spectrum. People's responses to these developments vary. Some see inequality trends in the same light that skeptics see data on global climate change, arguing that the present numbers, though stark and unsettling, are part of a normal, long-term pattern of variability. If we simply allow current trends to run their course, they claim, the numbers will eventually turn around and bring us back to lower levels of inequality. Others, by contrast, view the current situation as highly problematic. They would deem any further widening of the income gap both dangerous and unacceptable.

This chapter goes behind the numbers on U.S. income inequality to seek the underlying causes of the trend toward economic polarization. Several theories have been put forward—each is interesting; some are controversial. After considering possible reasons for the current trends, we will examine a whole range of policies that have been proposed by those who think the gap between rich and poor Americans has grown too wide and that something needs to be done about it.

The Wage Structure and Human Capital

Americans receive income in a variety of forms: wages, interest, dividends, alimony, rental income, pensions (including Social Security), and cash welfare, among others. Leading the list for most people is wages. If U.S. incomes are becoming more unequally distributed, therefore, it must be largely because of a similar trend in the wage distribution. And that is exactly what the data show. High earners in every major category—male, female, single, and married—are pulling farther and farther ahead of low earners. For example, over the period 1975 to 2002, the real (inflation-adjusted) hourly wage earned by the bottom one-third of male workers actually fell, while those in the top 5 percent saw their real hourly earnings increase by nearly 50 percent—a dramatic stretching of the wage distribution (Danziger and Gottschalk 2004, 15–16). This typifies the broad historical pattern of the second half of the 20th century, a pattern in which the well paid found ways to earn even better pay, while the poorly paid fell behind. It also represents a reversal from the first half of the 20th century, when trends toward a more equal, more "compressed" wage structure were in place (Goldin and Katz 2001).

How is it that some workers earn so much more than others? It is an age-old question to which standard economic theory has a simple answer: they produce things that have greater monetary value in the marketplace. Those things can range all the way from hand-harvested bunches of Riesling grapes to the management of critical aspects of an initial public offering (IPO) of securities on Wall Street. IPO specialists are paid more than vineyard laborers because what they, as individuals, produce on a weekly or yearly basis is worth more to their employers, and ultimately to consumers, than the harvest of the vineyard. High-wage workers in our economy tend to be well educated, well trained, skillful, and experienced. Low-wage workers generally lack these characteristics.

Economists use the term *human capital* to denote the earning capacity built up in a person through education, training, and experience. Like all capital, human capital is expanded through investment. Societies with sufficient resources invest in the education of their children and young adults to ensure that they will have the skills required to function successfully in the modern economy. Rates of return on educational investments have been measured time and again and are always found to be positive. Women with more education out-earn those with less education. Men with more education out-earn those with less. The same holds true for blacks, Hispanics, and other demographic categories.

Investment in human capital is not just social (tax-funded), however. In the United States, much of it is privately funded. Many companies invest heavily in the human capital of their employees through a variety of in-house programs, training subsidies, and even tuition grants. Individuals invest in their own human capital by paying, sometimes with help from their families, for education and training beyond what the government makes available to everyone. The question of who pays for human capital becomes critical at the level of college and graduate school, because higher education, unlike elementary and secondary education, must normally be paid for by the student.

Broadly speaking, then, we have reason to think that the wage gap in the United States is related to unequal rates of investment in human capital. We already saw, in chapter 1, that the educational playing field is far from level in the United States. Low-income children attend public schools that are inferior in almost every way to the ones attended by more affluent children, and when (or if) they graduate from high school, they are much less likely to attend college than the sons and daughters of the middle class. Several policies have been proposed to remedy the problem of unequal educational opportunity, and we will examine them later in this chapter. First, it will be useful to develop a fuller, more dynamic analysis of wage determination in the U.S. labor market.

Labor Skills, Labor Demand, and Technological Change

In theory, the wage in every labor market is determined by the interplay of supply and demand. The supply of labor expresses the willingness of workers to offer various amounts of their labor at varying wage rates. Other things equal, an increase in the supply of labor will lower the wage rate, and a decrease in labor supply will elevate the wage rate. The demand for labor comes from business firms, at least in the simplest models; government and nonprofit employers are added to the picture in more complete models. Firms base their hiring decisions on the productivity of labor, which, of course, is tied to human capital. If productivity rises, firms are likely to hire more workers and, in some cases, pay them better.

It should be pointed out that workers are not, generally speaking, interchangeable with one another. High school dropouts, for example, rarely find employment in engineering firms, and an assembly line worker cannot trade jobs with a radiologist. The limits on labor substitutability mean that workers in low-paying jobs cannot simply quit and take higher-paying jobs instead. A well-known British economist of the 19th century, John Stuart Mill, recognized that deficiencies in education, skills, training, or other attributes meant that workers in certain trades did not have the freedom to compete for better jobs in other trades. In his view, this accounted for the otherwise puzzling long-term persistence of wage differences across occupations (Mill 1999, bk. II, ch. XIV).

Mill's idea of non-competing groups sheds light on the question of why wages at the top of the job market have been rising faster than wages at the bottom. Suppose the demand for highly skilled labor grows faster than the demand for less-skilled labor. Wages for high-skill labor will rise, and (non-competing) low-skill labor will lack the ability to move into those high-skill jobs that now pay much better. The result will be a growing wage gap between the top and bottom of the labor market. That is the scenario presented in a recent analysis of the changing U.S. wage structure by David Autor, Lawrence Katz, and Melissa Kearney (2006). The authors contend that technological change in recent decades—specifically, the advent of computer technology—has impacted three categories of workers in divergent ways. Managers and abstract problem solvers, who tend to be college graduates, do the kinds of work that computers can leverage; accordingly, demand for these workers has risen significantly, and so have their wages. At the next lower rung of the ladder, where middle-wage workers perform more routine, repetitive tasks, computers can actually replace labor. Thus, demand for this kind of labor has fallen, and wages have been under pressure. The displaced mid-level workers find it difficult to shift upward to the top job category, as Mill might have predicted. They are more likely to drop into the lower ranks.

At the lower end of the job scale, manual tasks are performed by janitors, house cleaners, truck drivers, security guards, and others. These are not jobs for college graduates. They require more physical than managerial or high-level cognitive skills, and they might seem vulnerable to downward wage pressures. But compared to mid-level jobs, they are actually less vulnerable to technological unemployment because they involve non-routine tasks. The physical labor done by these workers cannot easily be substituted by a computer, no matter how cheap computing power becomes. At the lower end of the wage scale, therefore, the stress from technological change is less than in the middle range.

Autor, Katz, and Kearney give a fairly specific account of how technology is driving wage polarization. Other experts share these scholars' emphasis on technological change as a key force in determining relative income levels. The highly skilled top earners identified by Autor, Katz, and Kearney are essentially the same group singled out as critical new players in the economy by Robert Reich in his book *The Work of Nations*. Reich calls them "symbolic analysts" who "solve, identify, and broker problems by manipulating symbols." Most symbolic analysts, needless to say, are college educated (Reich 1991, 178–179). Frank Levy and Richard Murnane (2004) explore in depth the powerful role that computers have played in reshaping the skill sets desired by U.S. employers. They see the wage growth among college graduates since 1973 as clear evidence of growing demand for workers capable of "expert thinking" and "complex communication," while wage stagnation for high school graduates and dropouts suggests much less demand for lower-level job skills (Levy and Murnane 2004, ch. 3).

A top policy maker in the U.S. government supports the "skill gap" explanation of the growing wage (and income) gap. In congressional testimony, Federal Reserve chairman Ben Bernanke cited the rising skill premium—the extra wage paid to those with higher skills—as the "most important factor" behind rising income inequality during the past quarter-century. Equally significant was his further comment: given the problematic trend toward inequality, efforts to increase education and job training would be "a very positive thing" (Bernanke 2006).

International Competition

Historically, free trade has not been a consistent policy priority of the United States, but since the 1960s, the U.S. government has generally moved in the direction of trade liberalization. Indeed, the United States has become a leading proponent of globalization, which can be loosely defined as an international system allowing for the unrestricted movement of goods, capital, and ideas across national borders. Many observers are convinced that the increasing flow of certain types of imports into the United States, combined with increased rates of immigration in recent years (see next section), has contributed to the growing gap between rich and poor in the United States. Is there something to this?

Liberalized trade means fewer barriers to the free movement of goods into and out of a country. As tariffs and quotas are reduced, goods that can be produced more cheaply abroad start flowing into a country at higher rates than before. Industries that have been sheltered from foreign competition now must adapt to a more rigorous competitive environment. Companies in import-competing industries lose sales, which reduces their demand for resources, including labor. Workers feel the impact in plant closings, job losses, and lower wages and benefits. In the United States, much concern has been expressed for low-skilled workers in manufacturing industries, especially where products have to compete with imports from newly industrializing, low-wage countries like China, Indonesia, and Mexico. No one doubts that low-wage competition from abroad has done serious economic harm to such U.S. industries as apparel, textiles, athletic shoes, toys, and low-end electronics.

A shift to more open trade always creates both winners and losers. In a wealthy industrialized nation like the United States, free trade's losers tend to be low-skilled, less educated workers who, in some sense, must compete against workers in the Third World. It is an oversimplification to say that the unskilled wage rate in the United States today is set in China. Nevertheless, if low-skilled workers are producing the same items in the United States and in China, the fact that Chinese workers are paid only about 3 percent of what American workers are paid is certain to put downward pressure on the U.S. wage (Krugman 2007). Free trade's winners in the United States are likely to be found in high-tech, capital-intensive export industries—jet aircraft, computer software, machinery, and the like—where the workforce is characterized by high levels of human capital.

As far as overall efficiency is concerned, moving in the free trade direction is a plus, according to classic economic theory. The long-term benefits outweigh the costs. If tariffs are reduced on all sides, resource allocation improves. Job losses in import-competing industries may be matched or exceeded by the job *gains* in export industries. And of course, consumers everywhere enjoy the benefits of lower prices. But the implications for the rich-poor divide may not be so favorable: if the winners are already at the upper end of the skill and wage distribution, equipped with the human capital to take advantage of expanding opportunities in the export sector, while the losers are concentrated at the lower end of the skill and wage distribution, then the gap between rich and poor will grow wider. It is a troubling prospect that is only partially mitigated, in some people's minds, by a sense that the *world* distribution of income is becoming more equal as a result of markets in the wealthy nations opening up to imports of manufactured goods from Asia, Latin America, and Africa (see ch. 3 and Gilbert 2004, ch. 1–2).

Immigration

It is not hard to see how immigration on a large scale might affect the income structure of a country. If immigrants were mainly high-skilled and high-earning—think Sergey Brin, the Russian-born American cofounder of Google whose personal wealth exceeds $10 billion—then adding large numbers of them to the labor force would stretch the nation's income distribution at the upper end. If, on the other hand, most immigrants were low-skilled and low-earning, their influx would put a heavier weight on the lower end of the scale. And if the foreign-born came to the labor market with exactly the same proportions of human capital as the native-born population, measures of income inequality would barely be affected. This last scenario is one that we know for certain does not apply to the United States.

In recent years, the average skill level of immigrants to the United States has declined relative to native-born levels. The education data tell the story: in 2005, only 12 percent of U.S.-born residents age 25 or older had less than a high school education, while 32 percent of recently arrived foreign-born residents lacked a high school diploma (Martin and Midgley 2006, 18). This has meant that immigrants increasingly dominate the low-pay job ranks. In 1970, for example, foreign-born male workers were evenly distributed across all the deciles of the wage distribution, holding 5 or 6 percent of the jobs in each decile, from the highest paying to the lowest. By 2000, everything had changed. In the first place, there were many more immigrants in the labor force, with at least

10 percent of the jobs in every decile held by the foreign born. But more importantly, their distribution across the job ranks had become highly skewed. Foreign-born men in 2000 were slightly overrepresented in the top two deciles—again, think Russian-born, Korean-born, and Indian-born doctors, financial analysts, and Silicon Valley entrepreneurs—but *heavily* overrepresented in the bottom two deciles. Immigrants now do roughly 25 percent of the lowest-paying work performed by men in the United States (Borjas 2003a, 248–249).

Immigration's full potential for widening the gap between rich and poor in the United States cannot be gauged without considering the effects of immigration on native earnings and employment. This is a highly controversial topic politically, and one on which expert opinion is also divided. A standard argument runs like this: if you introduce large numbers of immigrant laborers into a job market, the native workers with whom they compete will experience depressed wages, and some of them will likely lose their jobs. It is a textbook example of supply and demand: an increase in supply results in a lower price. The real world, however, rarely matches up neatly with simple economic models. If immigrants bring a large amount of capital with them, for example, its infusion into the economy may indirectly lead to an increase in the demand for labor, which will tend to offset the wage-depressing effects of the increased supply of labor. This is just one of a large number of alternative assumptions that can be made, and alternative scenarios that can be explored, when one asks how immigration affects the well-being of unskilled natives.

The Harvard economist George Borjas, an immigrant himself, has consistently voiced a range of concerns about the economic harm done to native workers by the heavy immigrant inflow of the 1980s, 1990s, and early years of the 21st century. He argues that the influx of unskilled, heavily Hispanic labor in recent decades has probably worked to the advantage of more highly skilled labor, consumers, and employers, but not the least-skilled workers. He estimates, for example, that native-born high school dropouts saw their wage reduced by about 9 percent between 1980 and 2000 because of immigration (Borjas 2003b, 1368). In a 1999 book, he blamed immigration for roughly half the deterioration of dropouts' wages relative to other workers in the period 1980–1995, and went on to state a larger conclusion: "Immigration seems to have been an important contributor to the rise in income inequality in the United States, depressing the economic opportunities faced by the least skilled workers" (Borjas 1999, 11).

Borjas's negative findings on the size and extent of the impact experienced by low-wage native labor as a result of immigration have garnered considerable attention, but they have not gone unchallenged. The literature on this subject, much of it highly technical and complex, continues to expand rapidly. The New School's David Howell offers a concise, evenhanded review of that work, at the end of which he sums up this way: "On balance . . . the post-1980 surge in less skilled and heavily undocumented immigrants in largely unregulated labor markets contributes to downward wage and employment rates at the bottom of the labor market" (Howell 2007). If Howell is correct, it suggests that current U.S. immigration policy can be paired with the nation's trade policy in the vexing category of policies that simultaneously reduce *global* income inequality and raise *U.S.* income inequality.

Unions and the Wage Distribution

So far we have considered explanations for the growing wage gap that center on technology, trade, and immigration, each understood to be influencing labor markets through the ordinary forces of supply and demand. Some analysts believe that, aside from these fundamental forces, there are certain institutional factors affecting U.S. workers in ways that tend to widen the distance between top earners and those barely getting by on their weekly paychecks. Two that are commonly cited are the declining membership of U.S. workers in labor unions and the eroding real value of the minimum wage.

Historically, unions have given workers the opportunity to join together and bargain collectively with their employers to achieve better results, including higher wages, than they could have gotten as individuals. Few question the positive impact unions had, from the late 19th to the mid-20th century, on the earnings of at least part of the labor force. This is particularly true of workers at the lower end, the kind who joined the Congress of Industrial Organizations (CIO), for example. But union membership as a percentage of the labor force peaked in the early 1950s and has been in decline ever since. Unions are much weaker in the United States today than they are in Europe, and weaker than they have been in this country since the 1930s. The union membership rate was down to a mere 12 percent by 2006 (U.S. Department of Labor 2007).

Reasons offered for the strong deunionization trend have included a shift in the economy's structure from manufacturing toward services, a less supportive political environment beginning with the presidency of Ronald Reagan, and global competition that indirectly pits U.S. workers against low-paid workers overseas. Whatever its true cause, the shrunken share of workers covered by collective bargaining agreements is not good news for the low-paid end of the wage scale. Unions have traditionally been in the forefront of efforts to improve working conditions, wages, and benefits for the workers they represent, and this has been particularly beneficial for minorities and low-wage workers.

The wage advantage enjoyed by unionized over non-unionized workers is called the *union premium*. It is the higher pay, expressed as a percentage, that unionized workers receive compared to non-unionized workers in the same types of jobs, in the same regions and industries, with the same education and experience. The premium varies up and down the pay scale in ways that tend to compress rather than widen the dispersion of wages: it is only about 5 percent for college graduates but a whopping 35 percent for those with a high school diploma or less. Among low-wage workers, the union premium has been estimated at 28 percent, while among the highest-paid quintile it is about 11 percent (Mishel, Bernstein, and Allegretto 2007, 187–188). A point that should be stressed is that union benefits, along with their income-equalizing effects, extend beyond union members and even non-union members who are covered incidentally by collective bargaining agreements. Many not-yet-organized employers are so averse to unions that they will match the wages and benefits achieved by unions in their area in order to discourage union organizers.

The long-term decline of unions in the United States has a tendency to raise income inequality partly because membership losses are concentrated where union membership itself is concentrated—at the lower end of the wage distribution. The distributional impact is magnified by the fact that, as noted, the union premium is largest for the lowest-wage members. And there is something else to be considered: unions in the past have wielded substantial political clout in state capitols and in the halls of Congress. They have lobbied hard for passage of legislation favorable to working men and women. As the union movement weakens, so does its political influence on issues across the board, including those that may affect the distribution of income. One such issue is the minimum wage.

The Minimum Wage and Inequality

The minimum wage is the lowest hourly wage that employers, by law, are allowed to pay their employees. The United States has had a federal minimum wage since 1938, with Congress raising it from time to time since then, most recently in May 2007. By the summer of 2009, the federal minimum is scheduled to reach $7.25 an hour. Many states, including New York, California, Illinois, and Florida, have established their own minimum wages at levels above the federal rate. In such cases, the state minimum prevails; if the state minimum is below the federal, then the federal minimum prevails. Whether state or federal, these laws are commonly justified by the argument that low-wage labor needs to be protected from exploitation. While some workers who are paid the minimum wage would presumably earn the same wage in the absence of a legal minimum, others would certainly be paid less. To that extent, minimum wages are seen as nudging the income distribution in the direction of greater equality.

Critics of minimum wage laws contend that this type of government intervention into the labor market does more harm than good. If the government introduces a minimum wage that is higher than the equilibrium wage, it will result in some unemployment. Why? Because workers will want to work more hours at the higher wage, and employers will choose to hire fewer workers at that wage. (Employers will look for ways to economize on labor, possibly by replacing it with capital.) Thus, the benefits of having some low-paid workers earning better wages than they otherwise would are offset, to some degree, by the loss of income among those who are displaced from their jobs. Critics also point to the fact that only a few million U.S. workers are actually paid at the legal minimum. Millions more, however, earn wages that are linked informally to the legal wage floor; if the floor is lifted, they, too, will take home more pay. For example, workers whose jobs customarily pay $2 above the minimum wage can expect the 2007 legislation to increase their pay from $7.15 an hour to $9.25 by the summer of 2009.

Those who see a connection between rising U.S. wage inequality and the minimum wage usually focus on the real (inflation-adjusted) value of the federal minimum, arguing that workers at the low end of the wage distribution get hammered when inflation eats into the value of a given wage floor. This has happened repeatedly in the past. For long periods of time—typically when the Republican Party controls either the White House or Congress—the real minimum wage falls because the nominal rate is not automatically adjusted for inflation. The change in the federal minimum wage enacted by Congress in 2007 was the first increase in 10 years. During the preceding decade, the minimum wage of $5.15 an hour was so ravaged by inflation that its purchasing power fell to a 50-year low. It also shrank to a record low of 31 percent of the average U.S. hourly wage (Bernstein and Shapiro 2006, 2).

How much of the recent rise in inequality is attributable to the falling real value of the minimum wage remains an open question. The last (and only other) time the U.S. minimum wage was left unchanged for a decade was between 1981 and 1990. One study determined that the falling real value of the minimum wage in that period was a significant factor in the hefty increase of wage inequality that occurred in the 1980s, especially for women (Lee 1999). So far, no one has done the same math for the period 1997 to 2007. With the federal minimum wage now set to rise until 2009, both nominally and in real terms (unless there is a surge of inflation), we can expect a reduction of the wage gap at the lower end of the pay scale. The authors of *The State of Working America 2006/2007* calculated the impact of a $2.10 wage hike, and their results suggest that disproportionate benefits will flow to the lowest earners, as one would expect. They foresee 38 percent of the total gains generated by the wage increase going to the poorest quintile of households, and 57 percent going to the bottom two quintiles. This contrasts strongly with a mere 12 percent of the gains going to the top quintile (Mishel, Bernstein, and Allegretto 2007, 195–196).

Winner Take All?

At the very summit of the income distribution, where some individuals earn in a day what it would take years for the minimum-wage worker to earn, it seems that something more than education, training, and experience must be at work to account for relative incomes. Top entertainers, athletes, lawyers, and CEOs are much better paid today than was the case a generation ago, not only in inflation-adjusted terms but also relative to the *average* entertainer, athlete, lawyer, and CEO. There has never been a better time to be Number One in your field. The world's top-ranked tennis players now take home in excess of $20 million a year, if we include their commercial endorsements (Hodgkinson 2006). A few movie actors, like Will Ferrell and Johnny Depp, collect $20 million paychecks for each movie they make. A top TV and film producer, Jerry Bruckheimer, earns over $80 million per year. Something appears to have blown the top off the wage distribution in at least some U.S. industries and occupations.

Do "superstars" like the ones just named possess more human capital than their predecessors? More talent? Their fans may think so, but a better explanation for their jumbo-sized paychecks may lie in what the English economist Alfred Marshall, in his 1890 *Principles of Economics,* identified as a likely source of rapidly growing fortunes, namely, "the development of new facilities for communication, by which men who have once attained a commanding position are enabled to apply their constructive or speculative genius to undertakings vaster, and extending over a wider area, than ever before" (Marshall 1961, book VI, ch. XII). Athletic and acting performances today can be viewed not just by hundreds, as in the past, but by millions, thanks to advances in telecommunications. And the market system has found effective ways to charge national and global audiences for access to those performances. Since the public is far more interested in seeing the world's top-ranked tennis players, boxers, actors, etc., than others further down the list, even if the lower-ranked performers are, objectively speaking, almost as good, the top names in winner-take-all markets can command top dollar.

A direct application of Marshall's insight about the importance of scale ("vaster undertakings") as a basis for greater financial rewards can be seen in the world of investment banking during the 1980s. In that decade, the bonuses paid to Wall Street's top bond sellers—"masters of the universe," as they were called—shot up to unprecedented levels, and the reason was simple. The traders were not more skillful than before, but trading volumes in that decade exploded. According to one participant, the volume of business done by a typical trader went from about $5 million per week to $300 million per *day.* Hence, a salesperson of given talent and persuasiveness gained much more leverage and became worth much more to his or her employer than in previous decades (Frank and Cook 1995, 94–95). A similar logic may be applied to the whole issue of CEO compensation in the United States: the volume of sales and the level of profits for firms operating on a global scale mean that having the right executive at the top is of paramount importance. We return to the issue of CEO compensation later in the chapter.

Family Structure and Income Distribution

So far, we have focused on ways in which the growing divide between America's rich and poor might be accounted for by a growing polarization of earnings. The wage distribution has indeed been stretching wider across groups; thus, college graduates are widening the pay gap between themselves and high school graduates, and white-collar occupations are outdistancing blue-collar occupations. Within-group inequality also is growing: among male workers, for example, the gap between top and bottom earners has widened, and the same holds for female workers (to a lesser extent), as well as workers within industries, occupations, and ethnicities. The economic and technological factors that have been studied as possible causes of these developments are indeed a big part of the inequality story, but not the whole story. An important element in what has been happening with income inequality has to do with household arrangements in the United States. Demographic patterns have changed in ways that have a measurable impact on the distribution of income.

We can get a clear picture of how economic fortunes vary across different types of families by putting a spotlight on the lower end of the income distribution, that is, on those who fall below the poverty line. In 2005, only about one married-couple family in twenty had an income below the poverty line. The basic reason for such a low poverty rate is obvious: the traditional "nuclear" family structure is one that allows for two earners in the same household. If one spouse works full-time, even if the other works only part-time, it is difficult for the family's combined income to fall below the government's poverty threshold. The outlook is quite different for single-parent families. In those headed by a male with no wife present, the poverty rate was 13.0 percent in 2005. In families headed by a female with no husband present, the poverty rate was a staggering 28.7 percent (U.S. Census Bureau 2006, 58). The high vulnerability of mother-only families in the United States has long been a staple of poverty analysis and policy discussion.

Long-term changes in family structure become a force behind rising inequality if they result in more families experiencing extra-low or extra-high incomes. This has, in fact, been happening at the lower end of the distribution. In 1973, about 15 percent of American families were headed by a single parent; by 2005, that figure had risen to 25 percent. Thus, part of the overall increase in the U.S. poverty rate for families, from 8.8 percent in 1973 to 9.9 percent in 2005, can be attributed to a simple shift in the makeup of families, with more now in the vulnerable lone-parent category (U.S. Census Bureau 2006, 58). A specific calculation of the impact of evolving family structure on U.S. income inequality has been done by economist Gary Burtless. He finds that about one-fifth of the rise in the Gini coefficient (index of inequality) from 1979 to 1996 can be blamed on the declining percentage of Americans in husband-and-wife families (Burtless 2003, S189).

At the upper end of the income distribution, a different sort of demographic change has been intensifying inequality. It goes by the name "assortative mating" and involves the increasing likelihood that marriage partners will share common background characteristics, whether of income, education, or occupation. Couples already do themselves a financial favor just by tying the knot. When equally well-educated men and women do so, it elevates their prospects of moving quickly to the top income ranks. As Annie Paul has observed, "Once, it was commonplace for doctors to marry nurses and executives to marry secretaries. Now the wedding pages are stocked with matched sets, men and women who share a tax bracket and even an alma mater." She reports on a study that found a 43 percent drop, from the 1940s to the late 1970s, in the odds of a college graduate marrying a high school graduate, and another study that finds a strengthening association between women's pre-marriage earnings and the post-marriage earnings and occupational status of their husbands (Paul 2006).

How much has the growing concentration of earning power among couples contributed to rising income inequality in the United States? Gary Burtless credits the increasing similarity of husbands' and wives' earnings over the period 1979–1996 with about one-eighth of the rise in the Gini coefficient, making it a far from negligible factor (Burtless 2003, S189). This particular trend may now be played out, however. Historically, middle-class women began entering the labor force and bolstering their families' incomes during the 1960s. As time went on, women of higher educational attainment and earning potential joined the march into the workplace. As they added their earnings to those of their well-compensated husbands, the gap between rich and poor families tended to grow wider (Burtless 2003, S190). In recent years, the participation rate of women in the U.S. workforce seems to have peaked, which suggests that any further rises in inequality will have to come from other sources.

Political Perspectives on Income Inequality

Nearly everyone who has looked at the facts concerning income distribution in the United States has come to the same conclusion: the gap between rich and poor stretches wider today than at any time in decades. There is no similar unanimity on the exact causes of the polarization, although the explanations we have considered so far in this chapter are the ones most frequently cited. There is perhaps even less agreement about what, if anything, should be done about the current extent and trend of inequality. Those who mistrust government "meddling" in the economy argue that no action should be taken, at least by the government. In their conservative perspective, even the current degree of economic inequality falls within the normal bounds of historical variation. They point out that nearly all of the increase in statistical inequality can be accounted for by improvements at the top of the income distribution, rather than deterioration at the bottom. To begrudge the financially successful their gains—even outsized gains—is to indulge in the politics of envy.

A radical counterpoint to the conservative view on inequality would start from the premise that capitalism is what has created the vast gulf now separating the haves from the have-nots. The logical solution to the problem of inequality, therefore, is to sweep capitalism aside. And replace it with what? Radical critics of capitalism have generally proposed some form of socialism as a replacement. Although the varieties of socialism, both in theory and practice, are numerous, all have aimed to achieve a more equitable allocation of incomes than occurs under capitalism. Indeed, the promise to end poverty and inequality has always been counted among the most appealing aspects of socialism, at least on paper.

Between the two extremes sketched above lies a vast middle ground of positions on inequality occupied by moderates, centrists, liberals, and progressives. Most of them accept the premise that unequal incomes are a natural outcome of the capitalist economy, but they take this as a call to modify, not jettison, capitalism. Unlike conservatives, they are generally comfortable with using government to deal with social and economic problems, including inequality. This means they are prepared, at a minimum, to enlist the tax-and-transfer system to secure more equitable results for those left behind by the workings of the market economy. Rarely, if ever, do they call for a specific numerical change in an indicator such as the Gini coefficient or the 90–10 income ratio. What these scholars, activists, and politicians offer is a wide range of policies aimed at alleviating the worst, most deep-seated inequities generated by the U.S. economy. They do not necessarily worry about how realistic the chances are for acceptance of their proposals; even politicians have been known to float "trial balloons" that stand a good chance of being shot down. In the remainder of this chapter, we take up some of the most interesting and controversial policy proposals for countering the trend toward inequality.

Education as an Income Equalizer

If every five-year-old walking into kindergarten on the first day of school were put on a path of guaranteed educational success—assured that he or she would progress smoothly through elementary and middle school, graduate from high school, get accepted to college, and have the money to stay there for four years—much of the current gap between the rich and the poor would be closed. It would not disappear entirely, of course. The accidents of birth would continue to favor some and not others, with advantages like above-average IQs, social connections, and wealth. Some occupations would continue to pay more than others, as they always have. But over time, the distribution of incomes would almost certainly become more equal. This is not, however, the educational world we know. Children do not enter kindergarten on the same footing. They do not go home after school to the same family circumstances. Their schools are not identical because their neighborhoods are not. And college attendance is far from automatic for a majority of high school graduates.

If nothing is done to interrupt the typical growing-up experience of children from backgrounds of low socioeconomic status (SES), most will reach adulthood with far less human capital than their more advantaged peers, and their wages will lag accordingly. A number of policy interventions have been suggested to compensate for the social and cognitive deficits that low-SES children bring to school at every age. Some have been tested experimentally, and some implemented on a larger scale. In the next section we look at two famous examples; many more are described in Jonathan Crane's *Social Programs That Work* (1998). If educational investments are well timed and well carried out, excellent results are achievable. The rates of return on such investments can be remarkably high.

When a new public policy is contemplated, it often raises concerns about a trade-off between equity and efficiency—what helps the one may hurt the other. Nobel Prize-winning economist James Heckman notes that when it comes to educational interventions, particularly at young ages, there is no equity-efficiency trade-off to contend with. When these policies target low-income children and improve their life chances, they advance equity. They also build up much-needed human capital in the labor force, make our schools more productive, and "reduce crime, teenage pregnancy, and welfare dependency" (Heckman 2006, A14). Compensatory education has to be one of the prime tools employed by government if it is serious about addressing the nation's income gap.

The Effectiveness of Early Interventions

Two early childhood intervention programs have received a vast amount of attention from educators and social policy analysts: the 1962–1967 Perry Preschool (PP) program in Ypsilanti, Michigan, and the 1972–1977 Carolina Abecedarian (CA) program in North Carolina. Both studies were structured as randomized trials, and both tracked the participants for many years afterward to check on the long-term effects of the programs. The PP program started with a group of 123 low-SES African American children, ages three and four, who were randomly assigned to either a treatment group or a no-treatment group. The treatment group received high-quality preschool instruction for 2.5 hours each day, five days a week, eight months a year, for a two-year period. The teaching staff were trained in early childhood development and closely supervised. In addition to classroom sessions, they made weekly 90-minute visits to their pupils' homes (Schweinhart 2005).

The impact of the preschool program was substantial and long-lasting, as evidenced in data collected on PP participants every year until they were 11, and then again at ages 15, 19, 27, and 40. At age 40, for example, those who had been in the treatment group stood better than those who had been in the control group on a number of economic measures: they were more likely to be employed (76 percent vs. 62 percent); they had higher median earnings ($20,800 vs. $15,300); they had more savings accounts (76 percent vs. 50 percent); and they had higher homeownership rates. In many other ways, the PP program served the treatment group—and society—well. Those in the treatment group spent fewer years in special education, were much less likely to be classified as mentally retarded, graduated from high school at higher rates, received post-secondary education at higher rates, and had less involvement with crime. Cost-benefit calculations for the PP program have been highly favorable, mainly due to the estimated savings to society from lower crime rates among program participants (Schweinhart 2005).

A decade later, the CA program took an even more intensive approach to early childhood intervention than the PP program. Subjects were recruited into the program as infants; their average age at entry was 4.4 months. As with PP, the children were overwhelmingly African American, from low-SES backgrounds. The sample size, again, was small. By a randomized process, 57 infants were assigned to the treatment group and 54 to the control, or no-treatment, group. The former received high-quality child care eight hours a day, five days a week, 50 weeks a year, until they were three or four years old, at which time they were switched to a preschool program. During the five years children spent in the pre-kindergarten phase of the CA program, the curriculum emphasized age-appropriate play activities and language development. Upon entry to kindergarten, an extension of the Abecedarian program was made available to some treatment-group and some control-group children through second grade (Child Trends 2007).

The impact of the CA program on participants has been quite positive. Those in the treatment group, by comparison with no treatment, got better scores on reading and math tests, repeated fewer grades, were placed less often in special education, and at age 21 had either graduated from or were enrolled in four-year colleges at higher rates (35 percent vs. 14 percent). Among CA participants who had borne a child, the average mother's age at first birth was more than a year older for the treatment group than for the controls. Even IQ gains, which tend to fade out in childhood interventions, appeared to persist to age 21 among CA participants (Child Trends 2007).

The results achieved with Perry Preschool, Abecedarian, and a handful of other small-scale, model programs of early childhood intervention have convinced psychologists, educators, and even hard-headed economists that investing in young children from disadvantaged backgrounds makes sense (Heckman and Krueger 2003, 163–174). It can give participating children, and in some cases their mothers, a realistic chance of earning higher incomes over a lifetime, thus putting at least a dent in current levels of inequality. One might expect there to be an attempt at scaling up these promising efforts to a state or national level, but so far that has not happened.

What we have instead is Head Start, a vast Great Society-era program that annually serves more than 900,000 children, ages three and four, on a budget of roughly $7 billion. The goal of Head Start is to ensure that children from low-income families are ready for school. Head Start funding does not approach the per-child levels of the model programs, nor are its teachers as well qualified or well paid. In 2003, for example, only 31 percent of Head Start teachers had a BA degree or higher (Hart and Schumacher 2005, 3). Head Start children achieve modest IQ and other cognitive gains that tend to fade out in time, something that also happens in the model programs. James Heckman, among others, has stressed that cognitive measures (test scores) are not the sole gauge of program effectiveness. Noncognitive skills can be just as important as, or more important than, cognitive skills for those who come from a background of disadvantage. Self-discipline, perseverance, and cooperative skills can be critical to success at higher levels of education and in the job market, and preschool programs appear to develop these skills. Heckman reports on a recent long-term study of Head Start that finds solid benefits for its participants, whether in high school graduation rates, earnings, or lower crime rates, with the largest benefits going to those whose mothers had been high school dropouts (Heckman and Krueger 2003, 169–171).

U.S. Schools and Inequality

Most experts on poverty and inequality see a role for preschool intervention to help children from disadvantaged backgrounds have a better chance at success when they start school. But even with intervention and enrichment, children from low-SES families face daunting obstacles to success in the classroom. Many are being raised by a single parent whose own educational experience was limited and negative. Some have health issues related to poverty that can interfere with steady school attendance. Family instability causes many children to get moved from school to school, disrupting their educational progress in serious ways. For some children, the home environment is so chaotic that they cannot find the space or quiet to sit down and complete a homework assignment. If these are the personal challenges faced by a great many children from the lower end of the income scale, one may well ask: what can a school do to compensate? An even tougher question would be: what can society do to enable schools to be equalizing institutions, when children come to them with such diverse capacities and preparation?

As noted in chapter 1, most public schools in the United States are neighborhood-based and draw their funding, to a considerable extent, from local property taxes. U.S. residential patterns have become so segregated along class lines that many schools are essentially lower class, middle class, or upper middle class in terms of student enrollments. At the upper end, in leafy suburbs, one finds well-prepared, motivated children, supported by parents who know the value of education. Students are taught in well-maintained classrooms and state-of-the-art laboratories. They have a rich menu of extracurricular options. And long before high school, most understand that they are on the path to college. At the lower end, the situation can be much bleaker, from school locations in drug-infested neighborhoods and youth cultures that devalue academic achievement, to facilities and curricula that can only be called substandard. In settings like these, student expectations will not typically include automatic passage to college and a career.

In many public schools, of course, students are drawn from a mix of backgrounds. However, that diversity does not necessarily mean that the students mingle in the classroom or get the same education. Those with more advantage in their upbringing—that is, higher SES—usually take a different set of classes (college-prep) from the ones taken by students of less economic and social advantage. When we see such "tracking," which often begins well before high school, it can shake our confidence in America's schools as engines of opportunity and upward mobility. To some observers, it appears that the public schools serve an opposite function, as institutions for the entrenchment of current inequalities.

One view of how to change the system for the better would stress the importance of money. In *Savage Inequalities*, Jonathan Kozol paints a vivid picture of the underfunded school. The logical remedy for such schools would involve the injection of additional financial resources. Title I of the Elementary and Secondary School Act of 1965 has put federal money into high-poverty schools for the past 40 years. The great majority of the funds go to support children at the K–6 level, helping poorer districts hire more teachers and teachers' aides, purchase computers, and offer summer school. Title I was reauthorized in 2001 as part of the No Child Left Behind (NCLB) initiative of President George W. Bush.

Most school funding actually comes from states and localities; the federal share of total funding, including Title I, is only in the 6–8 percent range. Total expenditures per pupil in the United States have grown considerably over the decades, nearly doubling between 1970 and 1998 (Corcoran et al. 2004, 434). Local financing has diminished in importance, state funding has grown, and federal funding has edged up. The most notable change has been in state funding. Under political pressure and sometimes court order, the states stepped up aid to poorer districts enough to cause every measure of school spending inequality to fall significantly (20–30 percent) between 1972 and 1997 (Corcoran et al. 2004, 436–441). Per-pupil expenditures within states have been adjusted to the point where one can no longer claim that they show substantial inequality.

On other measures, however, inequality remains. A U.S. Department of Education survey in 1999 found that the schools with the highest numbers of poor students (that is, students eligible for free or reduced-cost lunches) were older, more crowded, and in worse shape in terms of roofing, plumbing, and heating than other schools. A 1994 survey found that teachers at high-poverty schools were less likely to be certified in their primary teaching field and much less likely to hold an advanced degree. Advanced placement courses, while more available in all schools in 1992 than in 1972, were offered less than half as often in high-poverty schools as in low-poverty schools. Computer access was more limited in high-poverty schools. In all of these dimensions of school quality, there remain differences—though they are narrowing—in the quality of educational resources available to the children of the middle class and the children of the poor (Cochran et al. 2004, 452–458).

Ways to Improve Low-SES Student Performance

Ironically, as the United States has been moving toward greater equalization of school expenditures, experts have reached no consensus on the efficacy of additional expenditures in producing better outcomes for less privileged students. Some say the extra dollars have little or no impact, a view originally expressed (or implied) in the famous Coleman Report of 1966. Others find that more spending produces positive results, and the balance of current research may be shifting in their direction (Rouse and Barrow 2006, 112–113). But even if we believe that more spending can improve student outcomes, we do not necessarily know how and where to spend those extra dollars. One possibility would be to create smaller classes for disadvantaged children. Would this help? A widely cited, rigorous, random-trial experiment conducted in Tennessee in 1985–1986 found that students performed better in class sizes of 13–17 pupils than in class sizes of 22–25, and the small-class advantage was greatest for students from less privileged backgrounds. Several other studies support the notion that lower pupil-teacher ratios make for better long-term outcomes, both in test scores and in adult earnings (Rouse and Barrow 2006, 113–114).

Another approach to improving the school performance of lower-SES children is to integrate them into classrooms with children from middle-class families. The idea is simple: lower-SES children benefit from the stimulating presence of classmates with larger vocabularies, higher aspirations, and other cognitive and attitudinal advantages. In a racial context, this was the core message of the *Brown v. Board of Education* decision by the Supreme Court in 1954, which ruled that "separate but equal" really was not equal at all. The court-ordered school busing that followed *Brown*, though politically untenable from the start, was based on the assumption that black children would achieve better educational results if they shared classrooms with white children. That belief got social science backing in the Coleman Report alluded to above. Johns Hopkins sociologist James Coleman, in trying to account for differences between black and white student outcomes in U.S. schools, concluded that student achievement had less to do with school quality per se—buildings, teachers, curricula—than with the SES of the students and their peers in the classroom.

To achieve the kind of SES mixing that promises to lift achievement levels for disadvantaged (and minority) kids, a number of school districts across the country have resorted to a strategy called income-based or economic integration. Four districts in particular have garnered considerable media attention for moving in this direction: La Crosse, Wisconsin; Cambridge, Massachusetts; San Francisco; and, most notably, Wake County, North Carolina. In 2000, Wake County school officials replaced a policy mandating racial balance among its schools with a new plan capping the share of low-income students permitted to attend any one school at 40 percent. Meeting this rule required a certain amount of busing, but since the school district sprawls out from Raleigh into rural areas, busing has been a normal experience for many students anyway. Busing within the city of Raleigh was made more palatable for middle-class families by the designation of certain schools as "magnet schools." The impact of the new policy to date has been remarkable. Student achievement across all groups has improved since 2000, and achievement gaps *between* groups, including high- and low-income students, have been narrowed (Kahlenberg 2006, 2–4). Many school officials around the country now are studying the Wake County program as a model of how to get low-SES students into middle-class schools, where they are known to perform better.

Raising the lagging achievement levels of minority and low-income students is a key motivation behind President Bush's No Child Left Behind Act of 2001. The law speaks of "meeting the educational needs of low-achieving children in our Nation's highest-poverty schools" and of "closing the achievement gaps between minority and nonminority students, and between disadvantaged children and their more advantaged peers" (U.S. Congress 2002, 115 STAT 1439–1440). NCLB calls for better teacher preparation and training, regular testing of students in math and reading, much more school accountability for educational results, and rising penalties for schools that fail to make timely progress. By 2014, *all* students are expected to meet their state's proficiency standards—an extremely ambitious goal. Supporters believe that holding schools and states accountable for results will force them to do a better job of educating all students, especially those from less privileged backgrounds. Critics, however, assail the regimen of frequent testing, the uneven proficiency standards from state to state, the punitive aspects of accountability, and the inadequate federal funding of some parts of the program. On one thing, all can agree: it will be years before we know whether NCLB is contributing to a reduction in U.S. inequality.

College: Ticket to the Middle Class

For at least a century, Americans have viewed their public school system as an essential part of what makes the "land of opportunity" work. While the role of the public school continues to be fundamental, vast changes in technology and industrial organization over the past half-century have made college degrees the new minimum requirement for entry into, or continued occupancy of, the middle class. This marks a sea change from earlier eras when a blue-collar job often provided a high school graduate with enough income for a comfortable middle-class lifestyle. Today, college graduates have skills that are much in demand in the so-called "knowledge economy," which means they receive an excellent return on their investment in higher education. But not all high school graduates feel they can afford that investment.

In the United States, post-secondary education is generally obtained at the expense of the individual student. There is a common belief that scholarships, loans, and grants make college affordable for everyone who really wants to go, but that notion stretches the truth. Students from higher-income backgrounds find the expense, including debt financing, easier to bear than those from poorer backgrounds. It has been estimated that in the early 1970s, it cost a low-income family 42 percent of its annual income to send a child to a public university; 30 years later, the cost had risen to nearly 60 percent (Haveman and Smeeding 2006, 137). Financial aid to needy college applicants has not kept pace with rising costs. Pell grants, the main type of federal assistance to low-income students, have shrunk in relation to total college costs. In 1976–1977, they covered 72 percent of average costs at a four-year college; by 2005, they covered only 34 percent (Draut 2005, 93). Colleges and universities themselves, as well as state governments, are making it harder for needy families to cover higher education costs by shifting need-based aid dollars into the status-enhancing category of merit-based financial assistance. High-SES applicants, who have had the benefit of high-quality public (or private) schools, summer science camps, stimulating travel, and expensive SAT prep courses, tend to receive most of the merit awards (Draut 2005, 93–94).

These cost factors are contributing to a widening "college gap" in the United States. In 1980–1982, 29 percent of the bottom income quartile of high school graduates went on to a four-year college, while 55 percent of the top quartile did so. By 1992, the bottom quartile figure had slipped to 28 percent, while the top quartile figure had climbed to 66 percent. Thus, the attendance gap had widened from 26 to 38 percent in just 10 years (Haveman and Smeeding 2006, 129–130). Viewed from the perspective of the nation's most selective colleges and universities, an even wider attendance gap has been reported: only 3 percent of students at those institutions come from the lowest income quartile, while nearly three-quarters are from the top quartile (Carnevale and Rose 2004, 106).

Policy analysts have come up with several solutions for the problem of unequal college access. First, put more resources into compensatory education at all levels from pre-K through high school; eventually, this should give lower-SES 12th-graders a fairer crack at college admission. Second, channel more federal aid to economically disadvantaged college students. The Pell grants, already mentioned, need more funding. The Hope and Lifetime Learning credits introduced in the 1990s could be made refundable so that their full benefits are available not just to families in higher tax brackets but also to those in the lowest brackets. Currently nonrefundable, these credits of as much as $2,000 a year are of little or no value to families with such low incomes that they owe no federal income taxes. Third, get colleges themselves to implement "economic affirmative action" in dealing with lower-SES applicants. Several universities have already moved in this direction, including the Universities of Florida, Washington, and California (Kahlenberg 2003, 2).

Less-advantaged students wanting to get into any of the nation's top colleges today face fierce competition for limited slots.

Tamara Draut, director of the Economic Opportunity Program at the think tank Demos, explains why: "As the spoils of our economy are increasingly spread among only a small group of top performers, getting into the winner's circle from the outset is imperative" (Draut 2005, 97–98). Unless we want the winner's circle in higher education closed to all but high-SES "insiders" who have enjoyed every advantage from infancy onward, our top schools—the ones serving as "gatekeepers" to the top jobs—will have to find ways to reach out to disadvantaged but high-potential applicants. Need-blind admissions policies have long been adopted at Ivy League schools and other premier colleges, yet low-income students are still grossly underrepresented. Devising creative ways to recruit and retain the brightest of these students is a continuing challenge.

Working on the Labor Market

The income inequality seen in the United States, insofar as it reflects an underlying wage inequality, arises chiefly from the fact that too many people are employed at low wages, and wage earners at the top are outdistancing those at every lower rung of the ladder. This awkward pattern does not prove that U.S. labor markets don't work; rather, it shows that they are responding to underlying forces that happen to be pushing them strongly in the direction of inequality. Those forces of technology, demography, custom, and political power act through supply and demand to yield a wage pattern that some find acceptable and others unacceptable, or at least worrisome. If the pattern is considered unsatisfactory, steps can be taken to modify it. In the next few sections, we consider a variety of policies that have the potential to alter the U.S. wage distribution over time.

One policy that can be taken off the table for now is the federal minimum wage. As noted earlier, the U.S. minimum wage has been cited as a contributor to growing wage inequality in the United States since its purchasing power has been allowed to drop for lengthy periods of time, including the decade following the increase of 1996. Given the minimum wage's role as an anchor wage, to which various other wage rates are attached or adjusted, the sinking of the real (inflation-adjusted) minimum wage over time may have exerted downward pressure across the entire lower end of the wage scale. The raising of the minimum wage in the spring of 2007, now set to reach $7.25 by 2009, probably removes this policy from further consideration until the mid-term election year of 2010, at the earliest. Proponents may work at the state level to keep lifting state minimum wages, but, barring an unexpected surge of inflation, the federal wage floor will not be looked at again for a number of years.

The Living Wage as a Boost to Low Wages

Frustration with the provisions of the federal and state minimum wage laws has sparked a movement across the United States to ensure that workers at city and county levels get paid a so-called living wage. The city of Baltimore passed the first living wage ordinance in 1994. It required that any private contractor doing business with the city pay its workers a minimum of $6.60 by 1996 (this at a time when the federal minimum wage was $4.25) and lift the minimum in stages to $7.70 by 1999. After 1999, the Baltimore living wage was to be adjusted annually in line with inflation. Other cities that have enacted similar legislation include Boston, St. Louis, Milwaukee, Detroit, San Francisco, Los Angeles, and at least 130 others. Dozens of campaigns are underway to extend the list (Gertner 2006, 39–42; Pollin and Luce 2000).

Living wage ordinances typically affect only a fraction of the workers in a city, namely, those employed by private firms doing business with the city or receiving financial assistance from it. The actual wage level varies from place to place, depending on the local cost of living and whether the contractor covers health benefits. A typical case is Manchester, Connecticut, which adopted a living wage ordinance in the spring of 2006. It applies to companies employing 25 or more workers and having service contracts of at least $25,000 with the city or receiving tax benefits of that amount. The wage is set at $11.06 an hour if health benefits are provided and $14 an hour if they are not (Living Wage Resource Center 2006). More ambitious living wage campaigns have attempted to extend wage floors to *all* workers in a given city. Santa Fe, New Mexico, is perhaps the best-known example. In 2002, the city passed a standard-issue living wage ordinance, but the next year, after huge controversy, it extended the city-wide wage floor to all firms employing 25 or more workers. By 2008, all Santa Fe employees will earn $10.50 an hour or more. A ballot measure to establish a similar wage floor in nearby Albuquerque, however, was defeated in 2005 (Gertner 2006, 62, 68, 72).

Opponents of living wage ordinances muster some of the same arguments against it as those used against the federal minimum wage: jobs will be lost, low-skill workers will be hurt the most, and there are more effective ways to reduce poverty and income inequality. They can make one additional argument that does not apply at the federal level: living wages, being local, can put businesses at a competitive disadvantage vis-à-vis other localities that have not passed such laws. So far, there is little evidence to support such a prospect. In general, the living wage appears to be delivering what its supporters promise. Two leading students of the economics of living wages, Scott Adams and David Neumark, of the Universities of Wisconsin and California, respectively, have looked at impact data for 1996–2002. They conclude that living wage laws raise the wages of low-wage workers but cost some jobs at the low-skill end; overall, these laws tend to cut urban poverty (Adams and Neumark 2005).

Stronger Unions as a Means to Lift Low Wages

Unionized workers in low-wage labor markets earn, on average, 28 percent higher wages than non-union workers (see above). If unions have a demonstrated capacity for boosting wages through collective bargaining, a prolonged decline in union density (less than 10 percent of the private sector is now unionized) is likely to place downward pressure on wage rates. Indeed, one of the reasons for the emergence of the living wage movement just discussed was the weakening and disappearance of the unions to which municipal workers once belonged. With the outsourcing of many city services to non-union private firms, workers found themselves earning wages inadequate to support their families.

There is no simple remedy for deunionization. It is a 50-year trend in the United States, driven by technological, political, and institutional forces. But one authority on labor economics, Harvard's Richard Freeman, believes that a turnaround in union membership, to 20 or 30 percent of private sector employment, would result in "a huge increase in pay and benefits at the bottom of the [income] distribution" (Freeman 1997). Even if Freeman is wrong, or overly optimistic, about the direct impact of higher union density on worker compensation, there could be significant indirect gains from union growth. Politically, a stronger labor movement might become a powerful ally of lawmakers trying to increase the frequency and size of minimum wage adjustments. It might also wield greater influence over future tax policy changes; in recent years, those changes have been skewed toward the high end of the income distribution.

For the labor movement to reverse its downward slide, there may need to be legal changes making it easier for workers to form a union. It is no secret that most employers actively oppose the introduction of unions. Wal-Mart is a famous example of a huge corporation that has consistently fended off all attempts to get its employees organized. In many workplaces, employees face delaying tactics, harassment, intimidation, and loss of their jobs when they try to gain union recognition. Companies have significant advantages in these confrontations, not least of which is the fact that labor law has been interpreted and enforced in employer-friendly ways since the 1980s. About one-third of the non-union workers in the United States would like to join a union, according to a 1994 poll. Why don't they? Because, according to the same poll, upwards of 40 percent fear that if they try to organize, they will lose their jobs (Pollin and Luce 2000, 189–190).

Earned Income Tax Credit

A program designed to bolster the wages of low-paid working Americans is the Earned Income Tax Credit (EITC), also known by the simpler term Earned Income Credit. It is a poverty-reducing measure that has had support from liberals and conservatives, Democrats and Republicans, since its passage in 1975. Only low-income workers are eligible for this refundable credit, and the size of one's refund depends on hours worked, total earned income, and family structure. The EITC is essentially a federal wage subsidy. Conservatives like it because it rewards work effort and cannot be confused with welfare. Liberals like it because it targets low-income people, especially low-income families. Both sides understand that it is an expensive program, with an annual price tag of roughly $40 billion, but presidents of both parties have helped lift the benefit rates from their initially low levels in 1975. At the same time that it reduces poverty, the EITC has an added benefit: it helps narrow the gap between rich and poor in the United States.

The mechanics of the EITC are fairly straightforward. Consider a family with two dependent children in 2006. (The same numbers would apply with any higher number of children.) On annual earnings up to $11,340, the EITC gives the worker a 40 percent refund, so if he or she earns, say, $8,000, a refund of $3,200 will be available. As earned income increases from $11,340 to $14,810, the EITC remains constant at its maximum amount, $4,536 (40 percent of $11,340). If the worker pushes earnings above the level of $14,810, the tax credit begins to decline from its maximum. For each additional dollar that is earned, 21 cents is deducted from the maximum benefit. If earned income reaches $36,348, the worker will be fully phased out, that is, the EITC will drop to zero. Why does there have to be a phase-out range of incomes in which extra dollars earned bring a reduction in the tax credit? Simply because without such phasing out everyone, from the poorest worker to the highest-paid, would be collecting EITC—a budget-busting, nonsensical situation.

Federal EITC income can be supplemented in about 20 states by state-level EITCs that offer qualified workers a refundable credit on their state income taxes, ranging from 5 percent to as much as 30 percent of the federal EITC. For example, in New York State, an individual who qualifies for a $1,000 federal refund can apply for an additional $300 from the state. A low-paid New York worker, in other words, can have wage income boosted by 52 percent—40 percent federal plus 12 percent New York—in the phase-in range.

In the majority of states, workers have only the federal EITC, but when $40 billion (plus billions more in state-level tax credits) are transferred from taxpayers in general to low-income workers, there has to be some equalizing impact on the U.S. income distribution. Presumably, if the EITC keeps getting made more generous, the impact will become even larger. There are a few policy downsides with the EITC, however. It is less generous to low-income workers with only one child and markedly less so to those with no children. Also, there is a distinct possibility that employers, mindful of the EITC, may be paying their employees less than they otherwise would, knowing that the tax credit will boost a low wage. And perhaps most seriously, there is the unavoidable fact that once a worker reaches a high enough wage income to start phasing out of the EITC, the program switches from being an incentive to a *dis*incentive to work, that is, it puts a marginal penalty on work effort of at least 21 percent (Schiller 2003, 266–269).

Limits on CEO Pay

The facts on chief executive officer (CEO) compensation in the United States have already been sketched in chapter 1, where it was noted that CEO pay at the biggest U.S. corporations is now about 250 times the pay of an average worker. This top-to-middle ratio was only one-tenth as large in 1965, and it greatly exceeds what is common in the rest of the industrialized world. But there are even more impressive numbers to illustrate high compensation at U.S. companies. Pay levels in the hedge fund industry in 2006, when announced in April 2007, made headlines around the world. In a listing of the top 25 hedge fund earners, the *lowest*-paid individual took home $240 million. The top three each earned at least $1 billion in a single year (Anderson and Creswell 2007, A1). Clearly the phenomenon of the highly compensated manager-executive contributes to overall income inequality in the United States, although top salaries in other parts of our "winner-take-all" society—sports, entertainment, law—have also rocketed to new heights in recent decades. The policy question is whether something should be done about it.

Logically, the gap between the rich and poor could be narrowed by raising the bottom (poor), lowering the top (rich), or some combination of the two. Liberals and progressives, with their strong dislike of inequality, would like to pull both extremes toward the middle. Conservatives, with their fundamental faith in the outcomes delivered by the free market, would leave things as they are. Capping CEO pay at some agreed-upon level is a top-reducing strategy that would partially satisfy liberals, though probably less than boosting low-end wages or incomes. It would be furiously opposed by the business community and conservatives. That no one has yet put this forward as a serious proposal is surely due to the fact that no one knows what the "right" level of compensation for a top executive should be. In theory, CEOs, like all employees, are paid an amount that reflects what they are worth to the company that employs them. In practice, CEO compensation is set by subcommittees of boards of directors, often composed of individuals who themselves were appointed by the CEO. Such personal ties can fortify CEO paydays (Larcker et al. 2005).

CEO compensation packages generally consist of base salary, bonus, perks, and stock options. The huge compensation amounts reported for some CEOs are nearly always dominated by the value of stock options, and that is exactly the point: corporate boards like to align their top managers' personal financial interests with those of the company and its stockholders. When the company prospers, so do the stockholders—and so does the CEO. Few would quarrel with this arrangement. But the record shows that many CEOs receive vast stock grants, options, and golden parachutes even when their companies perform poorly. Rank-and-file workers are rarely treated so kindly when company fortunes falter.

Although direct regulation of CEO pay is not on the legislative agenda, increasing attention is being given to pay at the top. Investor activists now regularly propose limits on CEO pay at stockholder meetings. Institutional investors, such as pension funds and mutual funds, are weighing in on the side of moderated executive compensation. Legislation to give shareholders some input or a "say on pay," rather than leaving compensation decisions entirely to boards of directors, was overwhelmingly approved by the U.S. House of Representatives in April 2007, though it faced uncertain prospects in the Senate and a veto at the White House if it ever got that far. One U.S. corporation, the insurer AFLAC, has adopted the shareholder "say on pay" idea voluntarily (Drawbaugh 2007); others may follow. In early 2007, the Securities and Exchange Commission announced that corporations would soon be required to disclose more clearly and fully the compensation of their top executives, including perks and stock options. Whether any of these actions will affect trends for CEO pay in the long run, or change institutional norms regarding such pay, is not yet apparent.

Immigrant Labor Supplies

A final labor market solution to the problem of a widening wage gap in the United States takes us back to the lower end of the distribution where, as noted before, the presence of large numbers of less-skilled immigrants puts downward pressure on wages. Two kinds of policies might relieve this pressure. First, the United States could legalize the undocumented workers currently in the country. (In what manner and on what schedule this would be done is a separate issue.) How might this boost low-end wages and thus reduce wage inequality? If we recognize that undocumented workers labor "in the shadows," where they are vulnerable to exploitation by employers, we can see that, in theory, the regularization of their status would free these workers to demand higher pay. Some labor unions already see undocumented workers as a pool of potential recruits. Probably for that reason, among others, the International Brotherhood of Teamsters, the Service Employees International Union (SEIU), and the Hotel Employees & Restaurant Employees International Union (HERE) have supported the legalization of undocumented immigrants.

The other immigration policy that might lift the lower end of the U.S. wage scale would be a restriction on further immigration by the low skilled. This would begin to reverse the pattern of recent decades when large numbers of immigrants, mainly from Mexico and other Latin American countries, have been unskilled. Even within the U.S. population of high school dropouts in 2000, immigrants came up short in terms of education—averaging only 6.9 years of school, compared to 9.7 years for U.S. native-born dropouts (Borjas 2003a, 247). Since their relative lack of human capital pushes so many immigrants to the low end of the U.S. job market, worsening income inequality, George Borjas has suggested one remedy: deny further immigration to persons lacking at least 10 years of education. This would deplete the numbers of immigrants in the lowest deciles of the wage distribution and, in his view, "drastically cut the number of low-income persons in the population" (Borjas 2003a, 250–251).

In the second term of George W. Bush's presidency, immigration reform became a contentious issue for Congress and the president. Not surprisingly, it got pinned down in a deadly crossfire of conflicting political interests. Both political parties recognized the need for reforming the system, but neither was internally unified on how to proceed. Questions of border security and amnesty for the estimated 12 million illegal aliens living in the country figured more prominently in the debate than any considerations of income inequality, although the latter issue was occasionally mentioned. The Senate bill that was the focus of debate featured a revision in the prioritizing of future visa applicants, making job skills a more important criterion and family ties less important. It was a slight shift in the Borjas policy direction.

Taxes and Transfer Payments

We have seen that inequality can be countered through measures aimed at boosting educational opportunities for disadvantaged youth, and also through labor market policies designed to make work more financially rewarding at the lower end (or less rewarding at the high end). With this assortment of tools at their disposal, policy makers, in theory, should be able to narrow the gap between rich and poor quite substantially. An additional set of policy tools—powerful, flexible, and simple to administer—can also be utilized to make the income distribution more equal. These are taxes and transfer payments. In a sense, taxes and transfers are the final means of modifying the pattern of incomes generated by market forces in our society.

When the government makes a monetary payment to an individual and asks for no goods or services in return, it is called a transfer payment. Examples include unemployment compensation, cash welfare, veterans' disability payments, and Social Security pensions. These kinds of payments tend to benefit people further down the income distribution more than those higher up. Therefore, if we wanted to make the income distribution more equal, one approach would be to increase transfer payments across the board. It would be essential, however, to fund the increased payments out of revenues raised from the affluent rather than from the kinds of people who typically receive transfer payments. Since this would not be the normal way of funding transfers, it would take an extraordinary change in the U.S. political climate to adopt such a policy.

Taxation offers a broader, more potent set of policy instruments than transfer payments for dealing with an issue like income inequality. The federal income tax is at the heart of the U.S. tax system. It imposes lower rates on those at the bottom of the income scale than on those at the top. In 2006, for example, single tax-filers with taxable incomes below $7,550 faced only a 10 percent marginal tax rate. At higher income levels, the marginal tax rates climbed to 15, 25, 28, 33, and 35 percent, with the 35 percent rate applying to all incomes above $336,550. On paper, then, the federal income tax is progressive, putting a heavier relative burden on those earning high incomes than on those earning low incomes. In the past, it probably did a better job of equalizing after-tax incomes, given that the marginal tax rates used to be much higher than they are today. The top marginal rate peaked during World War II at 94 percent, and as recently as 1971–1980, it was still 70 percent, twice the current rate (Tax Policy Center 2007).

The impact of the entire tax system on the distribution of incomes in the United States is a more complicated issue. There are other federal taxes to consider, especially the so-called payroll tax, and there are many state and local taxes on individuals as well. The payroll (FICA) tax, which pays for Social Security pensions, survivors' and disability benefits, and Medicare, has a regressive structure: its burden falls more heavily on low-income earners than on the well paid. In 2000, for example, it imposed an average 9.6 percent burden on households in the middle quintile; the burden on households in the top 1 percent was only 1.9 percent (Mishel, Bernstein, and Allegretto 2007, 70). For a majority of Americans, the FICA tax of 7.65 percent, when doubled to include the employer's share, is larger than their federal income tax liability. The overall impact of all taxes—federal, state, and local—on the populace of the United States is considered to be modestly progressive.

If we wanted to use the federal income tax to lessen income inequality, one way to do it would be to raise marginal tax rates at the upper end. Depending on the amount of the increase, this might roll back first the tax cuts of President George W. Bush and then those of President Ronald Reagan. Under Reagan, the top marginal rate was cut from 70 to 28 percent, while, after two other presidents, the top rate under Bush was cut from 39.6 to 35 percent (Tax Policy Center 2007). When the entire post-2001 Bush program of cuts in income, investment, and inheritance taxes is costed out, the largest tax savings by far have gone to those with the highest incomes. As of mid-2006, the average annual tax savings had been estimated at $63 per household in the bottom quintile, $363 in the second quintile, $665 in the middle quintile, and $1,113 in the fourth quintile. At the very top, tax savings to households in the top 1 percent are estimated to be $44,477 per year (Mishel, Bernstein, and Allegretto 2007, 75).

The other income-equalizing change that could be made to the federal income tax would be to cut tax rates and widen tax brackets at the lower end. If combined with hikes at the upper end, this would render the tax structure more progressive than it is today. Budget "hawks" might object that these changes would enlarge the federal budget deficit, but that need not happen. The changes could be calibrated so as to be revenue-neutral.

The payroll tax could also be adjusted to achieve greater after-tax income equality. The FICA tax rate itself could be lowered, although the resulting revenue losses would have to be recouped elsewhere to avoid damaging the already shaky long-term fiscal picture for Medicare and Social Security. Or there could be a change in the way the payroll tax is assessed. At present, the FICA tax is imposed on the very first dollars earned. That could be changed to exempt some initial amount of earnings from the tax, say, the first $5,000 or $10,000. Another modification of the payroll tax would be to lift the ceiling on taxable earnings. In 2006, the Social Security component of FICA (6.2 percent of the overall 7.65 percent tax) was assessed on only the first $94,000 of earnings. If the $94,000 ceiling were doubled, tripled, or simply removed, the payroll tax would become much less regressive. (The tax would also raise far more revenue and thus put off the day when Social Security runs out of money.)

We have looked at several ways to narrow the gap between rich and poor through modifications in the income and payroll tax structure. There is another, more radical way to use the income tax to reduce income inequality: adopt the negative income tax (NIT), as proposed by Milton Friedman more than 40 years ago. This NIT would use the existing income tax mechanism to channel funds—"negative taxes"—to those with incomes below a certain level. For example, if the line were drawn at $10,000 a year for a single person, and if Michael, a hypothetical taxpayer, had taxable income, from whatever sources, of only $4,000, the government would send him a check for some percentage of the $6,000 gap between his actual income and the official support level. With an NIT rate of 50 percent, his check from the government would be $3,000. Note: The NIT is not intended to fully close the gap between an individual's income and the support level. If it did that for Michael, he would have no incentive to earn more than $4,000, or indeed to earn anything at all up to $10,000 (Friedman 1962, 191–194). Like the EITC, the negative income tax offers a way to reduce poverty and income inequality. It could, however, be quite expensive unless, as in Friedman's original formulation, it replaced most other support programs. No politician since President Richard Nixon has seriously proposed the adoption of the NIT (Moffitt 2003).

Wealth and Estate Taxes

Because wealth is distributed so much more unevenly than income (see chapter 1), it would seem natural to consider the adoption of a wealth tax as a means to alleviate the rich-poor gap in the United States. Yet the nation has not so far adopted a broad tax on wealth comparable, in scope or revenues raised, to the federal income tax. The property taxes levied by counties and municipalities across the country are wealth taxes, of course, but they are a hodge-podge of uncoordinated local taxes of varying steepness, rarely designed to redistribute wealth. Their general impact is probably regressive rather than progressive, since much of the revenue is raised from seniors and farmers whose properties often have a value out of all proportion to their current income levels.

With a wealth tax, taxpayers must place a value on their real and financial properties and then pay a tax on the total value. Many European countries impose wealth taxes that could serve as models for the United States. Edward Wolff has studied some of them and simulated their effects if adopted in this country. His preference is for a Swiss-type wealth tax that would raise $55 billion of additional federal revenues each year. It would feature a $100,000 exclusion, with rising marginal tax rates on higher wealth amounts. For example, on household wealth between $100,000 and $200,000, the marginal tax rate would be 1/20 of 1 percent. For all amounts above $1 million, it would be 3/10 of 1 percent. Intermediate tax rates would apply to wealth amounts between $200,000 and $1 million. The same tax forms could be used by taxpayers for both their income and wealth taxes. Wolff concedes that there would be some risk of a disincentive to saving under such a wealth tax, but he believes it would be "very modest." And while he understands that a brand-new tax would not be popular, he notes that only 3 percent of U.S. families would see their combined income and wealth tax rise by more than 10 percent (Wolff 2002, 72–74).

One wealth tax that the federal government has imposed for most of the last century is the estate or inheritance tax. Historically this tax has been supported not so much because of the revenues it raises but because of the principle on which it rests: vast fortunes, if allowed to pass intact from one generation to the next, would endanger our democratic society. In the United States, the estate tax clearly operates in a progressive manner, since fewer than 1 percent of estates (those valued above $2 million) are subject to it. Under current law, the exemption rises to $3.5 million in 2009, the tax disappears completely in 2010, and in 2011 it comes back. The odd notion of a major tax making a return appearance the very year after its abolition tells us more about the political *legerdemain* needed to pass President Bush's 2001 tax bill than about the actual legislative preferences of Congress regarding the estate tax.

Some specific numbers gathered from the IRS by Citizens for Tax Justice (CTJ) help to clarify who pays the estate tax. In 2004, about 2.4 million Americans died, and of those, about 18,000 left a federal estate tax liability—fewer than 1 percent. The total amount collected by the government was almost $22 billion. Nearly two of every five dollars collected came from the 498 estates valued at over $20 million, and over half of the total revenue came from estates valued in excess of $10 million. Less than one-third of the tax revenue came from estates valued below $5 million. On paper, the top marginal tax rate was 48 percent in 2004, but in reality the actual estate tax burden on even the biggest estates (those over $20 million) averaged only 15.8 percent (CTJ 2007).

Support for the estate tax has come from those who worry about a growing concentration of wealth in the United States and who want to hold onto taxes that are clearly progressive. Opposition to the estate tax is found chiefly among Republicans, conservatives, businesspeople, and, of course, the wealthy (Gates and Collins 2003). Policy briefs in favor of its repeal have poured forth from think tanks on the right, that is, the Cato Institute, the Heritage Foundation, and the American Enterprise Institute. Opponents of the estate tax made a smart semantic move early on: they substituted the term "death tax" for estate tax. Who could be in favor of having tax collectors ringing the doorbells of the bereaved and demanding payment of a hefty proportion of the hard-earned savings of the deceased? Beyond semantics, the opponents of the estate tax have produced some serious arguments. They stress how crippling the estate tax is, or could be, to small business owners and family farmers. They point out that many countries around the world have no estate tax, including Canada, Australia, Sweden, and Switzerland. Of the countries that do impose this tax, most impose it at a lower rate than the United States. Perhaps the most compelling argument against the estate tax concerns economic efficiency: the extensive estate-planning and tax-avoidance activities engendered by the estate tax make this tax, ultimately, a very costly one. It is conceivable, in fact, that the efficiency losses from this tax exceed the revenues collected by the government, or so its opponents claim (Edwards 2006).

The saga of the federal estate tax is not over yet. It remains a ticking political time bomb. As the law now reads, the tax disappears in just a few years. But the following year it is reinstated, with the same high-end marginal rate (55 percent) and the same low exemptions as in 2001. An entire book has been written about the repeal campaign of 2001 (Graetz and Shapiro 2005). In a few years, when the upcoming battle over repeal versus reinstatement of the estate tax is over, there will no doubt be an audience for another book or two on the subject.

Asset-Building Policies

A new policy direction for dealing with economic inequality has slowly been gaining traction in the past decade and a half. It is grounded in a fundamental fact: financial assets are so unequally distributed in the United States, and passed on to succeeding generations so unequally, that young adults do not in any sense start out at the same point with the same advantages. This side of utopia, that of complete equality of opportunity, is unlikely to be realized, but there are ways we could do a better job of living up to that high standard. The history of the United States provides examples of bold national initiatives to broaden economic opportunity. The Homestead Act of 1862 offered up to 160 acres of land at no cost to anyone willing to settle on it, and the GI Bill of 1944 gave millions of returning veterans a chance to further their educations at government expense. In both cases, policies aimed at building up assets—whether productive land or human capital—left a legacy of expanded opportunity for millions of Americans. At a time when both political parties are searching for new ideas to address intractable problems of inequality and poverty, asset-based policies may soon be in the limelight.

Probably the boldest asset-based proposal to date is the one from Yale law professors Bruce Ackerman and Anne Alstott to provide every American, on reaching the age of 21, with a one-time "stakeholder grant" of $80,000. The money could be used to buy a house, pay off college loans, enter a trade, start up a small business, or do whatever the individual wanted, even if it were foolish. Ackerman and Alstott doubt that many would waste their stake, partly because high school graduation would be a prerequisite to receiving the money. (They envision new high school classes that would build up teenagers' financial literacy.) The price tag on this program would be about $255 billion, to be financed by an annual 2 percent wealth tax. At the end of life, those who could (or whose estates could) bear the cost would be expected to repay the original $80,000 plus interest. It would seem a near-certainty that this proposal, if enacted, would reduce the U.S. wealth gap considerably. Its rationale, however, is not so much to change a Gini coefficient as to provide each young American with "the wherewithal needed to pursue happiness on his or her own terms" (Ackerman and Alstott 1999, 13, 28, 34–41).

A less radical asset-building program that has already been implemented in localities across the United States is the individual development account (IDA). The program has its origins in the groundbreaking ideas of Michael Sherraden, a social policy analyst at Washington University (Sherraden 1991). An IDA is a savings account that permits a low-income individual to save up for educational costs, a down payment on a first house, the start-up of a business, or even retirement, with each dollar of savings getting matched by public or private funds, sometimes in ratios as favorable as 2:1. The idea is to motivate asset-accumulation among those who have traditionally been thought unable or unwilling to save but who, experience now shows convincingly, can do so on a regular basis. IDA programs have been set up in more than 40 states, and federal legislation to bolster funding for the program has had the support of both President Clinton and President Bush. The Savings for Working Families Act, aimed at adding almost a million people to the roughly 50,000 who now participate in IDAs, has been introduced for several years in Congress and still awaits passage.

An asset-building proposal that combines elements of the stakeholder grant and the IDA is the children's savings account, seeded with an initial deposit of, say, $500 provided by the government. For low-income children, an extra $500 might be deposited at birth. Until the child turned 18, additional deposits could be made to the account by parents, relatives, or the child, and those deposits might be matched by the government in some predetermined ratio. At age 18, the young adult would gain access to the accumulated funds but only for approved uses, such as education, a down payment on a house, or investment in a retirement fund. This policy proposal has been developed by the New America Foundation, a Washington, D.C.-based think tank, and a version of the proposal has been adopted in Great Britain, where it is known as the Child Trust Fund. A "Kids Account" plan was introduced into the California legislature in early 2007, where it ran into strong political headwinds and did not pass. Versions of the proposal have also been introduced into both the U.S. Senate and House, where the bill is known as the America Saving for Personal Investment, Retirement, and Education (ASPIRE) Act (Boshara, Cramer, and Parrish 2005, 3). The ASPIRE Act has not yet been put up for debate on the floor of either house.

What these three initiatives and many others like them have in common is the principle that families with financial assets make better, more confident choices about education, employment, saving, and retirement. People with assets have a stake in the future of their community and their nation. They have an interest in better understanding how credit works, how compound interest can multiply savings, and how rainy-day funds can sometimes make the difference between temporary hardship and financial collapse. Asset-building programs appeal to liberals with the promise of lifting up the disadvantaged and perhaps, over time, narrowing the gap between rich and poor. They appeal to conservatives as well, since they emphasize thrift, ownership, and personal responsibility. In most configurations, they do not involve massive redistributions of wealth, yet the funding flows that they entail are generally in a progressive direction, toward those at the lower end of the scale. Although some asset-building ideas, like the IDAs, have been implemented, many remain to be acted upon at all levels of government.

Summary

A considerable part of the widening U.S. income gap can be attributed to a widening *wage* gap. Some workers have much more human capital than others, and they have been in high demand given the nature of technological change in our society. Low-end workers, with low levels of human capital, are getting less wage protection from labor unions than in former times, and to make matters worse, they are facing stiffer competition from low-skilled immigrants. Meanwhile, they are also getting little help from minimum wage legislation. To boost wages at the lower end, some have recommended: programs to improve the educational opportunities of the disadvantaged; steps to strengthen labor unions; more restrictive immigration policies; and a more generous funding of the EITC program. At the upper end, it has been proposed that caps or other kinds of limitations be placed on CEO compensation. Beyond these labor-market changes, there have been proposals to help low-income families build up their assets. Certain tax changes could also moderate the inequality trend, whether through easing of taxes on poorer individuals or raising tax rates on high-end wealth and incomes.

References

Ackerman, Bruce, and Anne Alstott. *The Stakeholder Society.* New Haven: Yale University Press, 1999.

Adams, Scott, and David Neumark. "Living Wage Effects: New and Improved Evidence." *Economic Development Quarterly* 19, no. 1 (February 2005): 80–102.

Anderson, Jenny, and Julie Creswell. "Make Less Than $240 Million? You're Off Top Hedge Fund List." *The New York Times* (April 24, 2007): A1.

Autor, David H., Lawrence F. Katz, and Melissa S. Kearney. "The Polarization of the U.S. Labor Market." *NBER Working Paper No. 11986.* Cambridge, MA: National Bureau of Economic Research, 2006.

Bernanke, Ben. "Questions and Answers with Chairman Bernanke." Washington, D.C.: U.S. House Committee on Financial Services, February 15, 2006. Accessed at http://financialservices.house.gov.

Bernstein, Jared, and Isaac Shapiro. "Buying Power of Minimum Wage at 50-Year Low." Washington, DC: Center on Budget and Policy Priorities, and Economic Policy Institute, June 20, 2006. Accessed at http://www.cbpp.org.

Borjas, George J. "Comment," in Heckman and Krueger, 2003a: 241–251.

Borjas, George J. *Heaven's Door: Immigration Policy and the American Economy.* Princeton, NJ: Princeton University Press, 1999.

Borjas, George J. "The Labor Demand Curve Is Downward-Sloping: Reexamining the Impact of Immigration on the Labor Market." *Quarterly Journal of Economics* 118, no. 4 (November 2003b): 1335–1374.

Boshara, Ray, Reid Cramer, and Leslie Parrish. "Policy Options for Achieving an Ownership Society for All Americans." New America Foundation, Asset Building Program, Issue Brief #8 (February 2005).

Burtless, Gary. "Has Widening Inequality Promoted or Retarded U.S. Growth?" *Canadian Public Policy* 29 (January 2003 supplement): 185–202.

Carnevale, Anthony, and Stephen J. Rose. "Socioeconomic Status, Race/ Ethnicity, and Selective College Admissions," in Richard D. Kahlenberg, ed., *America's Untapped Resource: Low-Income Students in Higher Education.* New York: The Century Foundation Press, 2004.

Child Trends. "Carolina Abecedarian Program." Online information sheet (2007). Accessed at http://www.childtrends.org.

Citizens for Tax Justice. "Who Paid the Federal Estate Tax in 2005?" January 10, 2007. Accessed at http://www.ctj.org.

Corcoran, Sean, et al. "The Changing Distribution of Education Finance, 1972 to 1997," in Neckerman 2004: 433–465.

Crane, Jonathan, ed. *Social Programs That Work.* New York: Russell Sage Foundation, 1998.

Currie, Janet. "Early Childhood Education Programs." *Journal of Economic Perspectives* 15, no. 2 (Spring 2001): 213–238.

Danziger, Sheldon, and Peter Gottschalk. *Diverging Fortunes: Trends in Poverty and Inequality.* New York: Russell Sage Foundation, and Washington, DC: Population Reference Bureau, 2004.

Draut, Tamara. "The Growing College Gap," in James Lardner and David A. Smith, eds., *Inequality Matters: The Growing Economic Divide in America and Its Poisonous Consequences.* New York: The New Press, 2005: 89–101.

Drawbaugh, Kevin. "House Approves 'Say on Pay' for Shareholders." April 20, 2007. Accessed at http://www.earthtimes.org.

Edwards, Chris. "Repealing the Federal Estate Tax." *Tax & Budget Bulletin* 36 (June 2006). Washington, DC: Cato Institute.

Frank, Robert H., and Philip J. Cook. *The Winner-Take-All Society: Why the Few at the Top Get So Much More Than the Rest of Us.* New York: The Free Press, 1995.

Freeman, Richard. "Solving the New Inequality." *Boston Review* 21, no. 6 (December 1996–January 1997): 3–10.

Friedman, Milton. *Capitalism and Freedom.* Chicago: University of Chicago Press, 1962.

Gates, William H., Sr., and Chuck Collins. *Wealth and Our Commonwealth: Why America Should Tax Accumulated Fortunes.* Boston: Beacon Press, 2003.

Gertner, Jon. "What Is a Living Wage?" *The New York Times Magazine* (January 15, 2006): 38–45, 68, 72.

Gilbert, Geoffrey. *World Poverty: A Reference Handbook.* Santa Barbara, CA: ABC-CLIO, 2004.

Goldin, Claudia, and Lawrence F. Katz. "Decreasing (and Then Increasing) Inequality in America: A Tale of Two Half-Centuries," in Finis Welch, ed., *The Causes and Consequences of Increasing Inequality.* Chicago: University of Chicago Press, 2001: 37–82.

Graetz, Michael J., and Ian Shapiro. *Death by a Thousand Cuts: The Fight over Taxing Inherited Wealth.* Princeton, NJ: Princeton University Press, 2005.

Hart, Katherine, and Rachel Schumacher. "Making the Case: Improving Head Start Teacher Qualifications Requires Increased Investment." Center for Law and Social Policy, Policy Paper 1 (July 2005), Head Start Series.

Haveman, Robert, and Timothy Smeeding. "The Role of Higher Education in Social Mobility." *The Future of Children* 16, no. 2 (Fall 2006): 125–150.

Heckman, James J. "Catch 'em Young." *The Wall Street Journal* (January 10, 2006): A14.

Heckman, James J., and Alan B. Krueger. *Inequality in America: What Role for Human Capital Policies?* Cambridge, MA: MIT Press, 2003.

Hodgkinson, Mark. "Sharapova Looks Unbeatable in the Money Stakes." *Telegraph.co.uk* (August 17, 2006).

Howell, David R. "Do Surges in Less-Skilled Immigration Have Important Wage Effects?" in *Border Battles: The U.S. Immigration Debates.* Social Science Research Council Report. March 8, 2007. Accessed at http://borderbattles.ssrc.org.

Kahlenberg, Richard D. "Economic Affirmative Action in College Admissions." Century Foundation Issue Brief (April 2, 2003). Accessed at http://www.tcf.org.

Kahlenberg, Richard D. "A New Way on School Integration: An Update." Century Foundation Issue Brief (November 27, 2006). Accessed at http://www.tcf.org.

Kozol, Jonathan. *Savage Inequalities: Children in America's Schools.* New York: Crown Publishers, 1991.

Krugman, Paul. "Divided over Trade." *The New York Times* (May 14, 2007): A19.

Larcker, David, et al. "Back Door Links between Directors and Executive Compensation." Knowledge@Wharton (February 26, 2005). Accessed at http://knowledge.wharton.upenn.edu.

Lee, David S. "Wage Inequality in the United States during the 1980s: Rising Dispersion or Falling Minimum Wage?" *Quarterly Journal of Economics* 114, no. 3 (August 1999): 977–1023.

Levy, Frank, and Richard J. Murnane. *The New Division of Labor: How Computers Are Creating the Next Job Market.* New York: Russell Sage Foundation, and Princeton, N.J.: Princeton University Press, 2004.

Living Wage Resource Center. "City and County Campaigns." (May 2006). Accessed at http://www.livingwagecampaign.org.

Marshall, Alfred. *Principles of Economics.* 9th ed. New York: Macmillan, 1961 [1890].

Martin, Philip, and Elizabeth Midgley. "Immigration: Shaping and Reshaping America," rev. 2nd ed. *Population Bulletin* 61, no. 4 (December 2006).

Mill, John Stuart. *Principles of Political Economy.* New York: A. M. Kelley, in Reprints of Economic Classics series, 1999 [1848].

Mishel, Lawrence, Jared Bernstein, and Sylvia Allegretto. *The State of Working America 2006/2007.* Ithaca, NY: Cornell University Press, 2007.

Moffitt, Robert A. "The Negative Income Tax and the Evolution of U.S. Welfare Policy." *Journal of Economic Perspectives* 17, no. 3 (Summer 2003): 119–140.

Neckerman, Kathryn M., ed. *Social Inequality.* New York: Russell Sage Foundation, 2004.

Paul, Annie Murphy. "The Real Marriage Penalty." *The New York Times* (November 19, 2006): L22.

Pollin, Robert, and Stephanie Luce. *The Living Wage: Building a Fair Economy.* Rev. ed. New York: The New Press, 2000.

Reich, Robert. *The Work of Nations: Preparing Ourselves for 21st-Century Capitalism.* New York: A. A. Knopf, 1991.

Rouse, Cecilia Elena, and Lisa Barrow. "U.S. Elementary and Secondary Schools: Equalizing Opportunity or Replicating the Status Quo?" *The Future of Children* 16, no. 2 (Fall 2006): 99–123.

Schiller, Bradley. *The Economics of Poverty and Discrimination,* 9th ed. Upper Saddle River, NJ: Pearson Prentice Hall, 2003.

Schweinhart, Lawrence J., et al. *Lifetime Effects: The High/Scope Perry Preschool Project through Age 40.* Ypsilanti, MI: High/Scope Press, 2005.

Sherraden, Michael. *Assets and the Poor: A New American Welfare Policy.* Armonk, NY: M.E. Sharpe, Inc., 1991.

Tax Policy Center. "Historical Top Tax Rate." (2007). Accessed at http://www.taxpolicycenter.org.

U.S. Census Bureau. "Income, Poverty, and Health Insurance Coverage in the United States: 2005." *Current Population Reports: Consumer Income (P60–231)*, August 2006. Accessed at http://www.census.gov.

U.S. Congress. Public Law 107–110: "No Child Left Behind Act of 2001." January 8, 2002.

U.S. Department of Labor. "Union Members in 2006." Washington, DC: Bureau of Labor Statistics news release (January 25, 2007). Accessed at http://www.bls.gov.

Wolff, Edward N. *Top Heavy: The Increasing Inequality of Wealth in America and What Can Be Done about It.* New York: The New Press, 2002.

3

Worldwide Perspective

The widening gap between rich and poor seen in the United States in recent decades prompts a number of larger questions: Is economic divergence a trend peculiar to the United States, or is it part of a global pattern? Is the economic growth of the world's richer countries moving them ahead at a pace that leaves the poorer countries farther and farther behind? And on the related issue of *mobility*, does the United States lead the world—as Americans like to think it does—in the opportunity it offers its poor to rise to a higher rung on the economic ladder? These are a few of the important questions addressed in this chapter. The premise on which we proceed is that American trends are better understood when placed in a worldwide context. The forces driving U.S. inequality, after all, can hardly be unique to this country; in greater or smaller measure, they are undoubtedly being felt in many other parts of the world.

A World of Contrasts

Not unlike the gulf that separates low-income from high-income Americans, an economic, demographic, and educational gulf separates the world's poorest nations from its richest. Reams of statistics pour forth from the United Nations every year that enable us to document the dimensions along which global inequality is defined. In 2005, for example, the per capita incomes of 19 East African countries averaged $1,090, while the comparable figure for northern and western European countries was 28 times higher, and for the United States, 38 times higher (PRB, 2006).

One of the standard measures of absolute poverty employed by international agencies is the percentage of a country's population living on less than $2 per day. For the world's richest nations, that statistic is too small even to be reported, but elsewhere the picture is far different. In Asia, four of every five residents of India and Bangladesh, and three of every four Pakistanis—a total of 1.1 billion people on the subcontinent—subsist on less than $2 a day. In South America, two of every five Bolivians and Ecuadorians live on less than $2 a day. On the continent of Africa, home to more than 900 million people, fully two-thirds of the population fail to meet the $2 a day standard (PRB 2006).

Money is not the only gauge of cross-national differences in well-being, nor is it necessarily the most meaningful one. For confirmation of the enormous gap dividing the world's richest nations from its poorest, we can look to several alternative indices of material well-being: infant mortality rates, births attended by skilled health personnel, tuberculosis (TB) cases per 100,000 people, and the percentage of the population with access to clean water and sanitation. Worldwide infant mortality rates vary from around 4 per thousand in Western Europe to 102 per thousand in Western Africa. The West African nation of Sierra Leone has the world's highest rate, 163, which gives a newborn there a one-in-six chance of dying before her first birthday (PRB 2006). Virtually all births in Western Europe, North America, and Japan are attended by skilled health personnel. Such attendance falls to levels as low as 24 percent in Haiti, 16 percent in Niger, and 6 percent in Ethiopia (UNDP 2005, 236–239). The national incidence of tuberculosis correlates imperfectly but fairly strongly with economic status: rich nations like Norway, Australia, Canada, and the United States have rates in the single digits per 100,000 people, while poor nations in Asia and Africa can have rates 100 times higher. Cambodia and Congo, for example, have TB rates of 742 and 489 per 100,000, respectively (UNDP 2005, 246–249). Access to clean water and improved sanitation can spare adults and especially infants from deadly encounters with diarrhea, cholera, and other water-borne diseases. In the wealthy countries, access to improved sanitation and safe water supplies is universal. Among the poorer countries, such access is much more limited. Angola is not atypical, with only 50 percent of its population having access to an "improved water source" and 30 percent having access to "improved sanitation" (UNDP 2005, 240–243).

It does not minimize in any way the hardships of poor Americans to suggest that their material deprivations are of a different order of magnitude from what the poorest people on the planet experience. At the lower end of the U.S. wealth and income distribution, one finds economic insecurity, substandard housing, limited access to health care, and other manifestations of poverty that trouble the national conscience. At the lower end of the *world* distribution of wealth, one encounters life-threatening malnutrition, AIDS, malaria, tuberculosis, and life expectancies that are decades shorter than what is seen in Europe and North America. It is worth noting that the Millennium Development Goals adopted by the United Nations in 2000 do not call explicitly for reductions in wealth inequality either within or across nations. They do, however, call for the eradication of "extreme poverty and hunger," including a 50 percent reduction, by the year 2015, in the proportion of the world's population living on less than $1 a day (Gilbert 2004, 153). The United States, home to millions who are defined as poor by our government's standard, is expected to be a funding source for international poverty-reduction efforts, not a target of such efforts.

National Rates of Income Inequality

Economists have developed many statistical measures of income inequality. The most widely employed is the Gini coefficient or index. As noted in chapter 1, this coefficient can take on values anywhere from zero, indicating complete equality, to 100, indicating complete inequality. In the real world, the lowest Gini value seen in recent years has been 25. Five nations can claim that lofty degree of income equality: Belgium, the Czech Republic, Denmark, Japan, and Sweden. It is worth noting that all five are wealthy, industrialized countries. At the other extreme, one finds the world's highest Gini coefficients, and thus the widest gaps between rich and poor, in sub-Saharan Africa, with Namibia at 71 and Botswana, Lesotho, and Sierra Leone all at 63.

In its annual *Human Development Report,* the United Nations supplements the Gini index for each country with two ratio measures of inequality. One is the ratio of the income received by the richest 10 percent of a country's population to the income received by the poorest 10 percent; the other is the ratio of the top to the bottom 20 percent. Let us consider just the first ratio. The five countries rated most equal in the world according to the Gini index have top-to-bottom 10 percent ratios between 4.5 (Japan) and 8.1 (Denmark). Indeed, the majority of the 57 nations judged to have "high human development" by the United Nations have ratios under 10. At the other end of the spectrum, the four nations with the highest Gini indices and thus the worst inequality in the world—Namibia, Botswana, Lesotho, and Sierra Leone—also have among the highest ratios of top-to-bottom 10 percent income shares. These ratios range from 77.6 (Botswana) to 129 (Namibia). It is difficult to fathom how, in one of the world's poorest countries, the richest tenth of the population can command more than 100 times the income of the poorest tenth (UNDP 2005, 270–273).

There is no comprehensive theory to explain the wide variations of income inequality found across the globe. Politics, history, economic development, culture—all of these surely play a role, as do other factors. Even geography can be telling: the world's most unequal nations, as it happens, are found mainly in Latin America and sub-Saharan Africa (UNDP 2005, 270–273). That is among the few generalizations that can be made on this issue. One other is the following: countries judged to exhibit high "human development" by the United Nations tend to have more equal distributions of income than countries judged to exhibit only medium or low human development. The human development index (HDI) is a composite index of national well-being that incorporates measures of education effort, adult literacy, life expectancy, and per capita income. Income distribution is not explicitly factored into the HDI, yet the HDI seems to correlate fairly well with income distribution. Each of the top 20 high human development countries but one (the United States) has a Gini below 40, and three-quarters of the lowest-ranked countries in the "low human development" category have Gini coefficients above 40. Social and economic development appears to push nations, although not uniformly, toward income equality (UNDP 2005, 214–217, 270–273).

The placement of the United States in the global inequality rankings is anomalous. Its Gini coefficient of 41 puts it solidly in the middle third of worldwide Gini values reported by the United Nations. The nations with Gini values identical, or very close, to that of the United States are Turkmenistan, Ghana, Cambodia, Guinea, and Trinidad/Tobago. The Western industrialized nations to which the United States more routinely compares itself all have lower Gini coefficients, that is, greater income equality than the nation whose Declaration of Independence stated that "all men are created equal." The ratio of the top 10 percent to the bottom 10 percent of income received in the United States is 15.9, indicating a degree of income inequality significantly higher than is found among most other wealthy nations. It has sometimes been remarked that the world's English-speaking countries, for various historical and cultural reasons, tolerate more inequality than other advanced, industrialized countries. Even in the company of other Anglophone countries, however, the United States stands out with a higher Gini index, a higher 10 percent ratio, and a higher 20 percent ratio than what is found in the United Kingdom, Canada, Australia, or New Zealand (UNDP 2005, 270–273).

Income Inequality in Latin America and Africa

As skewed as wealth and incomes are in the United States, they are much more skewed in some other parts of the world. It has been noted above that the countries of Latin America and sub-Saharan Africa have some of the widest income disparities in the world. Why this should be so is not a question that lends itself to easy answers, but experts offer several conjectures worth examining. We begin with Latin America.

The six most populous countries in Latin America—Brazil, Mexico, Colombia, Argentina, Peru, and Venezuela—all have Gini coefficients that put them in the top (most unequal) one-quarter of the 124 countries for which the United Nations presents such data. Brazil ranks eighth in the world for income inequality, and Colombia and Chile are close behind. Even Latin America's least unequal country, Uruguay, has a Gini value (45) that is worse than that of the United States (41). Latin American inequality is stark, pervasive, and deeply rooted in its colonial past. When Spanish colonizers first came to the continent in the 15th and 16th centuries, their efforts at wealth-extraction centered on mining in Peru, Mexico, and Colombia. Indigenous *Indios* who survived contact with the diseases brought in by the Europeans were forced into the mines. Later, in other parts of South America, both Spain and Portugal found that higher returns could be achieved in their colonies through plantation agriculture, especially the growth and export of sugar. Slaves imported from Africa supplemented native populations in the workforce. Thus a legacy of extreme inequality developed between European-descended elites on the one hand and Afro-descended and indigenous people on the other, a legacy that survived the revolutions that liberated one nation after another from colonial rule in the early 19th century (UNDP 2005, 270–271; Perry et al. 2003, ch. 4).

The highly unequal distribution of income in Latin America mirrors a severely unequal distribution of resources (landowning inequalities are notorious) that favors the European-descended elites. Those elites also benefit from better access to water, health care, electricity, and education, public services that contribute directly to one's capacity to advance in society. Public funding for elementary education has traditionally been stinted in Latin America, while state funding for the universities to which only the elites send their children has been generous. Structures of privilege like these have embedded inequality so deeply that one does not expect to see significant changes in the near future. On a continent where the top 10 percent of the population receives 30 times the income of the bottom 10 percent, however, the future may instead hold considerable political turmoil. That appears all the more possible when one finds that over 80 percent of respondents in every Latin American country surveyed except one (Venezuela) judged the income distribution in their country to be either unfair or very unfair (Perry et al. 2003, Table A.9).

The poor quality of economic data for Africa limits what we can say with any certainty about the reasons for high inequality there, but several factors are often cited. First, Africa is a continent without a middle class: its national populations are comprised of small elites and large majorities of very poor people. The poorest Africans survive on less than $1 a day, mainly in rural areas where their small plots of land yield minimal subsistence crops. The richest Africans live in urban centers and have incomes based on trade, banking, government employment, and the like. Second, there are powerful structures of privilege in Africa, as in Latin America, that reinforce the high incomes of the elites. As in Latin America, the provision of public services is tilted toward the elites. Those at the top are also the beneficiaries of levels of corruption that can only be described as massive. Protectionist trade policies also work to the benefit of indigenous capitalist elites and to the detriment of impoverished consumers. Finally, nearly everyone agrees that ethnic fragmentation in Africa is a factor in the dominant positions of some groups and the marginalization of others. While the roots of African inequality are complex, the path to greater economic equality is as simple to specify as it is difficult to achieve. It requires above all a shift to higher rates of economic growth, and that can probably only come from a stronger engagement with the global economy.

Poverty in the Rich Countries

When we consider how people at the lower end of the income scale live their lives on opposite sides of the world, we have to admit that differences of culture and economic development may be so substantial as to make meaningful comparisons nearly impossible. How similar can the lives of the poor in Canada be to the lives of the poor in Cambodia or Cameroon? Feelings of powerlessness, insecurity, demoralization, and alienation may well be common to the poor of every continent, but material standards of living differ markedly, as do national methods of measuring poverty. To gain a meaningful perspective on U.S. poverty, therefore, it makes sense to restrict our comparisons to countries of similar economic standing. That is the approach Timothy Smeeding takes in a study published in the *Journal of Economic Perspectives* (Smeeding 2006). A well-known authority on the measurement of poverty internationally, Smeeding is a founder and former director of the Luxembourg Income Study (LIS), a nonpartisan research project that tries to harmonize the data gathered periodically from households in about 30 countries, mainly in Europe.

Smeeding takes a comparative look at several dimensions of poverty in the United States and 10 other wealthy nations. Three of those nations are English-speaking (United Kingdom, Ireland, Canada), two are Nordic (Sweden, Finland), four are in the heart of Europe (Germany, Belgium, Austria, Netherlands), one is southern European (Italy), and all are in the top tiers of international league standings for social and economic development. Smeeding finds poverty to be significantly more prevalent in the United States than in most other rich countries. If the poverty line is drawn at one-half the median income level of a country, and the count of people below that line is divided by total population to determine the poverty rate, then the United States ranks first in poverty among all 11 countries, with a poverty rate of 17.0 percent. (Finland has the least poverty, 5.4 percent.) The only other country with a poverty rate above 15 percent is Ireland, with 16.5 percent. When poverty rates for children are computed, the United States again tops the list, with a rate of 18.8 percent, well above the runner-up nation, Italy, with 15.4 percent (Smeeding 2006, 74).

Data from the LIS project make it possible, as Smeeding shows, to compare the effectiveness of government spending in each of the 11 countries in reducing poverty. This can be a useful exercise for policymakers—and for voters and advocates who want to educate themselves on the issue—as they think about the adequacy of the antipoverty efforts their governments are making. One begins by computing the poverty rate based on "market income" alone, meaning income from all private sources, like earnings, company pensions, investments, and child support, but excluding any cash or cash-like benefits from the government. On the basis of market incomes, about 23 percent of the U.S. population would fall below one-half the median income level and thus be considered relatively "poor." Surprisingly, based solely on market incomes, most of the other rich countries would have higher poverty rates than the United States. But other governments do much more than the U.S. government to modify market incomes for low-income individuals and families. Income enhancements can come in the form of social insurance or social assistance. Social insurance refers to benefits that are not means-tested, for example, Medicare, unemployment compensation, and Social Security. Social assistance refers to benefits going only to low-income individuals, such as welfare, Medicaid, and food stamps (Smeeding 2006, 78–80).

When social insurance and social assistance are taken into account, the U.S. poverty rate is reduced from 23.1 percent to 17.0 percent. This drop of 6.1 points represents little more than a one-quarter reduction from the poverty rate based on market incomes alone. No other rich country achieves so little poverty reduction by its government's efforts. In Canada and Ireland, government benefits cut the poverty rate by about 45 percent; in the United Kingdom and Italy, by about 60 percent; and in Austria, Belgium, Germany, and Sweden, by over 70 percent. When we focus on poverty reduction among families with children, the results are similar. For families with two parents, the U.S. government's efforts shave the poverty rate by 3.6 percent—a negligible amount compared to the 44.3 percent reduction achieved, on average, by all 11 rich countries. And for families with one parent, the U.S.

poverty reduction through government efforts is 10 percent, while the average for all the rich countries is 46.3 percent (Smeeding 2006, 79–81). Americans, it would seem, tolerate more poverty than people in rich societies elsewhere, and are content to have their government do less about it.

National Trends in Income Inequality

The current levels of poverty and inequality for any country can be thought of as the culminating end-points of past trends. Sometimes we can trace the historical roots of current patterns into the distant past, as with Latin America. If we want to track specific indicators of inequality over time, however, we face severe limitations in trying to assemble the necessary data. Statistical trend lines for inequality rarely can be extended more than a century into the past, and only for certain European nations and their colonial offshoots. For most countries, we have, at best, a mere 30 or 35 years of reliable data to work with. Still, a third of a century is more than enough time to discern broad patterns, such as the widening gap between rich and poor in the United States. That particular trend is now beyond dispute, and it raises a larger question: Is the trend toward higher levels of economic inequality unique to this country, or are similar trends to be seen in other regions of the world?

Bernard Wasow, a senior fellow at the Century Foundation, has studied the evidence on changing income patterns for 15 rich, mainly European countries—though the United States and Japan are included—over the quarter-century ending in 2005. His findings are presented in Figure 3–1. For each country, Wasow plots a point in the graph to indicate its Gini coefficient in 1980 and in 2005.

The heavy diagonal line separates countries that have experienced a rise in inequality (higher Gini in 2005 than in 1980) from those that have experienced a fall (lower Gini in 2005 than in 1980). With nine countries above the line, three below, and three essentially on the line, the broad picture seems to be that within-nation income inequality is trending upward. One should not, however, overstate the case. Only the labeled countries had Gini changes that were statistically significant, and those six countries were split evenly between upward and downward changes. Finland, the United Kingdom, and the United States became more

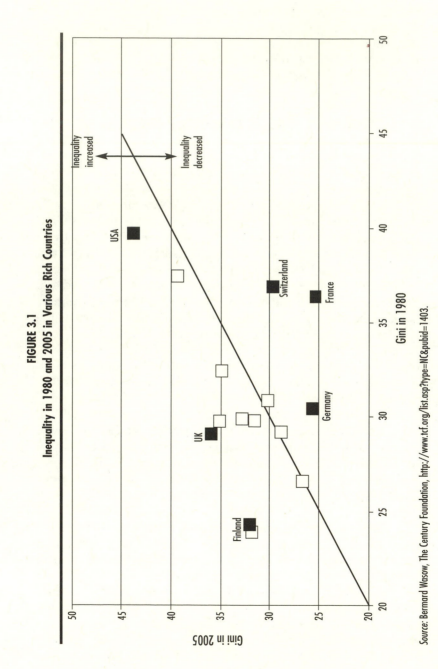

FIGURE 3.1
Inequality in 1980 and 2005 in Various Rich Countries

Source: Bernard Wasow, The Century Foundation, http://www.tcf.org/list.asp?type=NC&pubid=1403.

unequal; Germany, France, and Switzerland became more equal. Note that in both 1980 and 2005, the United States topped all the other rich nations in income inequality (Wasow 2006).

Glenn Firebaugh, a professor of geography at Penn State, offers a more detailed and geographically comprehensive account of global trends in income inequality in *The New Geography of Global Income Inequality* (2003). Firebaugh presents an ambitious theoretical and empirical analysis of worldwide income-distribution trends that leads him to a pair of strong conclusions: first, income inequality within six of seven regions of the world has been rising in recent decades, and second, income inequality, when measured across the entire global population, has been *falling*. The apparent contradiction between these two conclusions is an intriguing issue in itself and one to which we return later, but first it will be useful to focus on the regional trends. Firebaugh works with data from 1980 to 1995, computing two indices of inequality, the Theil index and the mean logarithmic deviation (MLD). These indices differ in certain technical respects from the Gini coefficient but are easier to compute from the income data that is most commonly available. Firebaugh defines his seven regions as Western Europe, Western offshoots, Southern Europe, Eastern Europe, Latin America, Asia, and Africa. The Western offshoots include Canada, the United States, Australia, and New Zealand. Even though the seven regions have experienced great diversity in their economic growth rates, every region except Africa saw income inequality rise between 1980 and 1995, with most of the increase occurring during the 1980s (Firebaugh 2003, ch. 9).

It is startling to see income gaps widening with such consistency across regions, but Firebaugh offers persuasive reasons for accepting the picture he paints. At the general level, he argues that structural changes related to economic development are the key driver of inequality. Poorer countries and regions are starting to industrialize, and this is something that historically has involved a major redeployment of workers from low-productivity (low-income) employments to higher-productivity (higher-income) employments. As we saw in chapter 1, Simon Kuznets theorized many years ago that this type of employment shift tends to raise income inequality, although not permanently. Meanwhile, in richer countries, Firebaugh believes that a trend toward increased employment in the service sector also is widening the dispersion of incomes because service jobs vary so greatly in their pay, from the low wages of fast-food preparers, daycare workers, and hotel maids up the scale to the lofty salaries of doctors, computer engineers, and financial analysts (Firebaugh 2003).

There are more specific reasons why inequality has increased in some regions. Eastern Europe, which recorded a huge jump in inequality between 1980 and 1995, made an epochal transition from communism to a system of market economics during that period. The resulting economic liberalization created big winners and losers, stretching the income distribution at both ends. The Asian region has grown more unequal simply because its two population giants, China and India, have been undergoing rapid industrialization, shifting millions of laborers toward higher-paying jobs. The so-called Western offshoots region has experienced a rise in income inequality because the richest and most populous member of that region, the United States, has recorded a significant increase in its inequality; Canada and Australia have also grown more unequal. Whatever the particular reasons, economic inequality has been on the rise within nations and regions for some time now, and this represents a reversal of the trend that much of the world, including the United States, followed during the greater part of the 20th century (Firebaugh 2003, ch. 9; Cornia and Kiiski 2001).

Income by Country: Divergence or Convergence?

Inequality trends *within* countries and inequality trends *across* countries are two separate issues. Both merit attention. We saw in the preceding section that within-country inequality is on the rise all over the world, except, possibly, in Africa. This does not imply, however, that average incomes among countries are spreading farther and farther apart. Some observers claim that such a trend is ongoing, with the rich nations getting richer and the poor nations getting poorer. Globalization, they say, is the main culprit. They contend that the breakdown of barriers to the free flow of goods, information, technology, and investment funds—globalization, in short—has enabled the more advanced, industrialized countries to not only maintain but lengthen their lead over the less developed ones, creating a degree of global inequality that, in their view, calls for urgent international action.

The debate over whether the economic fortunes of nations tend to converge or diverge over time has engaged deep thinkers as early as the 18th century (Firebaugh 2003, 173). Today, unlike then, we have the kinds of data that allow us to advance the debate beyond vague hunches and speculations.

Before industrialization, there was not much variation from one country to another in the average standard of living. In a sense, all countries were poor, at least on average. In the early 19th century, therefore, we would expect the Gini coefficient for inequality among nations to have had a relatively low value, meaning not much difference between the per capita GDPs of the "better-off" nations and the "worse-off" nations. Branko Milanovic, in his important study, *Worlds Apart: Measuring International and Global Inequality* (2005), puts the worldwide Gini coefficient in 1820 at 19.6. This figure is based on data for 26 countries encompassing 79 percent of the world's population, and gives each country equal weight in the computation. If instead we follow a procedure favored by most experts and give each country a weight proportioned to its population size, the Gini drops to a remarkably low value of 12 (Milanovic 2005, 140–142).

From 1820 onward, however, national per capita incomes took strongly divergent paths as industrialization and economic growth boosted the incomes of Western nations while leaving the others increasingly far behind. The period from 1820 to 1913, dubbed the "first century of globalization" by Milanovic, saw steady increases in both the Gini and Theil indices of inequality, with the unweighted Gini coefficient rising from 19.6 in 1820 to 30.8 in 1890 and 36.4 in 1913. The population-weighted Gini increased even more dramatically and for a longer time, from 12.0 in 1820 to 40.3 in 1929. It could truly be said that by the end of the 1920s, one's standard of living depended quite significantly on where in the world one was born, whereas a century earlier it would not have made much difference. After their century-long climb, between-country measures of inequality took a short pause and then resumed their climb. But from here the story has two endings. The unweighted Gini index reached its highest level ever, 54.3, in 2000. If one thinks it is appropriate to put exactly the same weight on every nation in a global inequality measure—giving Armenia's 3 million people the same mathematical representation as India's 1.1 billion, for example—then the steady rise of the unweighted Gini presents a rather bleak picture of ever-increasing global inequality. By contrast, the population-weighted Gini reached a peak value of 56.9 as far back as 1952, and thereafter subsided gradually to 50.2 in 2000 (Milanovic 2005, 140–143).

Where does this leave us on the issue of convergence versus divergence? Are the poorer countries of the world converging toward the incomes of the richer countries, or are they continuing a very long pattern of divergence? A partial answer comes from looking at standard statistical measures of inequality. When the Gini coefficient for between-country inequality rises, it implies that the income gap between rich and poor countries is widening; when it falls, it implies the opposite. The data assembled by Milanovic is quite comprehensive for 2000, based on 136 countries with 99 percent of the world's population (Milanovic 2005, 142). If we cannot offer a definitive answer to the convergence question, it is not for lack of data but for lack of universal agreement on the proper measure of inequality (weighted or unweighted Gini coefficient). For a century and half before 1950, national income levels grew farther apart. Since then, they have either diverged further (unweighted index) or begun a gradual convergence (weighted index). A split decision does not settle the issue, but an entirely new approach just might, and to that we now turn.

A New Concept of Global Inequality

We have considered two ways of measuring the divide between the world's rich and poor: within-country inequality and between-country inequality. Income gaps within many countries, including the United States, have been growing for decades. Income dispersion across countries, although far greater today than at the dawn of the industrial era, has begun to diminish during the past half-century, according to one index (the population-weighted Gini). So these two approaches give us mixed signals on the inequality trend. There is a third approach to the issue of global income inequality that has begun receiving attention in recent years. It involves treating everyone in the world as a "world citizen" rather than as a resident of any particular country. The world is reconceived as a borderless community of 6.7 billion individuals. The idea is neatly conveyed in the title of Surjit Bhalla's 2002 book, which helped inaugurate this new approach: *Imagine There's No Country: Poverty, Inequality, and Growth in the*

Era of Globalization. What Bhalla and others aim to do is gauge the extent of inequality across all of the world's people, wherever they may live, and to determine whether the global trend is toward more equality or more inequality.

Before we consider the specific findings of this third approach, it is worth noting the policy relevance of the three ways of thinking about inequality. Country-level inequality is an important concern for those who design, analyze, and advocate for policy changes within nations, whether in the area of taxation, income transfers, educational subsidies, or investment policies. National inequality levels also matter to voters, who may give support to, or withhold support from, candidates on the basis of their positions regarding the current degree of inequality. Inter-country levels of inequality are important to those whose concerns extend beyond their own national borders to issues of global equity. Often motivated by the plight of the world's most impoverished, these individuals have an interest in aid and trade policies that will benefit the least-developed countries. It is less clear who should take an interest, or feel they have a stake, in the abstract, borderless distribution of income. Academics, of course, have a professional interest in developing any new line of research that can shed fresh light on old questions. Another group taking an interest in the third approach to global income inequality consists of supporters of globalization; they have warmed to this approach because it tends to produce statistical results to their liking. We turn now to those results.

While several scholars (Bhalla 2002; Firebaugh 2003; Milanovic 2005) have depicted essentially the same trend for global inequality, Xavier Sala-i-Martin's 2006 article offers the most succinct and up-to-date presentation of the world distribution of income (WDI). It has the added advantage of addressing both the WDI issue and the related question of whether global poverty levels have shrunk in recent decades. The author integrates data from 138 countries for the time period 1970–2000. Statistically, what he does is tantamount to placing every household in the world on an income line that stretches from extraordinarily low (subsistence-level farmers in sub-Saharan Africa, perhaps) to nosebleed high (billionaire owners of computer software companies, for example), and then calculating how "spread out" those incomes are. Every person in the world is weighted equally under this approach, which means developments in China and India have a much larger impact on inequality measures than developments in

Peru or Latvia. Sala-i-Martin computes eight different inequality indices and finds a drop in global inequality *by every index*. The largest drop between 1970 and 2000 is for the ratio of the top 20 percent of income-recipients in the world to the bottom 20 percent: in 1970, that ratio was 10.3, and in 2000, it was only 8.2. The smallest change of a computed index is the 2.4 percent drop in the Gini coefficient (Sala-i-Martin 2006, 384).

A closer examination of Sala-i-Martin's results reveals some interesting details. It shows, in the first place, that none of the eight inequality measures moved steadily downward over the whole 30-year period, but most of the time the indices moved together, whether upward or downward. Second, it shows that the 1970s saw a slight increase in inequality, with real reductions of global inequality not beginning until the 1980s. And finally, a closer examination of the data shows the important role played by individual countries and regions in determining the global results. The United States and Africa both caused a worsening of global inequality from 1970 to 2000 in the following sense: U.S. citizens, already at the top of the global income distribution in 1970, pulled even farther ahead of the rest of the world's citizens by 2000, stretching the upper end of the distribution. Africans, already low on the income scale in 1970, dropped even farther by 2000, stretching the distribution in a downward direction. Outweighing the divergent impact of both the United States and Africa was the convergent impact of an economically dynamic China. Rapid economic growth in the world's most populous nation raised many millions of impoverished peasants into the middle ranks of the global income distribution. Had this not happened, the global Gini coefficient would have gone up rather than down, marking an increase in world income inequality (Sala-i-Martin 2006, 385–388).

Less Inequality, Less Poverty?

Which is the more urgent issue today, global inequality or global poverty? For most people, the question is easily answered. The term "poverty" suggests human misery in a way that "inequality" does not and thus appeals directly to our consciences. It would seem churlish to put a higher priority on unequal incomes than on *inadequate* incomes as a policy matter. Let the question be rephrased: Would you rather see a reduction in absolute poverty or a narrowing of the gap between the world's rich and poor? Put in this way, the question appears to require a choice, yet in reality it does not. Both outcomes can be achieved simultaneously. Not only is this theoretically possible, it is what the research of Bhalla and Sala-i-Martin has shown to be the case in recent decades. At the same time that the incomes of global citizens have become more equally distributed, the fraction, and probably the actual number, of the world's people living in absolute poverty has declined, say these economists.

Sala-i-Martin's estimates of poverty by world region, using a $1.50 per day standard of poverty, display a wide range of results for the period from 1970 to 2000. East Asia saw the number of people in poverty fall by 88 percent; the Middle East and North Africa, by 88 percent also; South Asia, by 84 percent; and Latin America, by 25 percent. Eastern Europe recorded a mere 4 percent reduction in the number of poor, and sub-Saharan Africa experienced an *increase* of 217 percent. Regional variations aside, the world as a whole saw the number of people in absolute poverty drop from around 700 million to around 400 million during those three decades, a remarkable 43 percent reduction. The same scholar gives alternative estimates of poverty reduction based on poverty lines of $2 per day and $3 per day, and they, too, show sizeable drops in the numbers of global poor. The prime mover in all of these glowing poverty-reduction results is China, where economic growth in recent decades has been little short of phenomenal (Sala-i-Martin 2006, 378).

In the fall of 2000, government delegates from around the world gathered at the United Nations to commit their countries to a set of so-called Millennium Development Goals (MDGs). Eight major goals were defined, all to be achieved by 2015. Greater income equality did not make the list of goals, although gender equality did. Probably the most cited goal was the first on the list: "eradicate extreme poverty and hunger." A specific target associated with this goal was to halve the proportion of the world's people living on less than $1 a day, with 1990 designated as the reference year (Gilbert 2004, 153). Sala-i-Martin notes that on the $1.50 per day standard, which he considers roughly equivalent to the World Bank's $1 per day standard, the world poverty rate in 1990 was 10 percent. By 2000, when the delegates in New York signed off on the MDGs, the poverty rate had already fallen to 7 percent. This meant, in effect, that the world was already three-fifths of the way to achieving its 2015 goal of a 5 percent global poverty rate. As Sala-i-Martin comments, "The world might just be in better shape than many of our leaders believe!" (Sala-i-Martin 2006, 374, 393)

Bhalla's projections of world poverty rates for 2015 support the optimism of his fellow economist. On a $2 per day poverty standard—an even higher standard than Sala-i-Martin's $1.50 per day—he projects a regional poverty rate for East Asia of *zero* by 2015. For South Asia, which includes India, Pakistan, and Bangladesh, he projects a drop in the poverty rate from 21.1 percent in 2000 to 3.5 percent in 2015. Other regions show smaller declines, but all should experience reductions in poverty, including sub-Saharan Africa. Bhalla believes that his forecasts are, if anything, on the conservative side, as they are based on economic growth rates that will probably be exceeded in most places. Both economists, therefore, see the globalization currently under way in a benign light: the world is moving toward a convergence of incomes while also enjoying a welcome reduction of absolute poverty (Bhalla 2002, 170).

Economic Mobility: The United States in Global Perspective

We saw in an earlier section that the income inequality now seen in the United States, as measured by the Gini coefficient, places it in the company of Ghana, Cambodia, and other countries that are not usually thought to bear much similarity to it. The wealthy industrialized nations that *are* similar to the United States have, in general, far more equal distributions of income. Many Americans, informed of this anomaly, would probably say that a high degree of inequality—a wide gap between rich and poor—is simply the price their country must pay for being a true "land of opportunity," where hard work, talent, and sheer grit are permitted to reap their full reward. The exceptional faith that Americans place in the value of hard work was confirmed by a 1999 survey, which found 61 percent of Americans agreeing with the statement that "people get rewarded for their effort" (Hertz 2006, 1). Among 27 countries where the same survey was conducted, there was no stronger endorsement of the work-gets-its-reward statement, except in the Philippines. We also have survey evidence, as noted in chapter 1, that Americans strongly (and increasingly) endorse the notion that anyone can "start out poor, work hard, and become rich." It is clear, therefore, that Americans prize the image of their country as a land of opportunity. But is the real extent of opportunity and mobility so high, by international standards, as to justify the very considerable income inequality that now exists in the United States?

A common way for social scientists to gauge long-term equality of opportunity is by seeing how one generation compares economically with its predecessor. Specifically, one may compare the wages earned by sons at a certain age with the wages their fathers earned at the same age. Daughters can likewise be matched up with their mothers. In a society of completely equal opportunity, one would find no correlation at all between the economic status of parents and that of their children. The offspring of poor fathers or mothers would be spread across the income distribution in a totally random fashion, with only 20 percent landing in the lowest quintile. The data needed to test for such an outcome are not easily obtained, however; only a couple dozen countries, mainly in Europe but including the United States, have good long-term mobility data. One study of intergenerational mobility in five European countries and the United States looked at the probability of sons and daughters ending up in the lowest income quintile, given that their fathers had been in the lowest quintile. Denmark proved to have the highest mobility, with 23.5 percent of daughters and 24.7 percent of sons of poor fathers ending up in the lowest quintile. The other European nations had somewhat lower mobility than Denmark, particularly the United Kingdom, with 30.3 percent of sons ending up in the lowest quintile. But the United States stood apart, with over 42 percent of sons in the lowest one-fifth of incomes. American daughters also had higher odds than their European counterparts of being in the poorest quintile, given a mother who had been in that quintile (Mishel, Bernstein, and Allegretto 2006, 100).

Another way that experts have quantified the ability of the younger generation to raise itself to a higher economic status is by estimating the intergenerational elasticity of earnings (IEE). This awkward-sounding term refers to the predictability of sons' (or daughters') wages based on their fathers' wages. The IEE can have a value between zero, meaning no correlation at all, and 1, meaning a 100 percent correlation between what the child earns and what his or her father earned. Put very simply, if a country has a low IEE, it means that sons have good prospects of out-earning their fathers; a higher IEE would mean that sons have worse prospects of out-earning their fathers. In a 2004 review of father-son earnings profiles in nine countries, the highest IEE values were found for the United Kingdom (0.50) and the United States (0.47), suggesting that poor sons faced the worst odds of bettering their condition in those two countries. Much lower IEE values were found in the other countries studied, including Denmark (0.15), Norway (0.17), Finland (0.18), and Canada (0.19), where fathers' wages were not especially predictive of their sons' wages (Hertz 2006, 2).

From the most recent evidence, therefore, it appears that long-term upward mobility is a more realistic prospect in the Nordic countries—Canada, Germany, and France—than in the United States—hardly what most Americans would want to believe about their land of opportunity. This evidence throws into doubt the familiar argument that a wide U.S. gap between rich and poor—wider than is seen elsewhere in the industrialized world—is just the price we pay for being such a fluid society. It now looks as if the United States is *more unequal* and, very possibly, *more rigid* in its income structure than most other high-income nations.

Top U.S. Incomes in Worldwide Perspective

As noted in chapters 1 and 2, the share of national income going to America's wealthiest families has been on the rise for at least three decades. This is a highly visible aspect of the growing income inequality in the United States. It is also a trend that has yet to show any sign of weakening. But does it set the United States apart from other countries? Is something really exceptional happening in the nation, or would we find, if we took a wider perspective that included countries similar to the United States, the same extraordinary redirection of income toward the very top? Economists Thomas Piketty and Emmanuel Saez provide some preliminary answers in a 2006 article on top incomes in the United States and a handful of other countries. What they find, in a nutshell, is that some countries are experiencing the same strong flow of income toward the top as the United States, while others show no such tendency (Piketty and Saez 2006, 204–206). The details are well worth examining.

An intriguing part of the story that Piketty and Saez tell is the stark divergence between the English-speaking countries and some non-English-speaking countries with regard to super-high incomes. If we focus on the former group, we see a sharply rising share of total income going to the top one-thousandth of income recipients (top 0.1 percent) from the late 1970s to the late 1990s. The rise is most pronounced in the United States but unmistakable in the United Kingdom and Canada as well. France and Japan, however, follow a completely different path: in those two countries, the share of income going to the top one-thousandth of the population has been essentially flat since the end of World War II. There is just as sharp a contrast between the English- and non-English-speaking countries with regard to the actual share of national income going to the top one-thousandth. In both Japan and France, the share has held steady at roughly 2 percent for over half a century—notable constancy in a basic social parameter when so much else was changing in both the Japanese and French economies. In Canada, on the other hand, the fraction of national income received by the top 0.1 percent has grown in recent decades to over 3 percent. In the United Kingdom, it has risen to over 5 percent; in the United States, to over 7 percent (Piketty and Saez 2006, 203).

It may strike some that a 2 percent, 3 percent, or even 7 percent share of national income is too small to merit concern or discussion. Bear in mind, however, that these are fractions of total national income going to a mere sliver (one-thousandth) of the population. To put this in perspective, if income flowed to the top 5 percent of the French population at the same proportional rate that it flows to the top 0.1 percent, there would be *no income left* for the bottom 95 percent. In the United States, income concentration is even more drastic: if income accrued to other top income recipients at the same rate that it now accrues to the top 0.1 percent, there would be no income left to support the lowest 98.5 percent of the population. This degree of income concentration at the top has not been seen in the United States since the end of the 1920s, nor in Canada and the United Kingdom for over half a century (Piketty and Saez 2006, 203).

CEO Pay and Income Inequality

The substantial difference among countries in both the shares and trends of income going to the very richest percentiles begs for an explanation. As yet, no one has come forward to do the explaining, but when that happens, the issue of compensation practices in various countries will surely be a decisive factor. Why? Because top-end incomes in most industrialized societies today are based more on earnings than on interest, dividends, or rents on property holdings. This is a huge change from a century ago. Top incomes at that time were obtained mainly from capital accumulations, typically in the form of stocks and bonds. But those "piles" of capital were heavily eroded by stock market meltdowns, the Great Depression, and steeply progressive wartime and postwar tax rates. Today's highest incomes, therefore, rarely come from "coupon-clipping"; more often they have to do with executive compensation packages. Executives at the world's biggest corporations have come to be paid handsomely for their services, and significantly better in some countries than others (Piketty and Saez 2006, 204).

The United States rewards its CEOs more generously than any other country, and by a wide margin. In 2005, the average compensation to U.S. chief executives was around $2.2 million. (There are, in any given year, some well-publicized individuals who receive $100 million or more, but those numbers are far above the average.) For the world's second-highest-paid CEOs, in Switzerland, average pay was about $1.4 million. Chief executives in France earned $1.2 million; in the United Kingdom and Germany, somewhat less than $1.2 million; and in Italy and Canada, about $1.1 million. Japanese CEOs, in contrast to their Western European and North American counterparts, make only about half a million dollars annually. From an income-distributional point of view, it is useful to see how CEO pay compares to the average pay of manufacturing workers. (The figures that follow are based on different income definitions and data sources than those cited in chapter 1, which accounts for their much lower levels.) In the United States, the CEO-to-average-worker pay ratio in 2005 was 39, and in the United Kingdom it was 32. Among the 14 countries considered, the median pay ratio was just under 20, or about half what is seen in the United States, and in Japan it fell below 11 (Mishel, Bernstein, and Allegretto 2007, 203–204).

If national differences in top incomes at present are the result of—or even heavily influenced by—CEO pay differences, the next question has to be how to account for those CEO pay differentials. Standard economic theory relates pay levels to individual productivity, implying that if American CEOs are paid much more than their counterparts in other countries, that is simply because they create more value for their employers and stockholders. It is a flattering explanation, to be sure, and one that would seem to reflect great credit on Wharton, Tuck, and other prestigious American business schools, but is it the right one? Much has been written about the non-transparency of CEO pay rates in the U.S. and the fact that they are set by compensation committees packed, as often as not, by friends and close associates of the top executive. High pay under these circumstances may reflect something other than a sterling job performance. Another line of analysis focuses on the grand scale of American enterprises (at least among the top 500 or 1,000) compared to those in other countries. Thus, a talented executive at a Dutch company may receive a modest compensation while an American executive of exactly the same talent may receive a proverbial king's ransom simply because the latter makes decisions on a bigger stage, with larger monetary consequences (Cowen 2006). Beyond issues of corporate scale and individual productivity, it may also be the case that in some societies—Japan, for example—there are well-established social norms that prevent companies from paying their CEOs at levels that greatly exceed what is considered seemly or customary. Keeping executive pay at a familiar multiple of average worker pay could be considered a requirement of the social contract in a number of European societies.

Wealth Taxes: A (So Far) Non-American Response to Wealth Inequality

The overwhelming weight of evidence now points to a dispersion of incomes, in the United States and many other countries, beyond what has been seen for at least a half-century. Trend lines suggest no slackening of the tendency of high incomes to pull away from middle- and lower-level incomes. It would seem reasonable, then, to give some consideration to policies that might be adopted in order to avoid what could become a destabilizing and politically unacceptable state of affairs. The range of policy options in any given society, including the United States, will always be a function of the historical, social, political, and cultural characteristics of that society, and an interesting case in point is the wealth tax. Americans historically have shown little appetite for a direct tax levied on an individual's or family's total wealth accumulation. (The only exceptions have been state and federal estate taxes.) Opponents call them "death taxes," and under the presidency of George W. Bush, the latter have been attacked and scheduled for eventual elimination.

In Europe, on the other hand, wealth taxes are relatively common. Switzerland, Germany, Sweden, Denmark, France, and the Netherlands are among the European nations where people are taxed annually on their wealth (although this is not the only tax they pay). The arguments in favor of a wealth tax are based on both equity and efficiency considerations. The fairness argument starts from the premise that people's tax liabilities should be based, to a great extent, on their ability to pay. Since ability to pay depends on both income and wealth, an income tax alone, even if it is progressive, fails the fairness test. It taxes individuals with equal incomes equally even if one has 50 times the wealth of the other. A fairer tax system would tax both income and wealth. On the efficiency side, a persuasive argument can be made that taxes levied on wealth will induce people to put their assets into more productive uses. For example, a wealth tax may encourage owners of low-yielding bonds to switch to higher-yielding bonds, and owners of idle land to convert their property to more productive, income-generating uses (Wolff 1996).

Edward N. Wolff, the preeminent American expert on wealth distribution, has studied the operations of European wealth taxes, particularly in Germany, Switzerland, and Sweden, and has considered how the adoption of similar taxes would impact the United States. In results reported in 2000, he found that a "very modest tax" on wealth, which included a $100,000 exemption and marginal tax rates ranging from 0.05 percent upward to 0.3 percent, would raise $50 billion of revenue for the federal government. On the plus side, these funds could be used to support a family allowance plan—the type of program many European governments use to help families with children—and other kinds of social transfers to benefit the poor and lower middle class. On the minus side, there would be a slight disincentive effect on savings, at least in theory. Wolff, however, has found "no deleterious effects" on either savings or economic growth from the modest wealth taxes that European countries have imposed, and he doubts that any such effects would be felt in the United States (Wolff 2000, 62–63).

A Caution on Wealth Taxes

Public policymaking becomes exceedingly difficult when new constraints and new policy goals are added to existing ones. Such is the prospect facing the industrialized world in the coming decades. Its population will be aging rapidly, and the resulting burden on fiscal systems will be tremendous. In Europe and Japan, especially, the costs of supporting a retired, elderly population will weigh upon labor forces that are either stagnating or shrinking in size. The financial resources of the state will be strained to the breaking point. To a lesser degree, the same pressures will be felt in the United States, with 78 million baby boomers set to begin retiring in 2011, and for that reason as much as out of any desire to narrow the growing gap between rich and poor, the U.S. political leadership may be forced to consider a wealth tax. Many dismiss that prospect as a fantasy: surely Americans would bridle at the idea of a direct tax on wealth. Yet most Americans already face local taxes on the value of their real estate, and that is a wealth tax. Also, estate (inheritance) taxes have been broadly accepted by the U.S. public until quite recently, and polls indicate continued acceptance by a majority of the population. Income taxes were once considered as unthinkable as a national wealth tax—until Congress passed the Sixteenth Amendment to the Constitution in 1909 and the states ratified it four years later (Alperovitz 2004, 23).

When tax revenues are no longer adequate to fund current outlays in the Social Security program (2017) or Medicare (2018), therefore, the U.S. government will have no way to avoid cutting entitlement benefits except by raising taxes, finding new taxes, or increasing its borrowing. Gar Alperovitz, a political economist at the University of Maryland, expects the coming fiscal crisis to be so severe that instituting a federal wealth tax will prove all but inevitable (Alperovitz 2004, 22–23). If he is right and a progressive wealth tax is adopted, it is highly unlikely that it will be justified to the electorate on any other grounds than fiscal necessity. A more balanced distribution of wealth may come to be seen as a positive side effect of the tax, but it is unlikely to be presented as the primary justification. Who, after all, can imagine an American president in the early 21st century railing against "malefactors of great wealth" as Theodore Roosevelt did in the early 20th century?

Any government contemplating a wealth tax will have to weigh not only a potential discouraging effect on the savings rate but also the possibility of capital flight. Individuals who find themselves subjected to steep new taxes have an understandable wish to deflect the blow. History offers many examples of people sending their money—and themselves—out of jurisdictions that have implemented heavy taxes on wealth or high incomes. Present-day France offers a case in point. Its wealth tax has been blamed for the self-exile of many rich families, most notably the Taittingers of champagne fame. According to tax experts, some well-off French citizens can find themselves paying more in wealth tax than their annual income. With the dubious distinction of ranking first on *Forbes* magazine's annual Tax Misery Index, France experiences capital flight in the form of a departing millionaire every day (Moore 2006, A12).

A national wealth tax might promote similar flight tendencies in the United States. It is a contingency to be studied and weighed carefully, since we know well that American families and businesses factor tax rates into their locational decision making. Experts believe that French entrepreneurs have found it relatively easy to flee to neighboring countries, particularly Belgium, thanks to the European Union's uniform business rules (Moore 2006, A12). Allowing for some essential differences between the way the European Union and the North American Free Trade Agreement (NAFTA) operate, policy makers contemplating a U.S. wealth tax may want to explore the risks and the consequences of wealthy American families relocating to Canada or Mexico. At present that does not seem likely to happen, but it cannot be ruled out either.

References

Alperovitz, Gar. "The Coming Era of Wealth Taxation." *Dollars and Sense* 254 (July/August 2004): 22–24.

Bhalla, Surjit S. *Imagine There's No Country: Poverty, Inequality, and Growth in the Era of Globalization.* Washington, DC: Institute for International Economics, 2002.

Cornia, Giovanni Andrea, and Sampsa Kiiski. "Trends in Income Distribution in the Post–World War II Period: Evidence and Interpretation." Discussion Paper No. 2001/89 (September), World Institute for Development Economics Research (WIDER). New York: United Nations University, 2001.

Cowen, Tyler. "A Contrarian Look at Whether U.S. Chief Executives Are Overpaid." *The New York Times* (May 18, 2006).

Firebaugh, Glenn. *The New Geography of Global Income Inequality.* Cambridge, MA: Harvard University Press, 2003.

Gilbert, Geoffrey. *World Poverty: A Reference Handbook.* Santa Barbara, CA: ABC-CLIO, 2004.

Hertz, Tom. "Understanding Mobility in America." Report prepared for Center for American Progress, Washington, D.C., 2006. Accessed at http://www.americanprogress.org.

Human Development Report 2005: International Cooperation at a Crossroads: Aid, Trade, and Security in an Unequal World. New York: United Nations Development Program (UNDP), 2005.

Milanovic, Branko. *Worlds Apart: Measuring International and Global Inequality.* Princeton, NJ: Princeton University Press, 2005.

Mishel, Lawrence, Jared Bernstein, and Sylvia Allegretto. *The State of Working America 2006/2007.* Ithaca, NY: ILR Press, 2007.

Moore, Molly. "Old Money, New Money Flee France and Its Wealth Tax." *The Washington Post* (July 26, 2006): A12.

Perry, Guillermo E., Francisco H. G. Ferreira, Michael Walton, and David M. de Ferranti. *Inequality in Latin America: Breaking with History?* Washington, DC: World Bank Publications, 2003.

Piketty, Thomas, and Emmanuel Saez. "The Evolution of Top Incomes: A Historical and International Perspective." American Economic Association, *Papers and Proceedings* 96, no. 2 (May 2006): 200–205.

Sala-i-Martin, Xavier. "The World Distribution of Income: Falling Poverty and . . . Convergence, Period." *Quarterly Journal of Economics* CXXI, no. 2 (May 2006): 351–397.

Smeeding, Timothy. "Poor People in Rich Nations: The United States in Comparative Perspective." *Journal of Economic Perspectives* 20, no. 1 (Winter 2006): 69–90.

Wasow, Bernard. "Standing Alone in Inequality." The Century Foundation, *News & Commentary* (September 22, 2006). Accessed online at http://www.tcf.org.

Wolff, Edward N. "Recent Trends in the Distribution of Household Wealth," in Ray Marshall, ed., *Back to Shared Prosperity: The Growing Inequality of Wealth and Income in America.* Armonk, NY: M. E. Sharpe, 2000: 57–63.

Wolff, Edward N. "Time for a Wealth Tax?" *Boston Review* (February/March 1996).

World Population Data Sheet. Washington, DC: Population Reference Bureau, 2006.

4

Chronology

This chapter highlights some of the key points of interest in our emerging sense of U.S. economic inequality. The entries are arranged chronologically from 1630 to the present. On the technical side, experts have developed various tools to measure and explain inequality, and our timeline records some of their key accomplishments. The degree of U.S. wealth inequality seems to have varied substantially through the centuries, and the public's response to the issue has likewise fluctuated. Our timeline reflects this: important political speeches, exposés, and other forms of commentary are noted. Because attitudes toward wealth inequality have often been shaped by public perceptions of individuals and families at the top of the income distribution, our chronology marks some of the key moments in the lives of those who, in an earlier era, were known as plutocrats. And, of course, the responses of government to poverty and inequality need to be taken into account. Redistributive federal programs have been proposed and then enacted or defeated, and the taxation of income and wealth has often been on the political agenda since early in the 20th century.

1630   In a sermon written on board the *Arbella* as it sails westward toward America, John Winthrop (1588–1649), the already-elected first governor of the Massachusetts Bay Colony, states: "God Almighty, in his most holy and wise providence, hath so disposed of the condition of mankind, as in all times some must be rich, some poor, some high and eminent in power and dignity; others mean and in submission." The sermon, "A Model of

1630   Christian Charity," is famous in later years for its com-
(*cont.*) parison of the Puritan colony to a "city upon a hill" (Bre-
        mer 2003, 176).

1662   Boston erects its first almshouse.

1758   Benjamin Franklin publishes *The Way to Wealth,* a com-
        pendium of proverbs extolling the twin virtues of indus-
        try and frugality. It is basically a repackaging of proverbs
        previously set forth in his *Poor Richard's Almanac* (see
        Franklin 1732–1758). A few examples: "What maintains
        one vice would bring up two children"; "If you would
        know the value of money, go and try to borrow some; for,
        he that goes a borrowing goes a sorrowing"; and "Dili-
        gence is the mother of good luck." As his posthumously
        published *Autobiography* makes clear, Franklin was the
        archetypal American striver, who, incidentally, died
        enormously wealthy in 1790.

1797   Thomas Paine (1737–1809), in his *Agrarian Justice,* remarks
        that society at present is "checkered with the extremes of
        affluence and want." He therefore proposes a "national
        fund" from which every person reaching the age of 21
        shall be paid a stakeholder sum. He also proposes a guar-
        anteed annual payment to the elderly out of the same
        fund, with revenues to be drawn from a 10 percent tax on
        inherited wealth. This is an early and often-cited example
        of a wealth-redistributive proposal (Paine 1797).

1802   Eleuthère Irénée du Pont, a recent immigrant from
        France, builds a gunpowder mill on the Brandywine
        River in Delaware. In later years, the family-managed du
        Pont company produces a variety of explosives and be-
        comes the world's largest munitions supplier. The fam-
        ily, prospering and growing larger with each generation,
        comes to be regarded as one of America's richest. (In the
        first *Forbes* listing of the 400 richest Americans, in 1982,
        there are 28 du Ponts.)

1806   Shoemakers in Philadelphia go on strike for higher
        wages. They not only lose the strike but are convicted of
        criminal conspiracy for joining together in a labor union.

1828   The wealthiest 4 percent of people in New York City own 49 percent of the city's non-corporate wealth, confirming what the New York merchant Philip Hone writes in his diary about the city which he serves as mayor during 1827–28: "The two extremes of costly luxury in living, expensive establishments and improvident waste are presented in daily and hourly contrast with squalid misery and hopeless destitution." Wealth becomes concentrated so quickly in the city that by 1845, the top 4 percent share of total non-corporate wealth has jumped from 49 to 66 percent. Similar trends are seen in Boston and Philadelphia (Pessen 1973, ch. 3).

Thomas Mellon, a 14-year-old Irish immigrant in Pennsylvania, finds inspiration in Ben Franklin's *Autobiography:* "Here was Franklin, poorer than myself, who by industry, thrift, and frugality [was] elevated to wealth and fame." At age 17, Mellon balks at following in his father's footsteps as a farmer, choosing instead to become a lawyer, judge, capitalist, and banker. In 1870, he founds what will eventually become the Mellon Bank in Pittsburgh. His son Andrew will later magnify the family fortune and also serve as Secretary of the Treasury under presidents Harding, Coolidge, and Hoover (Mellon 1996).

Workers at textile mills in Paterson, New Jersey, stage the first factory strike in U.S. history, demanding a reduction of the workday from 13.5 to 12 hours. They lose.

1829   The Boston Prison Discipline Society claims that 75,000 people each year are imprisoned for debt in the United States (Pessen 1973, 31).

1834   In New Hampshire, the Reverend Charles Burroughs sermonizes on the difference between honest poverty and degrading pauperism. "The former is an unavoidable evil, to which many are brought from necessity. . . . It is the result, not of our faults, but of our misfortunes." Pauperism, on the other hand, is the result of "willful error, of shameful indolence, of vicious habits." The poverty-pauperism distinction mirrors another, that between the "deserving" and the "undeserving" poor,

1834   which pervades much of American discourse on the
(*cont.*)   poor and how they should be dealt with (Katz 1989, 13).

1847   New Hampshire is the first state to set a legal limit of 10
hours of labor per day.

1853   Construction begins on Llewellyn Park, the first gated
community in the United States. The exclusive park is in
West Orange, New Jersey, about 15 miles west of New
York City. Luxurious homes in the development are designed by celebrated architects like Charles McKim and
Stanford White, and there is a guardhouse to ensure the
privacy and security of residents. Thomas Edison buys a
23-room mansion here in 1886; other residents include
members of the Merck and Colgate families.

1862   The first federal inheritance tax is approved by Congress
as a way to help pay for Civil War expenses. In 1874, the
Supreme Court upholds the constitutionality of the tax,
even though Congress had repealed it by then.

1863   President Abraham Lincoln issues the Emancipation
Proclamation, freeing slaves held in the southern states.
The long-term legacy of slavery, Jim Crow, and racial discrimination in hiring and housing is this: poverty rates
for African Americans are consistently higher than for
any other racial or ethnic group in the United States up
to the present day, and the black-white wealth gap is
enormous.

Congress authorizes the northern states to draft soldiers
into the Union army. Class differences are brought into
stark relief as wealthier men are permitted to buy "substitutes" to serve in their place, while working-class men
must put on the Union blues and go off to fight. (Mortality rates during the Civil War are horrendous, due to the
primitive state of battlefield medicine.)

1866   Horatio Alger (1832–1899) publishes *Ragged Dick*, the
first of his hugely popular rags-to-riches stories written
mainly for boys. In more than 100 such books, Alger promotes a single message: with hard work and good

morals, anybody can make a success of himself in the United States.

1868   Congress sets an eight-hour workday for federal employees. It will be 30 more years before the United Mine Workers of America win a similar workday for miners, and 70 years before the eight-hour day becomes the national rule in the Fair Labor Standards Act (1938).

1879   Journalist and economist Henry George (1839–1897) writes *Progress and Poverty,* one of the best-selling books of the 19th century. George offers a compelling explanation for the depressed condition of labor and the tendency of the economy to fall into periodic, painful downturns. He points to the fact that whenever the economic system becomes more productive, the resulting gains are captured by landowners, who hold a monopoly on the only fixed resource, land. Their rising rents are entirely unearned, and this suggests to George a suitable corrective policy. The government should put a heavy tax—he calls it a "single tax"—on land, and it should replace all other taxes.

1883   In *What Social Classes Owe to Each Other,* Yale sociologist William Graham Sumner (1840–1910) expresses the social Darwinist philosophy in its starkest terms: funds should not be redistributed from the rich to the poor, as this would amount to "coddling" the latter and would go against the laws of nature. The rule of survival of the fittest applies in the social realm just as it does in the natural.

1886   The Statue of Liberty is installed in New York Harbor. On its pedestal are inscribed the last five lines of "The New Colossus," an 1883 poem by Emma Lazarus. Lazarus is a member of New York's Jewish social elite. She writes movingly of the welcome to be extended to future generations of immigrants: "Give me your tired, your poor, / Your huddled masses yearning to breathe free, / The wretched refuse of your teeming shore."

1887   The novel *Looking Backward,* by Edward Bellamy (1850–1898), depicts an egalitarian United States of the future in

1887
(cont.)
which people live in harmony and comfort, their material needs met by an efficient, centrally planned economy. Sharp contrasts are drawn between this utopia and the harsh economic realities of late 19th-century America. The novel is a huge bestseller.

1889
Andrew Carnegie (1835–1919) publishes *The Gospel of Wealth,* in which he tackles the problem of how to maintain a harmonious relationship between the rich and the poor in a modern capitalist society. Great wealth accumulations, he argues, can be passed along privately to heirs; they can be taxed away upon death; or they can be "administered" for public purposes by rich individuals during their own lifetimes. Carnegie favors the third approach. He calls the wealthy man a "trustee for his poorer brethren." (See chapter 6.) Demonstrating the strength of his convictions, Carnegie, a great steelmaker, gives away some $350 million of his personal fortune before his death, mainly to public libraries and colleges.

Construction begins on Biltmore Estate, near Asheville, North Carolina, a grand residence for George W. Vanderbilt, grandson of "Commodore" Cornelius Vanderbilt. It is the largest house in the United States, with 250 rooms, including 34 master bedrooms and 43 bathrooms. Designed by Richard Morris Hunt and set in a park laid out by Frederick Law Olmsted, it takes six years to complete.

1890
Jacob Riis (1849–1914), a Danish immigrant to New York City, publishes *How the Other Half Lives,* an eye-opening account of life among the poorest slum-dwellers of his adopted city. Uniquely informed by Riis's own episodes of destitution and illustrated by his black-and-white photographs, the book is quickly recognized as a landmark in U.S. social history (Riis 1971).

1892
Cornelius Vanderbilt II, grandson of "Commodore" Vanderbilt, orders construction of The Breakers, a summer "cottage" in Newport, Rhode Island, with more than 70 rooms and 130,000 square feet of living space. Designed by Richard Morris Hunt and costing a staggering $7 mil-

lion, the mansion is completed in 1895. It features floors of Italian and African marble and whole rooms imported from chateaux in France. The Vanderbilts occupy The Breakers for two months each year.

1896   William Jennings Bryan gives one of the most famous speeches in American history at the Democratic National Convention in Chicago. Speaking in favor of a bimetallic monetary standard, which would tend to favor debtors (chiefly the poor), over the gold standard, which would favor creditors (chiefly the rich), Bryan declares, "You shall not press down upon the brow of labor this crown of thorns; you shall not crucify mankind upon a cross of gold." Bryan, an aspirant to his party's presidential nomination—which he receives on the strength of this speech—also declares, "What we need is an Andrew Jackson to stand, as Jackson stood, against the encroachments of organized wealth" (Bryan 1896).

1899   John Bates Clark, one of America's most respected economists, argues, in his *Distribution of Wealth: A Theory of Wages, Interest, and Profits,* that in a competitive economy, every factor of production is paid what it is worth to the employer. One implication of this theory is that however low the wage rate may fall, it cannot be called exploitative, since it reflects what the worker's productive efforts are worth to the employer, no more, no less. Such a theoretical framework puts neoclassical economics in the position of vouching for the essential fairness of the existing income distribution.

1904   Ida Tarbell (1857–1944) publishes *The History of the Standard Oil Company,* a carefully researched account of the business tactics, described by some as ruthless, employed by John D. Rockefeller in creating one of history's most lucrative monopolies. Rockefeller dismisses the book and its author, whom he derides as "Miss Tarbarrel." Seven years later, in 1911, the Supreme Court orders the Standard Oil trust dissolved.

1905   Max O. Lorenz, an American economist, introduces a simple graphical representation of wealth inequality that

1905
(*cont.*)
later becomes, along with the Gini coefficient, a vital part of the technical toolkit experts use to study wealth and income disparities in the United States and elsewhere. The Lorenz curve can be seen in any introductory economics textbook (Lorenz 1905).

1906 President Theodore Roosevelt proposes the introduction of a federal inheritance tax in his State of the Union address to Congress. "The man of great wealth," he asserts, "owes a peculiar obligation to the State because he derives special advantages from the mere existence of government." Roosevelt notes that the main purpose of the proposed tax should be to "put a constantly increasing burden on the inheritance of those swollen fortunes which it is certainly of no benefit to this country to perpetuate" (Roosevelt 1906).

1907 President Roosevelt attacks the "malefactors of great wealth" who, in his opinion, put their selfish financial interests above all other considerations, including the welfare of their workers and the stability of the marketplace. Roosevelt says that such individuals deserve to be punished. The "malefactors" phrase is often repeated in later years by critics of those who accumulate and then misuse great wealth (Hart and Ferleger 1941, 327–328).

1910 Gustavus Myers (1872–1942) publishes a three-volume work, *History of the Great American Fortunes,* which offers a hard-hitting exposé of the leading robber barons of the late 19th century. In Myers's view, all the great fortunes were founded on deceit, corruption, fraud, bribery, and exploitation, and he provides extensive details to bolster his case.

1912 Italian statistician Corrado Gini (1884–1965), in a journal article entitled "Variabilita e Mutabilita," presents a new quantitative measure of inequality. The so-called Gini coefficient is used extensively in later studies of income and wealth inequality around the world.

John D. Rockefeller's personal fortune reaches a peak of $900 million. In relation to the country's gross domestic product (GDP), this sum vastly exceeds the fortunes of either Bill Gates or the Walton family a century later.

1913   Ratification of the Sixteenth Amendment to the Constitution authorizes the U.S. government to levy an income tax. Congress proceeds swiftly to impose such a tax, setting the rate at 1 percent on incomes from $3,000 to $20,000. The marginal tax rate rises on incomes above $20,000, to a high of 7 percent on incomes over $500,000. Most Americans have incomes well below $3,000 and thus avoid taxation. Only about 2 percent pay any tax.

J. P. Morgan dies in Rome. The American financier famous for calming financial markets under pressure, for his deal-making prowess (he created the U.S. Steel Corporation out of the steel companies of Andrew Carnegie and others in 1901), and for his art-collecting exploits, is said to have left an estate of around $80 million. John D. Rockefeller, on learning of Morgan's worth, is quoted as saying, "And to think he wasn't even a rich man" (Strouse 2000, 15).

1916   In the year of her death, Hetty Green is America's wealthiest woman, with a fortune some estimate at $130 million. (At today's price levels, she would be a billionaire.) Never before—or since—has a woman in the United States had such a career at the very pinnacle of high finance. Often derided as the "Witch of Wall Street" for her preferred black attire and curmudgeonly manner, Green is also known for miserliness of epic proportions.

Congress reinstitutes a federal estate tax to offset costs associated with World War I. The top rate is 10 percent on estates over $5 million. By 1924, the top rate will be hiked to 40 percent on estates in excess of $10 million.

1918   The top marginal income tax rate hits 77 percent on incomes above $1 million, as the costs of World War I force the federal government to raise as much revenue as possible. Rates fall quickly after the war's conclusion.

1924   Congress enacts a federal gift tax. Its purpose is to prevent wealthy individuals from giving away their assets

1924
(*cont.*)
just before death to avoid the estate tax passed by Congress eight years earlier. The new tax is repealed in 1926 but permanently reinstated in 1932.

1926
An exchange between two American literary giants supposedly has F. Scott Fitzgerald telling Ernest Hemingway, "The rich are different from you and me," and Hemingway replying, "Yes, they have more money." The exchange is apocryphal, although it strongly echoes some lines in a short story by Fitzgerald ("The Rich Boy"). The 1920s are a decade of high and increasing wealth inequality in the United States, and the lavish lifestyles of the rich are captured memorably in Fitzgerald's novels and stories.

1934
President Franklin D. Roosevelt and Congress raise the estate tax to 60 percent on estates above $10 million. Unlike previous inheritance taxes, this one is justified on general redistributive grounds, as opposed to wartime revenue needs.

1936
Nominated on June 27 to run for a second term as president, Roosevelt uses his acceptance speech at the Democratic Convention to attack "economic inequality" in the United States. A small group of "economic royalists" has "concentrated into their own hands an almost complete control over other people's property, other people's money, other people's labor—other people's lives."

1938
Congress passes a federal minimum wage law: the Fair Labor Standards Act (FLSA). The minimum wage is set initially at 25 cents per hour but later raised in varying amounts at irregular intervals. By the end of the 20th century, some observers are convinced that the failure of the government since the late 1960s to maintain the real (inflation-adjusted) value of the minimum wage holds down wage levels at the lower end of the labor market, contributing to the growing inequality of income in the United States.

1939
John Steinbeck (1902–1968) publishes one of the most powerful accounts of Depression-era poverty in *The*

Grapes of Wrath. It tells the story of a family of Oklahoma farmers driven west by the Dust Bowl and barely hanging on to life and dignity. Steinbeck later wins the Nobel Prize for Literature (1962).

1944   The top marginal income tax rate hits 94 percent on incomes over $200,000. This is an all-time record high that Congress justifies on the basis of wartime revenue needs, and it lasts through 1945. After the end of World War II, the top marginal rate varies between 82 and 91 percent until the Tax Cut of 1964 reduces it to 77 percent on incomes over $400,000. The top rate remains in the 70 percent range through the 1960s and 1970s (Wilson and Jordan, 2002).

Congress passes the Servicemen's Readjustment Act of 1944, otherwise known as the GI Bill of Rights. It entitles servicemen returning from World War II to education and training benefits; offers loan guarantees to veterans for the purchase of a home, farm, or business; and provides weekly cash benefits to unemployed veterans for up to one year. Over half of all veterans receive training of some kind under the bill, and in 1947 veterans account for roughly half of all college admissions. The GI Bill is later seen as one of the most successful pieces of social legislation in U.S. history, making it possible for vast numbers of ordinary Americans, including many poor (as long as they have served in the military), to raise themselves to a higher economic and social status than would otherwise have been the case. New versions of the GI Bill are passed in the wake of the Korean War and the Vietnam War with overwhelming public support.

1953   Union membership as a share of the total U.S. labor force peaks at about 35 percent. Thereafter, the union share falls steadily, and in 2006 it is a mere 12 percent. This is significant because some explanations of the growing rich-poor gap in the United States point to the role of unions in helping workers achieve higher wages. Weaker unions, in this view, can cause a lowering of labor incomes relative to the incomes of business owners, managers, and professionals.

1958   John Kenneth Galbraith (1908–2006), a Harvard econo-
        mist, publishes *The Affluent Society*, in which he observes
        that "in the United States, the survival of poverty is re-
        markable. We ignore it because we share with all soci-
        eties at all times the capacity for not seeing what we do
        not wish to see" (Galbraith 1998, 242). American poverty,
        he asserts, is a disgrace that cannot be excused or toler-
        ated. Galbraith makes the case that public investments—
        in schools, parks, mass transportation, and so on—will
        not only help correct a systemic imbalance between pub-
        lic and private consumption in the United States but will
        do much to alleviate poverty. His book is later seen as an
        antidote to Eisenhower-era complacency and a harbin-
        ger of the Kennedy-Johnson commitment to tackle U.S.
        poverty.

1962   The economist Milton Friedman (1912–2006), in his
        highly influential book *Capitalism and Freedom*, advocates
        a guaranteed annual income to every household as a
        way to replace the existing hodge-podge of government
        programs for the poor. Friedman proposes that those
        earning very low (or no) incomes be provided with a
        check from the U.S. government through the income tax
        system; he calls it a "negative income tax." Some are
        shocked by such a radical idea, especially coming from a
        conservative, but Friedman points to the superior effi-
        ciency and expanded freedom of choice promised by his
        proposal.

        Michael Harrington (1928–1989) publishes *The Other
        America: Poverty in the United States*, a now-classic ac-
        count of the extensive destitution coexisting with afflu-
        ence in mid-century America. Harrington, a prominent
        socialist, describes rural poverty, racial and ethnic
        poverty, urban poverty, and the poverty of many older
        people, venturing a guess that the number of poor in the
        United States may total 50 million. The book is often de-
        scribed by middle-class readers as revelatory, and histo-
        rians credit it as one of the key intellectual forces behind
        the War on Poverty initiated by President Lyndon John-
        son in 1964.

1963– Mollie Orshansky (1915–2006), a Social Security Admin-
1964   istration statistician, constructs the official poverty
       thresholds still used by the U.S. government more than
       40 years later. Her poverty yardstick is based on Agricul-
       ture Department estimates of what it costs to feed a fam-
       ily on a "thrifty" food plan. Since American families in
       this time period spend, on average, about one-third of
       their income on food, Orshansky multiplies the food cost
       by three to arrive at the poverty threshold, that is, what
       it would cost to meet all of a family's basic needs. She
       calculates an array of threshold figures appropriate to
       various family sizes, ages, and rural/urban locations. In
       later years, the figures are adjusted upward annually to
       take inflation into account.

1964   President Lyndon B. Johnson (LBJ) uses the occasion of
       his first State of the Union address on January 8 to de-
       clare "unconditional war on poverty in America." In
       March, he submits his Equal Opportunity Act of 1964 to
       Congress, and in August, he signs the bill into law. An
       Office of Economic Opportunity (OEO) is established to
       run the war on poverty, with Robert Sargent Shriver Jr.,
       brother-in-law of the late President John F. Kennedy, as
       its first director. OEO oversees several programs, includ-
       ing Job Corps, Volunteers in Service to America (VISTA),
       and Neighborhood Youth Corps.

       LBJ, in a speech in May, outlines his "Great Society" ini-
       tiative, which will come to include the Medicare, Medi-
       caid, and Head Start programs (passed by Congress in
       1965). Near the end of his speech, LBJ asks the audience:
       "Will you join in the battle to give every citizen an escape
       from the crushing weight of poverty?"

       Warren Buffett (b. 1930) takes control of Berkshire Hath-
       away, an old-line New England textile company that he
       soon transforms into an all-purpose investment com-
       pany through which he is able to build up an immense
       personal fortune. By 2006, he is worth $44 billion (on
       paper) and is the second-richest person in the United
       States.

1968 Dr. Martin Luther King Jr. (1929–1968) writes, "The time has come for us to civilize ourselves by the total, direct and immediate abolition of poverty." Previous government efforts to alleviate poverty, he says, have been "fragmentary" and "spasmodic." What is needed now is a comprehensive attack on poverty. He comes out in favor of the Milton Friedman plan for a guaranteed annual income, without mentioning Friedman by name. The two economists he does refer to are Henry George and John Kenneth Galbraith (King 1967, 161–166).

1969 Just six months into his presidency, Richard Nixon proposes his Family Assistance Plan (FAP), a modified version of Milton Friedman's negative income tax. Nixon stresses that the FAP will replace the existing welfare program, Aid to Families with Dependent Children (AFDC), but will be structured in a way that leaves no family worse off than before. After the House of Representatives passes the FAP bill in 1970, Milton Friedman speaks out publicly against it for being a mere add-on to, rather than replacement for, existing programs. The plan dies in a Senate committee.

1970 Arkansas Community Organizations for Reform Now (ACORN) begins to organize welfare recipients and low-wage workers in Little Rock. Its leadership comes from a well-established national group, the National Welfare Rights Organization (NWRO), and its agenda ranges from obtaining clothes and furniture for welfare families to securing better social services for Vietnam vets, the unemployed, and blue-collar families. ACORN expands beyond Little Rock and eventually beyond Arkansas, to Texas and South Dakota in 1975 and to 20 states by 1980. Renamed as the Association of Community Organizations for Reform Now, ACORN becomes a grassroots political force and a major backer of the living wage movement in the United States. By 2006 it is the "largest neighborhood-based antipoverty group in the country" (Eckholm 2006).

1973 The poverty rate in the United States hits its lowest recorded level ever: 11.1 percent.

1975   Microsoft Corporation is founded by Harvard dropout
        William Henry (Bill) Gates III and his friend Paul Allen.
        The company will eventually make Gates the richest per-
        son in the United States, if not the world. Paul Allen
        ranks eleventh in the 2007 *Forbes* listing of the richest
        people in the United States.

        Congress passes and President Gerald Ford signs the
        Earned Income Tax Credit (EITC) bill, under which low-
        income workers can receive a wage subsidy from the
        federal government. The EITC program becomes one of
        the most expensive, but also one of the most effective, of
        all the federal efforts to fight poverty. It consistently
        draws bipartisan support in Congress and the White
        House.

1981   President Ronald Reagan signs into law the Economic
        Recovery Tax Act of 1981, which cuts federal income tax
        rates by 23 percent in three yearly stages. The top mar-
        ginal tax rate falls from 70 percent to 50 percent. By the
        end of the decade, the top rate has dropped to 28 percent.

1982   *Forbes* magazine launches its annual listing of the richest
        400 Americans.

1983   The Federal Reserve Board begins conducting a triennial
        Survey of Consumer Finances (SCF) that offers for the
        first time a semi-official government overview of the U.S.
        wealth distribution.

1985   *Forbes* ranks Samuel Walton, founder of the Wal-Mart
        Corporation, as the country's richest man, a title he car-
        ries for several years until the magazine decides to split
        credit for the Wal-Mart fortune among Sam, his wife, and
        his children. Unlike fellow billionaires Bill Gates and
        Warren Buffett, Walton puts a lifetime into building a
        business and making money, showing little interest in se-
        rious philanthropic endeavors. At his death in 1992, the
        great bulk of Walton's personal fortune passes to his wife
        and children, not to charitable causes. More than 20
        years later, the Walton family remains America's richest.

1988   In his January 25 State of the Union address to Congress, President Reagan says, "My friends, some years ago, the Federal Government declared war on poverty, and poverty won." He then describes the "fifty-nine major welfare programs" on which the federal government spends $100 billion a year, bemoans the "dependency" they have created among America's poor, and praises the states for their many innovative programs aimed at getting welfare recipients back to work. He urges that the states be given more flexibility to pursue tougher child-support and welfare-to-work policies.

1990   The Immigration Act of 1990 lifts the ceiling on annual (legal) immigration from 500,000 to 700,000 persons annually. "Family reunification" now accounts for the largest number of legal immigrants into the country. *Illegal* immigration grows steadily during the 1990s and in the first years of the new century. Some observers link an influx of lower-skilled workers into U.S. labor markets to downward pressures on wage rates, thus causing—or worsening—poverty (Samuelson 2006).

1993   The Omnibus Budget Reconciliation Act of 1993, signed into law by President William J. Clinton, raises the top marginal tax rate to just under 40 percent, where it remains throughout his two terms in office.

1996   Congress approves a two-stage increase in the federal minimum wage, from a level of $4.25 (set in 1991) to $4.75 in 1996 and then to $5.15 in 1997. Liberals urge a higher rate in order to benefit low-paid workers and their families; conservatives argue that minimum wages burden small businesses with added costs and create unemployment.

2001   A Boston-based group, Responsible Wealth, speaks out vigorously against President George W. Bush's proposal to repeal the federal estate tax (see next item). The group—which includes Warren Buffett, George Soros, several Rockefellers, and William Gates Jr., father of Microsoft billionaire Bill Gates—places an ad in *The New York Times* on February 18, warning that revenues lost from the repeal of the estate tax will either force increases in other taxes or result in reduced funding for government programs like Social Security and Medicare.

President Bush signs into law the Economic Growth and Tax Relief Reconciliation Act of 2001. The law lowers the income tax rate applicable to the wealthiest Americans from about 40 percent to 35 percent. It also lowers the top marginal tax rate on estates from 55 percent in 2001 to 45 percent by 2009, and increases the individual tax-exempt amount from $675,000 in 2001 to $3.5 million ($7 million for married couples) in 2009. Under the law, federal estate taxes will disappear completely in 2010—and then be reinstated in 2011 at the tax rates prevailing in 2001.

2004   *Forbes* inaugurates an annual listing of the nation's most expensive gated communities. The magazine observes, "As long as there have been rich people, there have been gates to keep everyone else out." In the initial listing, more gated communities are found in Boca Raton, Florida, than anywhere else in the country, although high-end developments are also found in California, Connecticut, Nevada, and Hawaii (Clemence 2004).

2005   Hurricane Katrina devastates New Orleans and much of the Gulf Coast. The nation's media, politicians, and pundits belatedly "discover" poverty in America. *Newsweek* magazine, for example, runs a cover story entitled "The Other America," consciously echoing the title of Michael Harrington's groundbreaking book of 1962. Calling the kind of poverty the storm revealed in New Orleans's Ninth Ward and the rural counties of Louisiana and Mississippi "an enduring shame," the article notes that "Hurricane Katrina exposed the harsh disparities between rich and poor in this country. Despite recent economic growth, poverty rates have risen for four straight years" (Alter 2006, 46).

2006   Bill Gates, the richest man in the United States for over a decade, announces that he will be stepping down from major business responsibilities related to Microsoft in the summer of 2008. From then on, he will devote his time and energy to the philanthropic projects of the Bill &

2006   Melinda Gates Foundation that have already earned him
(*cont.*) high praise, particularly in the field of international pub-
          lic health. Gates is a few years younger than John D. Rock-
          efeller was when he withdrew from active engagement in
          running the Standard Oil Company in 1896, devoting the
          remainder of his long life to philanthropic pursuits.

          Warren Buffett announces that he will give the bulk of
          his fortune—about $31 billion at current Berkshire Hath-
          away stock prices—to the Bill & Melinda Gates Founda-
          tion. This reverses earlier declarations by Buffett that his
          charitable donations would not occur until his death.
          Observers credit the relationship of trust that has devel-
          oped between Buffett and Gates since the two met in
          1991 for this change in Buffett's plans. For an individual
          of Buffett's wealth to donate most of it to another foun-
          dation rather than establishing his own is unprecedented
          (O'Brien and Saul 2006).

          The results of the Federal Reserve's 2004 SCF survey are
          released, and in the carefully worded conclusion of the
          survey report, they reveal that from 1989 to 2004, "the
          distribution of family wealth shifted higher." The Gini
          coefficient in 2004 was significantly higher than it had
          been in 1989, 1992, or 1995, although little changed from
          1998 or 2001. Also, the share of net household wealth
          held by the poorer half of the population fell between
          1995 and 2004, from a paltry 3.6 percent to an even pal-
          trier 2.5 percent (Kennickell 2006, 46).

2007   The official U.S. poverty rate is 12.3 percent.

          Congress passes, and President Bush signs into law, an
          increase in the federal minimum wage that will lift it, in
          stages, to $7.25 by mid-2009.

References

Alter, Jonathan. "The Other America." *Newsweek* (September 19, 2005):
42–48.

Bremer, Francis J. *John Winthrop: America's Forgotten Founding Father.* New York: Oxford University Press, 2003.

Bryan, William Jennings. "Cross of Gold" speech (1896).

Clemence, Sara. "Most Expensive Gated Communities in America." *Forbes* (2004). Accessed at http://www.forbes.com.

Eckholm, Erik. "City by City, an Antipoverty Group Plants Seeds of Change." *The New York Times* (June 26, 2006): A12.

Fitzgerald, F. Scott. "The Rich Boy," in *All the Sad Young Men.* New York: Charles Scribner's Sons, 1926.

Franklin, Benjamin. *Poor Richard's Almanac.* Published annually; originally published 1732–1758.

Galbraith, John Kenneth. *The Affluent Society,* Fortieth Anniversary Edition. Boston: Mariner Books, 1998 [1958].

Hart, Albert Bushnell, and Herbert Ronald Ferleger, eds. *Theodore Roosevelt Cyclopedia.* New York: Roosevelt Memorial Association, 1941.

Katz, Michael B. *The Undeserving Poor: From the War on Poverty to the War on Welfare.* New York: Pantheon Books, 1989.

Kennickell, Arthur B. "Currents and Undercurrents: Changes in the Distribution of Wealth, 1989–2004." Federal Reserve Board, *SCF Working Papers* (2006). Accessed at http://www.federalreserve.gov.

King, Martin Luther, Jr. *Where Do We Go from Here: Chaos or Community?* New York: Harper and Row, 1967.

Lorenz, M. O. "Methods of Measuring the Concentration of Wealth." *Publications of the American Statistical Association* 9, no. 70 (1905): 209–219.

Mellon, Thomas. *Thomas Mellon and His Times.* Pittsburgh: University of Pittsburgh Press, 1996 [1885].

O'Brien, Timothy L., and Stephanie Saul. "Buffett to Give Bulk of His Fortune to Gates Charity." *The New York Times* (June 26, 2006): A1, A15.

Paine, Thomas. *Agrarian Justice* (1797). Accessed at http://www.ssa.gov/history/paine4.html

Pessen, Edward. *Riches, Class, and Power before the Civil War.* Lexington, MA: D. C. Heath, 1973.

Riis, Jacob. *How the Other Half Lives.* New York: Dover Publications, 1971 [1890].

Robbins, Gary. "Estate Taxes: An Historical Perspective." The Heritage Foundation, *Backgrounder* 1719 (January 16, 2004).

Samuelson, Robert. "We Don't Need 'Guest Workers.'" *The Washington Post* (March 22, 2006): A21.

Strouse, Jean. *Morgan: American Financier.* New York: Random House, 2000.

U.S. Department of Veterans Affairs. "History of the G.I. Bill." Accessed at http://www.gibill.va.gov.

Wilson, Robert A., and David E. Jordan. "Personal Exemptions and Individual Income Tax Rates, 1913–2002 (Rev. 6–02)," Internal Revenue Service, *Statistics of Income Bulletin* (Publication 1136), Spring 2002: 216–225.

5

Biographical Sketches

This chapter offers thumbnail sketches of 27 individuals whose lives or ideas shed light on economic inequality in the United States. Some, like Warren Buffett, Bill Gates, and Sam Walton, give us a sense of what it means—and what it takes—to be at the very top of the income distribution, to have wealth that can be equated to the GDPs of small nations. Some, like Chuck Collins, Marian Wright Edelman, and Dolores Huerta, have been notable advocates on behalf of those at the lower end of the income distribution. Several economists are included for the work they have done to fashion tools for measuring the gap between rich and poor, or for their contributions to the actual measurement of the gap. Another group of individuals featured in the chapter are experts on wealth or poverty in the United States, people like Paul Schervish, Sara McLanahan, and Timothy Smeeding. And finally, there are individuals who have legendary and mythologic stature in the annals of American wealth: John D. Rockefeller, Hetty Green, and Horatio Alger. Taken together, they constitute a fascinating gallery of men and women who, in one way or another, help us grasp the meaning of highly disparate economic fortunes in the United States.

Horatio Alger Jr. (1832–1899)

The belief that anyone can rise from poverty to wealth through hard work, honesty, and sheer persistence is often seen as characteristically American. Although the creed of "strive and succeed" did not originate with Horatio Alger—think, for example, of Benjamin Franklin's *Autobiography*—Alger undoubtedly drove it much deeper into the popular consciousness with the best-selling dime novels that he produced by the scores, beginning in 1867. The son of a Unitarian minister, Alger attended Harvard and then Harvard Divinity School, and served briefly as a parson on Cape Cod before moving to New York City and becoming a full-time writer. He was struck at once by the vast numbers of orphaned and abandoned children living on the streets. His first rags-to-riches story, *Ragged Dick*, was so successful that it became the template for more than a hundred similar tales with titles like *Bound to Rise, Sink or Swim,* and *Making His Way, or, Frank Courtney's Struggle Upward.* Nearly all featured a penniless youth who, by dint of luck and pluck—and often with the timely assistance of a mentoring adult—pulled himself up to respectability and financial success. In the era of the robber barons, when the gap between rich and poor yawned wider than at any other time in U.S. history, the Horatio Alger stories found a huge readership, selling as well as the works of Mark Twain. What they offered young readers was the promise that anyone, however humble his origins, could climb the ladder of success if he was diligent and industrious enough.

Further Reading

Horatio Alger, *Ragged Dick and Mark, the Match Boy: Two Novels by Horatio Alger,* New York: Touchstone, 1998; Stefan Kanfer, "Horatio Alger: The Moral of the Story," *City Journal* (Autumn 2000), accessed at http://www.city-journal.org.

Anne L. Alstott (b. 1963)

Faced with the facts about U.S. income and wealth disparities, some observers shrug and find nothing amiss. Others, like Anne Alstott, argue for redistributive efforts by the government to move society in a more egalitarian direction. Alstott and Bruce Ackerman, coauthors of *The Stakeholder Society,* have said that they would not object to an unequal distribution of wealth if all Americans enjoyed genuine equality of opportunity from birth to adulthood. But since that is far from the case, Alstott and Ackerman have advanced a radical proposal: every American reaching adulthood should be given an $80,000 "stake" to be used for any good purpose, such as going to college, starting a business, buying or making a down payment on a house, or enrolling in a training program. This stakeholding program would cost around $250 billion a year. It could be financed by a 2 percent wealth tax to be imposed on the top 40 percent of wealth-holders and, when possible, by a payback of each person's original stake upon death.

In her 2005 book *No Exit: What Parents Owe Their Children and What Society Owes Parents,* Alstott offers another bold proposal that would tend to lessen economic inequality in the United States. Arguing that society has a clear interest in ensuring that parents have the resources they need to rear their children, and that the costs of childrearing are now higher than ever, she favors a government award of $5,000 to every parent of a child under 13. The "caregiver grant" could be used to pay for child care, education, or even retirement savings. Alstott holds an AB degree from Georgetown University (1984) and a law degree from Yale (1987), where she is now a deputy dean and the Jacquin D. Bierman Professor of Taxation.

Further Reading

Bruce Ackerman and Anne Alstott, "$80,000 and a Dream," *The American Prospect* 11, no.16 (July 17, 2000): 23–25; Bruce Ackerman and Anne Alstott, *The Stakeholder Society,* New Haven, CT: Yale University Press, 1999; Anne Alstott, *No Exit: What Parents Owe Their Children and What Society Owes Parents,* New York: Oxford University Press, 2005.

Warren E. Buffett (b. 1930)

Often referred to as the greatest investor in the world—possibly the greatest of all time—Warren Buffett has been the second-richest American for a number of years. *Forbes* magazine estimated his wealth in 2007 at $52 billion, somewhat behind Bill Gates's $59 billion but far ahead of third-ranked Sheldon Adelson's $28 billion. Buffett is a generation older than Gates, and he built his fortune by acquiring much more traditional companies than Microsoft. He is a "value investor" who sizes up the intrinsic value of a company, checks the price at which its shares are selling in the stock market, and acts accordingly. If the value is greater than the share price, the company is worth buying; otherwise, it is not. In his youth, Buffett studied this investment strategy in a class taught by the legendary Benjamin Graham at Columbia University. By the mid-1950s, he was back in his hometown of Omaha,

Nebraska, managing investment partnerships. His own savings and those of many partners enabled him to achieve control of Berkshire Hathaway by the middle of the 1960s. He proceeded to turn this old-line textile company into a holding company through which he could buy and control a whole range of businesses that he deemed to be undervalued, with good market share and solid growth potential. Some of Buffett's most important (and profitable) investments over the years have been in industries that are anything but high-tech: insurance, soft drinks, candy, underwear, and manufactured houses. The popular press depicts Buffett as someone who lives simply in the same house he bought 45 years ago, drives a pickup truck, eats burgers and steaks, drinks Coca-Cola, and, as the "Oracle of Omaha," dispenses simple yet astute investment advice to Berkshire Hathaway stockholders at their annual meetings. Colorful he may be, but Buffett has a track record unrivaled anywhere—a 22 percent compound annual return on Berkshire Hathaway stock since he gained control of the company more than 40 years ago.

Further Reading
Warren E. Buffett, *The Essays of Warren Buffett: Lessons for Corporate America*, New York: L. Cunningham, 2001; Roger Lowenstein, *Buffett: The Making of an American Capitalist*, New York: Random House, 1995.

John Bates Clark (1847–1938)

Everyone knows the expression, "You're paid what you're worth." The plausibility of that statement probably helps many people accept, without too much grumbling, a distribution of personal income that is far from equal in the United States. If some individuals are paid poorly, it is because they are less productive and therefore worth less to the employer, and if some are paid much better, it is because they are more productive. The notion that we are all paid according to how productive we are goes back to a theory developed by one of America's great economists, John Bates Clark. In *The Distribution of Wealth: A Theory of Wages, Interest, and Profits* (1899), Clark set out his marginal productivity theory of income distribution. In essence, he argued that in a free-market economy, labor will be paid according to its productivity, and capital (tools, machines, and so on) will likewise be rewarded according to *its* contribution to total output. No individual or social class will have any good reason to complain. In particular, the radical claims of Karl Marx (1818–1883) and Henry George (1839–1897) that capitalists and landlords were hogging too much of society's income were, in Clark's view, refuted by his theory. In later years, however, Clark came to recognize that the proliferation of monopolies and trusts—Rockefeller's Standard Oil Company, for example—posed a serious problem for his theory. Only if the economy were competitive, and not marred by monopoly, could the distribution of incomes be considered "natural" and fair.

Clark graduated from Amherst College in 1875 and got his graduate training at universities in Switzerland and Germany. Upon his return to the United States, he received teaching appointments at Carleton College, then Smith, Amherst, Johns Hopkins, and finally, Columbia University. In 1883, he served as president of the American Economic Association (AEA), of which he had been a co-founder three years earlier. Since 1947, the AEA has awarded the John Bates Clark Medal every two years to outstanding young economists, many of whom go on to win the Nobel Prize in economics.

Further Reading

Stanley L. Brue, *The Evolution of Economic Thought*, New York: Dryden Press, 2000: 281–291; John Henry, *John Bates Clark: The Making of a Neoclassical Economist*, New York: St. Martin's Press, 1995; Steven Pressman, *Fifty Major Economists*, New York: Routledge, 1999: 73–77.

Chuck Collins (b. 1960)

When Chuck Collins, great-grandson of meatpacking magnate Oscar Mayer, inherited his share of the family fortune in 1986 at the age of 26, it amounted to a little under half a million dollars. He promptly donated all the money to charity. The idea of coasting through life on inherited wealth does not appeal to Collins, nor does the prospect of an entire society becoming more and more divided between the rich and the poor. In 1995, he co-founded United for a Fair Economy (UFE), a Boston-based organization committed to shining a bright light on the growing inequality of wealth and income in the United States, and doing something about it. UFE works on many fronts to try to narrow the income gap. It encourages corporate philanthropy, holds seminars for religious and business groups, drafts shareholder resolutions aimed at narrowing the pay gap, lobbies against tax cuts for the wealthy, and organizes rallies. In 1997, Collins co-founded Responsible Wealth, a spin-off of UFE that enlists wealthy individuals and corporate leaders to work together in opposition to national policies, especially tax policies, that widen the gap between the haves and have-nots. One would not expect America's most affluent citizens to show much enthusiasm for activism that runs counter to their own interests, but Collins has made some powerful friends. William H. Gates Sr., father of the world's richest man, worked with Collins on a petition drive in early 2001 aimed at defeating a Republican proposal to abolish the federal estate tax. More than 100 of the country's richest individuals signed the ad, which appeared in *The New York Times*. Collins is a 1984 graduate of Hampshire College, with an MBA in community economic development from New Hampshire College (1987).

Further Reading
Chuck Collins and Felice Yeskel, *Economic Apartheid in America: A Primer on Economic Inequality and Insecurity,* revised and updated edition, New York: The New Press, 2005; Bill Gates Sr. and Chuck Collins, *Wealth and Our Commonwealth: Why America Should Tax Accumulated Fortunes,* Beacon Press, 2003; David Cay Johnston, "Dozens of Rich Americans Join in Fight to Retain the Estate Tax," *The New York Times* (February 14, 2001): A1.

Marian Wright Edelman (b. 1939)

Children have the highest poverty rate of any age group in the United States, far higher than adults or the elderly, and far above the child-poverty rates seen in other wealthy, developed countries. One might almost say that being young is a risk factor for poverty in the United States. One of the loudest voices calling attention to the plight of children in this country belongs to Marian Wright Edelman, founder and long-time president of the Children's Defense Fund (CDF). Born in Bennetsville, South Carolina, Edelman experienced racial prejudice as an African American child, but she also learned lessons of social service and commitment to equality from her parents. (Her father was a Baptist minister and a great admirer of civil rights pioneer A. Philip Randolph.) After graduating from Spelman College in Atlanta, Edelman earned a law degree from Yale in 1963. Her career began in Mississippi, where she worked on civil rights issues for the

NAACP Legal Defense Fund. In 1968, she moved to Washington, D.C., to provide counsel to the Poor People's Campaign, a project begun by Dr. Martin Luther King Jr.

In 1973, Edelman founded the CDF, and she has been its vigorous, outspoken leader ever since. The CDF advocates for children in many ways but primarily through lobbying efforts. It supports, and often urges expansion of, such programs as Head Start, child nutrition, children's health insurance, childhood immunization, foster care, and welfare. Because of the toll that guns have taken on children's lives, Edelman supports gun control. And because so many black youths end up in prison, she works for reform of the criminal justice system. Edelman never tires of reminding audiences that the United States is the world's richest nation. Why then, she asks, can it not provide a safe, healthy, and nurturing environment for its children? Edelman has written many books, received more than 100 honorary degrees, and been awarded the Presidential Medal of Freedom.

Further Reading

Marian Wright Edelman, *The Measure of Our Success: Letter to My Children and Yours,* New York: Harper Paperbacks, 1993; Marian Wright Edelman, commencement remarks, Colgate University, May 15, 2005, accessed at http://www.colgate.edu; "Marian Wright Edelman" page at Children's Defense Fund Web site, accessed at http://www.childrensdefense.org.

John Edwards (b. 1953)

In recent years, no politician running for national office in the United States has spoken as passionately about poverty as John Edwards. His "Two Americas" stump speech was easily the most memorable of the 2004 presidential primary season. In that speech, Edwards spoke of "one America that does the work, another America that reaps the reward," and of "one America that is struggling to get by, another America that can buy anything it wants, even a Congress and a President." Although the Kerry-Edwards ticket lost to Bush-Cheney in 2004, Edwards did not let go of the poverty issue. In early 2005, he helped create the Center on Poverty, Work and Opportunity at the University of North Carolina at Chapel Hill and became its first director. In the fall of that year, his campus speaking tour, Opportunity Rocks, drew enormous audiences across the country. "You can make ending poverty in America the cause of your generation," he told them. "It's the right thing to do. This is not about charity—it's about justice!"

John Edwards strikes many as uniquely qualified to speak about wealth disparities. His father was a textile mill worker in North Carolina; his mother was a postal worker. Edwards's own career took him from working-class origins to the heights of financial success as a trial lawyer. He received his undergraduate degree, the first in his family to do so, from North Carolina State University (1974). His law degree is from the University of North Carolina at Chapel Hill (1977). Edwards won his first political contest by beating North Carolina's incumbent Republican senator, Lauch Faircloth, in 1998. Two years later, he had made the short list to be Al Gore's running mate in the presidential election of 2000, just behind Joe Lieberman.

Further Reading

David Kusnet, "Stumped: Edged Out," *The New Republic Online* (July 29, 2004); Bob Moser, "Cornbread and Roses," *The Nation* (November 28, 2005); Peter Slevin, "Edwards Builds New Platform," *The Washington Post* (June 15, 2005): A03.

Barbara Ehrenreich (b. 1941)

A rite of passage for college freshmen across the country is to read, during the weeks before their arrival on campus, a book selected by their college faculty for reflection and discussion. Barbara Ehrenreich's *Nickel and Dimed* has become a familiar entry on such reading lists. The book gives middle-class young adults a glimpse—for some, their first—into what life is like for America's low-wage workers. Ehrenreich's first-person account of her experiences cleaning houses, waiting on restaurant tables, and straightening ladies' garments at a Wal-Mart store is sharp, angry, funny, and eye-opening. To the surprise of many, including Ehrenreich, the book has sold over a million copies since its publication in 2001.

Born in Butte, Montana, Ehrenreich had well-established credentials as a writer, social critic, and radical long before she went "undercover" to investigate the world of low-paid wage labor. An undergraduate degree from Reed College (1963) and a PhD in cell biology from Rockefeller University (1968) equipped her with the research skills to undertake a wide range of projects. Her books and articles have dealt with student activism, women's health issues, welfare policy, the psychological roots of war, and class divisions in the United States. Beyond her dozen books, she has written prolifically for, among others, *The New York Times, The Atlantic Monthly, Time,* and *The Progressive*.

Further Reading

Robert Birnbaum, "Interview with Barbara Ehrenreich," *identity theory* (2001), accessed at http://www.identitytheory.com; Barbara Ehrenreich, *Nickel and Dimed: On (Not) Getting by in* America, New York: Henry Holt and Company, 2001; Scott Sherman, "Class Warrior: Barbara Ehrenreich's Singular Crusade," *Columbia Journalism Review* 42, no. 4 (November/December 2003): 34–41.

Victor R. Fuchs (b. 1924)

The poverty line adopted by the U.S. government in 1964 and still used today is sometimes called the Orshansky index, in honor of Mollie Orshansky, who devised it. Based on what it costs for a household to barely subsist, it is an absolute poverty standard. If general living conditions improve, the poverty line does not rise accordingly; it rises only with inflation. The economist Victor Fuchs proposed a different poverty standard in 1967. He argued for drawing the poverty line at one-half the national median income level. In 1967, the median household income in the United States was around $6,000, meaning there were as many households receiving more than that income as there were receiving less. Fuchs's proposal would have counted any household below $3,000 as poor. Coincidentally, in the mid-1960s, the Orshansky and Fuchs poverty lines both stood at roughly $3,000, but as time passed, the two lines spread apart, with the Fuchs standard rising faster. Thus, today we would count more Americans as poor if we applied the Fuchs standard than we do using the official (Orshansky) standard. Most other countries measure poverty in the relative manner that Fuchs proposed.

Fuchs did his undergraduate work at New York University, then earned his PhD at Columbia University (1955). He went on to become one of the country's leading experts on the economics of the health care industry. His 1974 classic *Who Shall Live? Health, Economics, and Social Choice* is widely read in medical schools around the nation; it was revised and reissued in 1998 (Singapore: World Scientific Publishing). Fuchs has taught at Columbia University, New York University, City University of New York, and Stanford University. He served as president of the American Economic Association in 1995.

Further Reading
Victor R. Fuchs, "Redefining Poverty and Redistributing Income," *The Public Interest* 8 (Summer 1967): 88–95; Joseph P. Newhouse, "Distinguished Fellow: In Honor of Victor Fuchs," *Journal of Economic Perspectives* 6, no. 3 (Summer 1992): 179–189.

William H. Gates III (b. 1955)

Bill Gates has been the richest man in America, and probably the world, for over a decade. Although his name is not quite the byword for super-wealth that "Rockefeller" and "Vanderbilt" once were, Gates's fortune of $50–$60 billion is regularly compared to the gross national products of entire countries. By one calculation, his net worth exceeds that of the bottom 40 percent of all Americans combined.

Gates was born, grew up, and still lives in Seattle, where his company, Microsoft is headquartered. The son of a lawyer and a schoolteacher, he got hooked on computers at the age of 13. He was able to master the skills of computer programming so quickly that he ended up teaching programming to other students. He and a young friend, Paul Allen, even formed a small programming business as teenagers; it folded when Gates departed for college at age 18. At Harvard, he began developing software for personal computers (PCs), and in his junior year, he dropped out of college to devote himself full-time to the business of designing and marketing software. He and Paul Allen founded Microsoft in 1975, with partnership shares of 60 and 40 percent, respectively.

The patents and royalties on various Microsoft products, like Windows, Word, PowerPoint, and Excel, as well as the promise of future innovations in PC technology, are what give the Microsoft Corporation its enormous market value and, thereby, make Bill Gates the world's wealthiest man. Gates's entrepreneurial qualities—his extreme competitiveness, intensity, strategic vision, and ability to attract talented people to work for him—no doubt factor into Microsoft's success. (Business rivals have pointed to a "ruthless" streak in Gates, and the government's antitrust division has had serious problems with some Microsoft practices.) In recent years, however, Gates has taken a growing interest in philanthropic endeavors. In 2000, he and his wife established the Bill & Melinda Gates Foundation "to help reduce inequities in the United States and around the world." With assets of $29 billion in 2005, it is by far the most richly endowed U.S. charitable foundation, and its global health programs are winning considerable praise, especially its initiatives to combat AIDS and tropical diseases.

Further Reading

Bill Gates biography page at http://www.microsoft.com; The Bill and Melinda Gates Foundation Web site at http://www.gatesfoundation. org; "Profile: Bill Gates," *BBC News* (January 26, 2004), at http://news. bbc.co.uk.

Corrado Gini (1884–1965)

In discussions about income distribution, the measure of income inequality that is cited most frequently is the Gini coefficient. The calculation of this measure—also called the Gini index or Gini ratio—can be technically challenging, but the interpretation of the number itself is relatively straightforward. If incomes are perfectly equal throughout society, the Gini coefficient is zero. If the income distribution is perfectly unequal, with all income going to just one individual or family, the Gini coefficient is 100. Since the real world is more complicated than these two theoretical extremes, actual values of the coefficient always lie somewhere between zero and 100. The Gini coefficient for the United States stands at around 47. What concerns some observers, however, is the fact that the Gini coefficient has moved upward during the past few decades. This strongly suggests that the gap between the rich and the poor has been growing.

The Gini coefficient was developed by an influential Italian statistician and fascist political theorist, Corrado Gini. Born in a small town near Venice, Italy, Gini studied law, statistics, economics, and biology at the University of Bologna. In a long academic career, he taught, successively, at the Universities of Cagliari, Padua, and Rome. Beyond the academy, he also reorganized the national statistical office in Rome and devised a plan for reforming the Italian Senate along lines agreeable to the Fascist Party. Gini was elected to national and international scientific bodies, served as a consultant to the League of Nations, and received honorary degrees from four universities, including Harvard (1936) and the University of Geneva (1934). The scientific study of population was one of his strong interests, and the demographic journal *Genus,* which he founded in 1934, continues to be published today. Gini's famous inequality coefficient was presented in a 1912 paper, "Variabilita e Mutabilita."

Further Reading

"Biography of Corrado Gini," *Metron* (n.d.), accessed at http://www.metronjournal.it; Corrado Gini, "The Scientific Basis of Fascism," *Political Science Quarterly* 42, no. 1 (1927): 99–115.

Hetty Green (1834–1916)

Hetty Green was described in her day as the richest woman in America, if not the world—and also the most miserly. At her death in 1916, Green was probably worth at least $130 million, a sum that would exceed $2 billion in today's prices. Daughter and granddaughter of New Bedford, Massachusetts, whaling merchants, Green learned the elements of finance from her father. A lonely Quaker childhood with minimal schooling seems to have formed her character along unsociable and frugal lines. On her father's death in 1865, Green received a substantial inheritance, which she promptly invested in government notes that were deeply discounted in the aftermath of the Civil War. Her faith in the government's ability to pay its debts rewarded her handsomely, and she continued making savvy investments for decades to come. Real estate and railroads, she once said, were more attractive to her than mines, factories, or trade. She also made many loans to municipalities—her loan to Tucson, Arizona, in 1900 financed the construction of that city's water system, and more than once she rescued New York City from financial straits.

Hetty Green's reputation in the world of finance reached its zenith during the Panic of 1907. When two trust companies in New York City were threatened with ruin by massive deposit withdrawals, the banker J. P. Morgan summoned the city's top moneymen to an all-night session at his private library. A solitary woman wearing a black veil (a standard feature of Green's wardrobe) was reported to have joined the men for several hours, and reporters concluded that it had to be Green. By this time, her personal quirks were considered as newsworthy as her financial exploits. Tales of her stinginess multiplied. She migrated among apartments in Brooklyn, New York, and Hoboken, New Jersey, to avoid the taxes she would have faced by living in more permanent, spacious dwellings. She dressed in rags when visiting a doctor so as not to be recognized and charged the full medical fees. She once spent two days hunting for a two-cent stamp she had misplaced. Eccentric in these and many other ways, Green was nonetheless as skilled and determined as any man of her era when it came to high-stakes finance.

Further Reading

Charles Slack, *Hetty: The Genius and Madness of America's First Female Tycoon*, New York: Ecco, 2004.

Dolores Huerta (b. 1930)

Some of the worst-paid American workers are those who labor in the fields, orchards, and vineyards. Their low wages and minimal family incomes result, in part, from the fact that so many are undocumented immigrants, hesitant to organize themselves for better wages and working conditions. For decades, Dolores Huerta has been striving to change this. Born to a father who was a farm worker, miner, and union activist, and a mother who was first a cook and later a businessperson and community activist, Huerta grew up in the San Joaquin Valley of California. After becoming the first in her family to graduate from college, she took an elementary school teaching job, but soon gave it up because, in her words, "I couldn't stand seeing farm worker children come to class hungry and in need of shoes. I thought I could do more by organizing the parents than by trying to teach their hungry children."

Mainstream U.S. labor leaders were not interested in organizing a group of workers who were mainly Latino, so in 1962 Huerta and César Chávez decided to establish the National Farm Workers Association (NFWA). The fledgling NFWA soon joined forces with the Agricultural Workers Organizing Committee (AWOC), a labor group primarily for Filipinos, in the epic five-year Delano

(California) Grape Strike. The NFWA and AWOC merged to form a group that evolved into the United Farm Workers (UFW). Dolores Huerta became deeply engaged in recruiting workers to join the union, negotiating contracts, assisting with grievance and arbitration processes, and lobbying state lawmakers, even as she raised 11 children. Her lifelong advocacy on behalf of low-paid, mainly Latino, workers has earned her widespread recognition. She has received half a dozen honorary degrees; schools have been named after her in three western states; and President Clinton presented her with the Eleanor Roosevelt Human Rights Award in 1998.

Further Reading

"Biography" at the Dolores Huerta Foundation Web site, accessed at http://www.doloreshuerta.org/dolores_huerta_foundation.htm; John Gregory Dunne, *Delano: The Story of the California Grape Strike*, New York: Farrar, Straus, & Giroux, 1967.

Jonathan Kozol (b. 1936)

Common sense suggests that in any society with substantial variations in wealth and income, those with the most financial resources will have the most appealing choices when it comes to private goods like clothing, cars, travel, and housing. Should these same high-income individuals also be placed ahead of everyone else when it comes to *social* goods, such as health care and education? Many democratic theorists would say no, but reality often differs from our democratic ideals, as social critic Jonathan Kozol has been documenting with regard to America's public schools over the past four decades. After graduating from Harvard in 1958, going on to Oxford as a Rhodes Scholar, and spending several years in Paris writing a novel, Kozol took a teaching job in one of Boston's poorest neighborhoods. His book describing that experience, *Death at an Early Age: The Destruction of the Hearts and Minds of Negro Children in the Boston Public Schools* (1967), won a National Book Award. In 1991, Kozol confronted the issue of disparate educational opportunities for rich and poor children head-on in *Savage Inequalities: Children in America's Schools*. Through extensive travel and research, he uncovered many stark contrasts between conditions in inner-city and suburban schools. The former were often characterized by overcrowding, dilapidated buildings, and grossly inadequate funding, while the latter featured well-equipped, spacious campuses, staffed with well-paid teachers and administrators. More recently, in *The Shame of the Nation: The Restoration of Apartheid Schooling in America* (2005), Kozol has called attention to the resegregation of America's public schools long after the landmark 1954 *Brown v. Board of Education* decision outlawing the doctrine of "separate but equal" schooling for minority children.

Besides the inequalities of the U.S. educational system, two related issues on which Kozol has written are homelessness (*Rachel and Her Children*) and illiteracy (*Illiterate America*). Kozol has received a number of honors in his career, including fellowships from the Guggenheim, Rockefeller, Ford, and Field foundations. Several colleges and universities have bestowed honorary degrees on him, and he is much in demand as a speaker before college and community groups.

Further Reading

Jonathan Kozol, *Savage Inequalities: Children in America's Schools*, New York: Harper Perennial, 1992; Jonathan Kozol, *The Shame of the Nation: The Restoration of Apartheid Schooling in America*, New York: Crown Publishers, 2005; Jonathan Kozol, "Still Separate, Still Unequal: America's Educational Apartheid," *Harper's Magazine* 311, no. 1864 (September 2005): 41–54.

Simon Kuznets (1901–1985)

During some periods of American history, the gap between the rich and poor has grown wider, while in other periods it has narrowed. Are these long-term fluctuations in income distribution merely random, or is there some logic behind them? Do economists have any theories about this? One notable economist who contributed to both the theory and the measurement of income inequality was Simon Kuznets. Born in Russia, he and his brother immigrated to New York City in 1920. By 1923, Kuznets had learned English and received a BS degree from Columbia University, where he went on to earn a PhD in economics three years later. During his long and productive career, Kuznets taught at the University of Pennsylvania, Johns Hopkins University, and Harvard. But much of his most notable research was done at the National Bureau of Economic Research (NBER), including his pioneering work on the construction of the U.S. national income accounts during the 1930s. Kuznets won the Nobel Prize for economics in 1971.

In a classic 1955 article, Kuznets hypothesized that the distribution of incomes depended on the stage of a nation's economic development. As a country advanced economically, he said, its incomes would become more unequal, in part because of the migration of workers from rural areas, where incomes tended to be more equal, into urban areas, where they were less equal. But as time went on, the trend would reverse itself: the skills required to earn higher urban incomes would gradually be spread through the population, reducing inequality. These ideas came to be represented by the Kuznets U-curve, which depicts a decline in income equality followed by a rise in equality as nations grow richer and more industrialized. For most of his professional life, Kuznets's theory had the support of empirical data. (He was, in fact, a pioneer in the gathering of statistics on U.S. income distribution, especially for the top 1 percent and 5 percent of income earners.) During the 1970s, however, U.S. incomes started becoming more unequal again—reversing a long-term trend toward equality that dated back to around 1929. This was not supposed to happen under Kuznets's theory. But as he would have been the first to say, if the facts change, we have to revise our theories.

Further Reading

Simon Kuznets, "Economic Growth and Income Inequality," *American Economic Review* 45, no. 2 (March 1955): 1–28; Steven Pressman, *Fifty Major Economists*, New York: Routledge, 1999: 120–124.

Bhashkar Mazumder (b. 1966)

Our intuition tells us that a society with a wide gap between rich and poor will tend to be one in which a person's economic status is substantially determined at birth. In other words, the children of the rich have a far better chance of ending up (or staying) rich than the children of the poor. Most Americans would resist applying these ideas to their own society. They generally think of their country as one in which, regardless of the existing distribution of wealth, anyone can climb the ladder of success. Bhashkar Mazumder, a senior economist at the Federal Reserve Bank of Chicago, has been doing sophisticated research that bears directly on this question. He focuses on measures of intergenerational mobility, and what he finds runs counter to some of our "Horatio Alger" beliefs. His econometric work indicates that sons and daughters tend to earn incomes quite similar to their fathers' incomes in the previous generation. Hence, economic mobility is considerably lower than previous studies have suggested. This is particularly true of the period since 1980. Mazumder's findings, when plugged into a simple model of economic advancement over time, imply that a family on the poverty line today might need five to six generations, or 125 to 150 years, to work its way up to the *average* U.S. income level. Mazumder holds bachelor's and master's degrees from New York University and a PhD in economics (2001) from the University of California, Berkeley.

Further Reading

Bhashkar Mazumder, "The Apple Falls Even Closer to the Tree Than We Thought," in Samuel Bowles, Herbert Gintis, and Melissa Osborne Groves, eds., *Unequal Chances: Family Background and Economic Success*, New York: Russell Sage Foundation, 2005: 80–99; Bhashkar Mazumder, "Fortunate Sons: New Estimates of Intergenerational Mobility in the United States Using Social Security Earnings Data," *Review of Economics and Statistics* 87, no. 2 (May 2005): 235–255.

Sara S. McLanahan (b. 1940)

It is an oversimplification to say that poor children grow up to be poor adults, but it is not flat-out wrong. Social scientists have spent the past few decades trying to understand (and even quantify) the various ways in which a disadvantaged childhood impairs one's life chances. Princeton sociologist Sara McLanahan has become a leader in this field of research. The main focus of her work has been the impact of nontraditional family structures on children's well-being. In collaboration with Gary Sandefur, she has found that children growing up in single-parent households perform less well on academic tests, are more likely to become pregnant as teens, and have lower school completion rates than children raised by married biological parents. Even when the lower average income levels of single-parent households are taken into account— "controlled for," in the jargon of the statistician—these effects still weigh upon children raised by single parents. More recently, McLanahan (2004) has expressed concern about U.S. demographic trends since the 1960s that have worsened inequality among mothers and therefore among children. The offspring of young, single mothers are coming up short in terms of the parental resources available to them compared to the children of older, married, more educated, and higher-earning mothers. As the gap in parental resources widens, McLanahan sees a role for public policy in providing support to low-income mothers and fathers. She also sees merit in the "marriage initiatives" proposed by the Bush administration—if they are designed correctly.

McLanahan earned her BA in sociology from the University of Houston (1974) and her doctorate (1979) from the University of Texas, Austin. At Princeton University, she is the founder and director of the Center for Research on Child Wellbeing at the Woodrow Wilson School of Public and International Affairs. She is editor-in-chief of the journal *The Future of Children*, and she oversees a major national study of "fragile families" that began in the late 1990s and will last for many years.

Further Reading

Sara McLanahan, "Diverging Destinies: How Children Are Faring Under the Second Demographic Transition," *Demography* 41, no. 4 (November 2004): 607–627; Sara McLanahan and Gary Sandefur, *Growing Up with a Single Parent*, Cambridge, MA: Harvard University Press, 1994.

Mollie Orshansky (1915–2006)

The U.S. government has never defined an income level that qualifies someone as rich, but it has defined an income level below which someone is considered poor. Major credit for establishing the official poverty line belongs to Mollie Orshansky. In 1963, while employed as a researcher in the Social Security Administration, she pursued the following logic: if a family could subsist on about $1,000 worth of food in the United States, and if, as surveys indicated, families tended to spend about one-third of their incomes on food, then in theory a family needed $3,000 of income to avoid being in poverty. Hence, $3,000 was the poverty threshold. (Bear in mind the lower price levels of the 1960s.) This figure was quickly adopted by the Lyndon B. Johnson administration as a handy round number that could be used for marking progress in its War on Poverty. Orshansky developed a whole matrix of poverty thresholds, based on family size, elderly or non-elderly status, and urban or non-urban location. Although it has often been criticized over the decades, the Orshansky index, as it is sometimes known, remains the official yardstick for poverty in the United States. It rises with inflation but not for any other reason. Data released in 2007 placed the 2006 poverty line for a family of two adults and two children at $20,444, and the poverty rate for the nation at 12.3 percent. Orshansky, a 1935 Hunter College graduate and lifelong public servant, retired from the Social Security Administration in 1982. Among friends and former co-workers, she was known affectionately as "Miss Poverty."

Further Reading

David Brady, "Lies, Damned Lies, Poverty Statistics," *Duke Magazine* 92, no. 1 (January-February 2006), accessed at http://www.dukemagazine. duke.edu/dukemag; Gordon M. Fisher, "The Development and History of Poverty Thresholds," *Social Security Bulletin* 55, no. 4 (Winter 1992): 3–14; Robert D. Hershey Jr., "The Hand That Shaped America's Poverty Line as the Realistic Index," *The New York Times* (August 4, 1989): A11; U.S. Census Bureau, "Income, Poverty, and Health Insurance Coverage in the United States: 2006," accessed at http://www.census.gov.

John D. Rockefeller (1839–1937)

The Rockefeller name evokes an era of ruthless capitalism, robber barons, muckraking journalism, trust-busting, and dynastic privilege, as well as philanthropy on a massive scale. John D. Rockefeller came of age at a time when whale oil was no longer sufficient to light America's lamps and a refined petroleum product, kerosene, was just beginning to offer a good alternative. (Later, the automobile industry would spur a rapidly growing demand for another petroleum derivative, gasoline.) Oil drilling was a chancy business at best, but Rockefeller was smart enough to leave that aside and focus instead on the refining end of the industry. He and his associates formed the Standard Oil Company in 1870; they soon controlled nearly all refining activities in the Cleveland area. Over time, Rockefeller built up Standard Oil to the point where it completely dominated the domestic oil-refining industry. By 1896, when he was 57 years old, Rockefeller was ready to retire from active management of Standard Oil. For the remaining 40 years of his life, he occupied himself with giving away money.

There was much to give away, since Rockefeller was by far the richest man of his time. The fortune he had accumulated by 1913 ($900 million) represented a share of the U.S. gross domestic product that today would translate to about $200 billion, vastly more than even Bill Gates can claim. Estimates vary, but it appears that by the end of his life Rockefeller had given away roughly half of his fortune. Objects of his philanthropy included the University of Chicago, the Rockefeller University, and various other colleges and universities, notably several historically black colleges. One of these, Spelman College in Atlanta, is named for Rockefeller's wife, Laura Celestia Spelman.

Further Reading

Ron Chernow, *Titan: The Life of John D. Rockefeller, Sr.,* New York: Random House, 1998; Michael Klepper and Robert Gunther, *The Wealthy 100: From Benjamin Franklin to Bill Gates – A Ranking of the Richest Americans, Past and Present,* Secaucus, NJ: Citadel Press, 1996.

Paul G. Schervish (b. 1946)

Paul Schervish is one of the nation's best-known philanthropy experts, which of course implies that he is also an authority on those who engage in philanthropy, namely, the wealthy. Trained in both theology and sociology, Schervish has conducted many interviews with wealthy individuals to try to understand what motivates their giving. The 1994 book *Gospels of Wealth* is an important product of that research. Schervish was in the news in 1999 for an estimate he and John Havens made of the amount of wealth that Americans were likely to transfer to heirs and charity in the first half of the 21st century—$41 trillion at a minimum. This was shaping up to be, as they put it, the largest intergenerational wealth transfer in history. The unprecedented magnitude of the wealth to be transferred and its concentration in the hands of a relatively small segment of the population led Schervish and Havens to speculate that the United States would soon be entering a "golden age of philanthropy." By their estimate, at least $6 trillion was likely to be donated to charitable causes.

Schervish holds degrees in literature, theology, and sociology, including a doctorate in sociology from the University of Wisconsin (1980). He is currently the director of the Center on Wealth and Philanthropy at Boston College. A senior advisor to the John Templeton Foundation and to the Wealth & Giving Forum, Schervish consults widely on issues of philanthropy.

Further Reading
John J. Havens and Paul G. Schervish, "Millionaires and the Millennium: New Estimates of the Forthcoming Wealth Transfer and the Prospects for a Golden Age of Philanthropy," accessible at http://www.bc.edu; Paul G. Schervish, Platon E. Coutsoukis, and Ethan Lewis, *Gospels of Wealth: How the Rich Portray Their Lives*, New York: Praeger, 1994.

Thomas M. Shapiro (b. 1947)

In 1999, African Americans in the United States earned about 60 cents for every dollar earned by whites. This income gap is significant, but its size cannot compare to the wealth gap the same year, when African Americans had only about 10 cents of accumulated wealth for each dollar of wealth held by whites. As Thomas Shapiro explains in his book *The Hidden Cost of Being African American*, wealth confers many tangible and intangible advantages. It improves one's chances of being able to buy a home, allows one to live in a better (safer) neighborhood, provides access to higher-quality public schools, and furnishes an all-important safety net. Because whites are so disproportionately wealthy compared to blacks, they enjoy a racial economic advantage that carries forward from generation to generation. Shapiro argues that social justice requires us to pursue policies that might narrow the gap, such as children's savings accounts, individual development accounts (as pioneered by Michael Sherraden), and estate taxation. These asset-based policies would be race-neutral in design, but over time they should work to shrink both the rich-poor and the black-white economic divides.

Shapiro had a fruitful collaboration with fellow sociologist Melvin Oliver on the 1995 book *Black Wealth/White Wealth*, which won several prestigious awards. He is a 1969 graduate of the University of Wisconsin and holds a PhD in sociology from Washington University in St. Louis (1978). Currently, he is the Pokross Professor of Law and Social Policy at Brandeis University.

Further Reading
Melvin Oliver and Thomas Shapiro, *Black Wealth/White Wealth: A New Perspective on Racial Inequality*, New York: Routledge, 1995; Thomas

Shapiro, *The Hidden Cost of Being African American: How Wealth Perpetuates Inequality,* New York: Oxford University Press, 2004.

Michael Sherraden (b. 1948)

Michael Sherraden's 1991 book *Assets and the Poor: A New American Welfare Policy* lived up to its title by introducing a genuinely new idea for helping low-income Americans start the climb to a better life. Sherraden proposed that the government help the poor *save* for such life goals as the purchase of a house, post-secondary education, a business start-up, or a more secure retirement. Low income earners could put their savings into individual development accounts (IDAs), and the government would match their savings at a one-to-one or two-to-one ratio. As Sherraden has often pointed out, a program of this kind would not be so different from a number of existing programs, like individual retirement accounts (IRAs) and 529 college savings plans, through which the government already subsidizes socially beneficial activities. The big difference would be that IDAs would mainly benefit the poor, rather than the middle and upper classes. IDA programs are now being tried out—or "piloted"—in many states. The results so far indicate that the poor can be successful at saving when offered a structured program with incentives. Sherraden believes that IDA programs yield other behavioral benefits, too: they encourage hard work, deferral of consumption, and more positive attitudes toward planning for the future.

Sherraden is a professor of social development at Washington University in St. Louis and the founder, as well as long-time director, of the Center for Social Development there. He has advised the White House, the Treasury Department, and the governments of several other countries, including the United Kingdom, Taiwan, and Canada. He was an undergraduate at Harvard and holds a PhD from the University of Michigan.

Further Reading

Mark Schreiner and Michael Sherraden, *Can the Poor Save? Saving and Asset Building in Individual Development Accounts,* Somerset, NJ: Transaction Publishers, 2006; Michael Sherraden, *Assets and the Poor: A New American Welfare Policy,* Armonk, NY: M. E. Sharpe, 1991; Judy H. Watts, "Helping the Poor Build Assets," *Washington University in St. Louis Magazine* (Fall 2000), accessed at http://magazine.wustl.edu.

Ronald J. Sider (b. 1939)

Politically speaking, Ron Sider is nobody's idea of a typical evangelical Christian. Evangelicals are commonly viewed as core constituents of the Republican Party base, dependably supporting the most conservative positions on social and economic issues. Sider breaks the mold, at least in part. Founder and president of Evangelicals for Social Action (ESA), he calls upon his fellow Christians not to ignore the huge gap between the rich and the poor, but to follow Jesus's words and example in providing for the "least among us." His influential *Rich Christians in an Age of Hunger,* first published in 1977, challenged people of faith in the wealthy industrialized nations to do more—much more—for the world's poor. In his 1999 book *Just Generosity,* Sider laid out an ambitious program for reducing U.S. poverty through such measures as a federally mandated living wage, equal per-student funding of all schools, and universal health insurance.

While the liberal tilt of his antipoverty agenda is undeniable, Sider defies easy labels. He is, for example, a supporter of school voucher experiments, faith-based initiatives, and a constitutional ban on same-sex marriage. An ally of President George W. Bush on social issues, he is a strong dissenter from the president's tax cuts and his plan to abolish estate taxes. Taxes, Sider believes, should be levied according to people's ability to pay. The Bush tax cuts have disproportionately benefited the wealthy, when they could and should have been directed to the middle class and the working poor. Sider also parts ways with the president on environmental issues. God expects us to be good stewards of the Earth, and the Bush record of environmental stewardship has been, as Sider sees it, "abominable."

Raised in rural Canada the son of a pastor, Sider earned his BA in European history from the University of Waterloo (Ontario). He went on to Yale University, where he received a Master of Divinity degree and a PhD in history. In addition to directing the ESA, Sider is a professor of theology, holistic ministry, and public policy at the Palmer Theological Seminary of Eastern University, outside Philadelphia.

Further Reading
Ronald J. Sider, *Just Generosity: A New Vision for Overcoming Poverty in America,* Grand Rapids, MI: Baker Books, 1999; Ronald J. Sider, *Rich Christians in an Age of Hunger: Moving from Affluence to Generosity,* 5th ed.,

Nashville: W Publishing Group, 2005; Tim Stafford, "Ron Sider's Unsettling Crusade," *Christianity Today* (March 13, 2000).

Timothy M. Smeeding (b. 1948)

When people want to compare the income distribution within the United States with what is seen in other countries, they often turn to the work of Timothy Smeeding, an economist and professor of public policy at Syracuse University. For many years, Smeeding has studied income patterns in both the United States and Europe. He was instrumental in the establishment of the Luxembourg Income Study (LIS) in 1983 and served as its overall director until retiring in 2006. Smeeding and others have used the data yielded by the LIS to draw a much clearer picture of where the United States stands relative to other industrialized nations, such as Sweden, Germany, France, and Canada, on various measures of income inequality. When looking at incomes generated by the market—before the government either taxes or provides benefits to families—the United States is just behind the United Kingdom as the most *unequal* in its income distribution. After taking into account taxes and transfers by the government, the United States overtakes Britain as the most unequal of all. In related research, Smeeding and Lee Rainwater have found that the United States lifts many fewer children out of poverty through government action than other wealthy nations do. Smeeding has also studied international public opinion regarding income distribution. In unpublished research with Lars Osberg, he finds Americans to be increasingly polarized in their attitudes toward inequality, with a more accepting attitude toward inequality at the poor end, but a less accepting attitude toward inequality at the wealthy end of the spectrum. Smeeding is a 1970 graduate of Canisius College with an economics doctorate from the University of Wisconsin (1975).

Further Reading
Lars Osberg and Timothy Smeeding, "'Fair' Inequality? An International Comparison of Attitudes to Pay Differentials," unpublished (June 2005); Lee Rainwater and Timothy M. Smeeding, *Poor Kids in a Rich Country: America's Children in Comparative Perspective*, New York: Russell Sage Foundation, 2003.

Samuel Walton (1918–1992)

In his 1992 autobiography, Sam Walton recounts how shocked he was one day in 1985 to learn that he had been named the richest American by *Forbes* magazine. Older by three decades than Bill Gates was when *he* reached the top of the *Forbes* list some years later, Walton was an acknowledged business innovator of the first rank. His Wal-Mart chain of retail stores (the first was opened in 1962) thrived on a combination of "everyday low prices" and rapid inventory turnover. Wal-Mart struck ferociously tough bargains with suppliers, established a tight distribution network, installed the most advanced computerized merchandise-tracking system ever seen, and fended off labor unions. Walton presided over his corporate domain with a folksy manner that never quite masked the ruthless competitor within. Even detractors conceded that he knew how to motivate his workers—he introduced the term "associates"—to high levels of performance. Some of them managed to retire very comfortably with their Wal-Mart stock holdings, even though they had never earned much more than the minimum wage. After the company went public in 1970, Walton chose to retain about 40 percent of the stock for his family. His five main heirs were collectively worth over $60 billion in the fall of 2005, making them the nation's wealthiest family. Contrary to popular belief, Sam Walton was born in Oklahoma, not Arkansas, but Wal-Mart's corporate headquarters have always been in Bentonville, Arkansas. The company he built is now the largest in the world.

Further Reading

Bob Ortega, *In Sam We Trust: The Untold Story of Wal-Mart, the World's Most Powerful Retailer,* New York: Times Business, 2000; Sam Walton, with John Huey, *Sam Walton: Made in America,* New York: Doubleday, 1992.

Richard Wilkinson (b. 1943)

No one is surprised to learn that richer nations have better health statistics—lower infant mortality, longer life expectancy, and so on—than poorer nations. For example, health measures for Germany today are generally higher than those for Guatemala, as one would expect from the large disparity between the two countries' average income levels. What may come as a surprise is the fact that health tends to be worst in countries where the gap between rich and poor is widest, regardless of the average wealth or poverty of the country. Richard Wilkinson, a professor of social epidemiology at the University of Nottingham (England), has been a pioneer in sorting out the effects of inequality on social health. He and his co-researchers have found that rates of homicide and other types of violent crime, heart disease, infant mortality, and many other dimensions of social well-being are statistically correlated with income inequality. This holds true across nations, states, and counties. In other words, inequality is harmful to people's health, in and of itself. Why? Wilkinson believes that when people see themselves on the lower rungs of a stretched-out social ladder, they are likely to experience a sense of deprivation, unworthiness, depression, and lack of control. In short, they feel stressed, and the stress takes a toll on their minds and bodies. Therefore, if we want to achieve broad advancements in social well-being, it would be a mistake, according to Wilkinson, merely to treat the psychosocial symptoms of inequality with more prisons or doctors or counseling programs. A better solution, he thinks, would be to deal with the structural causes of the problem, which means taking steps to reduce inequality and increase social cohesion. Richard Wilkinson was a senior research fellow at the University of Sussex before assuming his present position at the University of Nottingham.

Further Reading

Richard Wilkinson, *The Impact of Inequality: How to Make Sick Societies Healthier,* New York: The New Press, 2005; Richard Wilkinson, *Unhealthy Societies: The Afflictions of Inequality,* London: Routledge, 1996; R. G. Wilkinson and K. E. Pickett, "Income Inequality and Population Health: A Review and Explanation of the Evidence," *Social Science and Medicine* 62, no. 7 (2006): 1768–1784.

Edward N. Wolff (b. 1946)

A New York University professor of economics, Edward Wolff is generally considered the nation's top expert on U.S. wealth inequality. Wolff has been studying American wealth patterns for over a quarter-century; his primer on the subject, *Top Heavy,* went into its third edition in 2002. Broadly speaking, Wolff has found, and so far no one has seriously disputed, that wealth in the United States has become more concentrated since the 1970s. Indeed, the wealth gap has grown wider than at any time since the late 1920s. In no other advanced economy for which we have data, whether Japan, Germany, France, or the United Kingdom, is wealth as unequally held as in the United States. Wolff has proposed a number of suggestions for alleviating the disparity between rich and poor: raise the minimum wage, make the earned income tax credit (EITC) more generous, help low-income families build up assets, and implement a wealth tax. It is the final suggestion that stirs the most controversy. Wolff points to Switzerland as a prime example of an affluent country that assesses a modest tax on wealth accumulations; he suggests that a similar tax in the United States could easily raise over $50 billion of tax revenue each year.

A Harvard graduate (1968) with a PhD from Yale (1974), Wolff is the author of many scholarly articles and a number of books. He has written on income and wealth distribution, alternative measures of living standards, regional variations in economic well-being, and labor productivity trends. Besides his primary affiliation with New York University, he is a research associate at the National Bureau of Economic Research and a senior scholar at the Levy Economics Institute.

Further Reading
Edward N. Wolff, "The Rich Get Richer: And Why the Poor Don't," *The American Prospect* 12, no. 3 (February 12, 2001): 15–17; Edward N. Wolff, *Top Heavy: The Increasing Inequality of Wealth in America and What Can Be Done About It*, 3rd ed., New York: The New Press, 2002.

6

Data and Documents

The metrics of economic inequality in the United States are varied, but they tell a fairly consistent story of a wide—and widening—gap between the rich, especially the super-rich, and the poor over the past few decades. This chapter presents a range of statistics on both income and wealth inequality, drawn mainly from government sources. The aim is to offer a ready reference place for some of the data most frequently cited in discussions about U.S. poverty and wealth levels. The chapter also features several document excerpts and short essays dealing with particular aspects of inequality, such as CEO compensation levels and inheritance taxes. Issues such as the two just mentioned tend to be controversial, with advocates staking out strong pro and con positions. The excerpts offered below can be, at the very least, a starting point for anyone who wants to become better informed about inequality-related topics. Many additional sources of information are provided in chapters 7 and 8.

U.S. household income has been slowly shifting toward the top quintile for several decades, as seen in Table 6.1. In 1967, the poorest quintile had 4.0 percent of total income; it maintained or increased its share through 1984 but then underwent a gradual reduction to 3.4 percent in 2005. The second and third quintiles also shrank between 1967 and 2005, and did so more steadily. The second-from-highest quintile has been shrinking gradually since the mid-1980s. Only the top quintile's share of income has actually increased over the full 38-year period from 1967 to 2005, rising from 43.6 to 50.4 percent.

The Gini coefficient or index is the most commonly cited single number reflecting overall income (or wealth) inequality for a

TABLE 6.1
U.S Household Income Shares by Quintile, 1967–2005
(All figures in percent)

Year	Lowest Quintile	Second Quintile	Middle Quintile	Fourth Quintile	Highest Quintile
2005	3.4	8.6	14.6	23.0	50.4
2004	3.4	8.7	14.7	23.2	50.1
2003	3.4	8.7	14.8	23.4	49.8
2002	3.5	8.8	14.8	23.3	49.7
2001	3.5	8.7	14.6	23.0	50.1
2000	3.6	8.9	14.8	23.0	49.8
1999	3.6	8.9	14.9	23.2	49.4
1998	3.6	9.0	15.0	23.2	49.2
1997	3.6	8.9	15.0	23.2	49.4
1996	3.6	9.0	15.1	23.3	49.0
1995	3.7	9.1	15.2	23.3	48.7
1994	3.6	8.9	15.0	23.4	49.1
1993	3.6	9.0	15.1	23.5	48.9
1992	3.8	9.4	15.8	24.2	46.9
1991	3.8	9.6	15.9	24.2	46.5
1990	3.8	9.6	15.9	24.0	46.6
1989	3.8	9.5	15.8	24.0	46.8
1988	3.8	9.6	16.0	24.2	46.3
1987	3.8	9.6	16.1	24.3	46.2
1986	3.8	9.7	16.2	24.3	46.1
1985	3.9	9.8	16.2	24.4	45.6
1984	4.0	9.9	16.3	24.6	45.2
1983	4.0	9.9	16.4	24.6	45.1
1982	4.0	10.0	16.5	24.5	45.0
1981	4.1	10.1	16.7	24.8	44.3
1980	4.2	10.2	16.8	24.7	44.1
1979	4.1	10.2	16.8	24.6	44.2
1978	4.2	10.2	16.8	24.7	44.1
1977	4.2	10.2	16.9	24.7	44.0
1976	4.3	10.3	17.0	24.7	43.7

continues

TABLE 6.1   Continued

Year	Lowest Quintile	Second Quintile	Middle Quintile	Fourth Quintile	Highest Quintile
1975	4.3	10.4	17.0	24.7	43.6
1974	4.3	10.6	17.0	24.6	43.5
1973	4.2	10.4	17.0	24.5	43.9
1972	4.1	10.4	17.0	24.5	43.9
1971	4.1	10.6	17.3	24.5	43.5
1970	4.1	10.8	17.4	24.5	43.3
1969	4.1	10.9	17.5	24.5	43.0
1968	4.2	11.1	17.6	24.5	42.6
1967	4.0	10.8	17.3	24.2	43.6

Source: U.S. Census Bureau. 2006. *Current Population Reports,* P60-231, "Income, Poverty, and Health Insurance Coverage in the United States: 2005," 40–41.

nation. It can range from a low value of zero, indicating complete equality, to a high value of 100, indicating complete inequality. As we see in Table 6.2, the Gini coefficient for the United States has risen (moved in the inequality direction) fairly steadily since about 1974. Two other measures in the same table confirm what the Gini and the income quintile data suggest: growing inequality

TABLE 6.2
Selected Measures of Income Inequality in the United States, 1967–2005

Year	Gini Index	90th/10th percentile	95th/50th percentile
2005	46.9	11.17	3.61
2004	46.6	11.08	3.57
2003	46.4	11.22	3.57
2002	46.2	10.75	3.54
2001	46.6	10.63	3.57
2000	46.2	10.58	3.46
1999	45.8	10.42	3.52
1998	45.6	10.44	3.41
1997	45.9	10.60	3.43

continues

TABLE 6.2 Continued

Year	Gini Index	90th/10th percentile	95th/50th percentile
1996	45.5	10.33	3.40
1995	45.0	10.11	3.32
1994	45.6	10.57	3.41
1993	45.4	10.64	3.37
1992	43.3	10.34	3.27
1991	42.8	10.22	3.21
1990	42.8	10.12	3.17
1989	43.1	9.99	3.17
1988	42.6	10.21	3.16
1987	42.6	10.23	3.11
1986	42.5	10.09	3.10
1985	41.9	9.69	3.05
1984	41.5	9.55	3.06
1983	41.4	9.61	3.04
1982	41.2	9.48	3.00
1981	40.6	9.22	2.91
1980	40.3	9.09	2.86
1979	40.4	9.14	2.87
1978	40.2	8.90	2.80
1977	40.2	8.74	2.80
1976	39.8	8.70	2.76
1975	39.7	8.53	2.74
1974	39.5	8.58	2.76
1973	40.0	8.86	2.78
1972	40.1	8.99	2.75
1971	39.6	9.08	2.68
1970	39.4	9.22	2.67
1969	39.1	8.93	2.62
1968	38.6	8.68	2.58
1967	39.7	9.23	2.70

Source: U.S. Census Bureau. 2006. *Current Population Reports,* P60–231, "Income, Poverty , and Health Insurance Coverage in the United States: 2005," 40–41.

of income. The 90th-10th percentile ratio is a measure of top-to-bottom income disparity. Thus, the figure of 11.17 for 2005 means that the average household that was one-tenth below the top of the income distribution had more than 11 times as much income as the average household that was one-tenth above the bottom. In 1967, the ratio had been much less unequal at 9.23. In the last column, we have an index of top-to-middle income disparity. Naturally, this ratio is lower than the 90th-10th ratio, but what is telling is the fact that it climbed from 2.70 in 1967 to 3.61 in 2005—a relatively bigger stretch than occurred in the top-to-bottom income gap. This statistic hints at the way the very top of the U.S. income scale has been pulling away from everyone below it.

To gain some international perspective on the degree of income inequality in the United States, one needs to have comparable measures of inequality for other nations. That is provided in Table 6.3, a listing of Gini coefficients for nations across the globe. The six highest Ginis, indicating the most extreme income inequality, have values of 60 or above, and all except one are nations in Africa: Botswana, Central African Republic, Lesotho, Namibia, and Sierra Leone; the only non-African nation is Bolivia. These are countries that stand out not only for the inequality in their income distributions but also for their low per-capita income levels. European countries tend to have much narrower income spreads; the Scandinavians in particular boast low Gini coefficients, in the 20s. The United States, with a Gini of 45, borders a more equal nation on the north (Canada: 33.1) and a less equal nation on the south (Mexico: 54.6). The country often cited as the greatest economic rival of the United States, both in the present and the future, is China, which now has a Gini coefficient that is essentially the same (44) as the U.S. coefficient. This represents a significant departure from Maoist egalitarian ideals, to say the least, but it is consistent with the emergence of a dynamic capitalist economy in China since around 1990. The shift to a market economy has been taking a similar toll on the vaunted Soviet-era equality of Russia; that nation now has a Gini (40.5) that could match the United States in a few more years.

As noted in chapter 2, growing income inequality has its roots in growing wage inequality, since wages are by far the most important source of income for Americans. Tables 6.4 and 6.5 provide useful statistics on U.S. wage patterns over time. Table 6.4 looks at wage trends since 1973, tracing the changes for each decile. What is especially notable over the period from 1979 to

TABLE 6.3
Global Gini Coefficient

Albania	26.7 (2005)	Egypt	34.4 (2001)
Algeria	35.3 (1995)	El Salvador	52.5 (2001)
Argentina	48.3 (June 2006)	Estonia	33 (2003)
Armenia	41 (2004)	Ethiopia	30 (2000)
Australia	35.2 (1994)	European Union	31.3 (2003 est.)
Austria	31 (2002)	Finland	26.9 (2000)
Azerbaijan	36.5 (2001)	France	26.7 (2002)
Bangladesh	31.8 (2000)	Georgia	38 (2003)
Belarus	30.4 (2000)	Germany	28.3 (2000)
Belgium	25 (1996)	Ghana	30 (1999)
Bolivia	60.6 (2002)	Greece	35.1 (2003)
Bosnia/Herzegovina	26.2 (2001)	Guatemala	59.9 (2005)
Botswana	63 (1993)	Guinea	38.1 (2006)
Brazil	56.7 (2005)	Honduras	55 (1999)
Bulgaria	31.6 (2005)	Hong Kong	52.3 (2001)
Burkina Faso	48.2 (1998)	Hungary	26.9 (2002)
Burundi	33.3 (1998)	India	32.5 (2000)
Cambodia	40 (2004 est.)	Indonesia	34.8 (2004)
Cameroon	44.6 (2001)	Iran	43 (1998)
Canada	33.1 (1998)	Ireland	35.9 (1996)
Central African Rep.	61.3 (1993)	Israel	38.6 (2005)
Chile	53.8 (2003)	Italy	36 (2000)
China	44 (2002)	Jamaica	38.1 (2003)
Colombia	53.8 (2005)	Japan	38.1 (2002)
Costa Rica	46.5 (2000)	Jordan	36.4 (1997)
Côte d'Ivoire	45.2 (1998)	Kazakhstan	31.5 (2003)
Croatia	29 (2001)	Kenya	44.5 (1997)
Czech Republic	27.3 (2003)	Korea, South	35.8 (2000)
Denmark	23.2 (2002)	Kyrgyzstan	29 (2001)
Dominican Republic	47.4 (1998)	Laos	37 (1997)
East Timor	38 (2002 est.)	Latvia	35 (2003)
Ecuador	42 (2003)*	Lesotho	63.2 (1995)

continues

TABLE 6.3   Continued

Lithuania	32.5 (2003)	Russia	40.5 (2005)
Macedonia	28.2 (1998)	Rwanda	28.9 (1985)
Madagascar	47.5 (2001)	Senegal	41.3 (1995)
Malawi	50.3 (1997)	Sierra Leone	62.9 (1989)
Malaysia	46.1 (2002)	Singapore	42.5 (1998)
Mali	50.5 (1994)	Slovakia	25.8 (1996)
Mauritania	39 (2000)	Slovenia	28.4 (1998)
Mauritius	37 (1987 est.)	South Africa	59.3 (1995)
Mexico	54.6 (2000)	Spain	32.5 (1990)
Moldova	33.2 (2003)	Sri Lanka	50 (2004)
Mongolia	44 (1998)	Sweden	25 (2000)
Morocco	40 (2005 est.)	Switzerland	33.1 (1992)
Mozambique	39.6 (1996–97)	Tajikistan	34.7 (1998)
Namibia	70.7 (2003)	Tanzania	38.2 (1993)
Nepal	37.7 (2005)	Thailand	51.1 (2002)
Netherlands	30.9 (2005)	Tunisia	40 (2005 est.)
New Zealand	36.2 (1997)	Turkey	42 (2003)
Nicaragua	55.1 (2001)	Turkmenistan	40.8 (1998)
Niger	50.5 (1995)	Uganda	43 (1999)
Nigeria	50.6 (1996–97)	Ukraine	31 (2006)
Norway	25.8 (2000)	United Kingdom	36.8 (1999)
Pakistan	41 (FY98/99)	United States	45 (2004)
Panama	56.4 (2000)	Uruguay	45.2 (2006)
Papua New Guinea	50.9 (1996)	Uzbekistan	26.8 (2000)
Paraguay	56.8 (1999)	Venezuela	49.1 (1998)
Peru	49.8 (2000)	Vietnam	36.1 (1998)
Philippines	46.1 (2003)	Yemen	33.4 (1998)
Poland	34.1 (2002)	Zambia	52.6 (1998)
Portugal	38.5 (1997)	Zimbabwe	56.8 (2003)
Romania	28.8 (2003)		

* Ecuador's data are for urban households.

Source: U.S. Central Intelligence Agency, *The World Factbook*, "Distribution of Family Income—Gini Index," updated on June 19, 2007. Accessed at https://www.cia.gov/library/publications/the-world-factbook/fields/2172.html.

TABLE 6.4
Unequal Wage Growth, 1973–2005 (2005 dollars)
Wage by percentile*

Year	10	20	30	40	50	60	70	80	90	95
Real hourly wage										
1973	$6.79	$8.20	$9.74	$11.33	$12.99	$14.91	$17.31	$19.80	$24.88	$31.21
1979	7.37	8.40	9.86	11.60	13.13	15.22	17.99	20.96	25.64	31.31
1989	6.33	7.88	9.45	11.29	13.13	15.33	18.24	21.81	27.54	33.85
1995	6.44	7.87	9.41	11.07	12.89	15.25	18.18	22.01	28.44	35.67
2000	7.15	8.81	10.29	11.90	13.88	16.42	19.47	23.66	30.92	39.44
2005	7.20	8.84	10.21	12.12	14.29	16.82	19.86	24.44	32.49	41.70
Percent change										
1973–79	8.4%	2.4%	1.2%	2.4%	1.0%	2.1%	3.9%	5.9%	3.1%	0.3%
1979–89	-14.1	-6.2	-4.2	-2.7	0.0	0.7	1.4	4.0	7.4	8.1
1989–2000	13.0	11.8	8.9	5.4	5.7	7.1	6.7	8.5	12.3	16.5
1989–95	1.8	-0.1	-0.5	-2.0	-1.8	-0.5	-0.3	0.9	3.3	5.4
1995–2000	11.1	11.9	9.4	7.5	7.7	7.7	7.1	7.5	8.7	10.6
2000–05	0.6	0.3	-0.8	1.8	3.0	2.4	2.0	3.3	5.1	5.7
1979–2005	-2.3	5.2	3.5	4.4	8.9	10.5	10.4	16.6	26.7	33.2

*The Xth percentile wage is the wage at which X% of the wage earners earn less and (100-X)% earn more.

Source: Mishel, Bernstein, and Allegretto, *The State of Working America 2006/2007*, p. 121.

2005 is that the hourly wages of those near the top increased much faster than wages for any other group. At the 90th percentile, the gain was 27 percent in real terms, and for those at the 95th percentile, it was a robust 33 percent. Although these are not spectacular increases by historical standards, they are far bigger gains than workers farther down the ladder experienced. One way to illustrate the divergent experiences of low-paid and highly paid workers is this: in 1979, a worker at the 10th percentile had to work about 4.5 hours to earn what a worker at the 95th percentile earned in an hour. In 2005, it took the low-paid worker 5.8 hours to equal the hourly wage of the 95th percentile worker. The big picture is clear: in the bottom half of the wage distribution, American workers had only single-digit gains between 1979 and 2005, with the lowest-paid decile actually experiencing an absolute *drop* of 2.3 percent in real wages, while in the top half of the distribution, workers enjoyed double-digit gains.

The worst wage setback shown in Table 6.4 is the 14.1 percent drop for the first decile during the 1980s. It is probably no coincidence that this was a decade, starting in 1981, when the federal minimum wage did not change at all, since many low-level wage rates are keyed to the minimum wage. Table 6.5 provides data on the minimum wage back to 1947, with columns for the minimum and inflation-adjusted minimum wage and for the fraction (the nominal wage) represented of the average private-sector nonsupervisory wage. This table is relevant background to the congressional action taken in the spring of 2007, when, after a decade at $5.15, the federal minimum wage was finally raised, in stages, to $7.25, effective the summer of 2009. In real or inflation-adjusted terms and as a fraction of the average U.S. wage, the minimum wage had fallen to levels not seen in half a century. Supporters of the raise argued that it was long overdue.

The inequality of wealth holdings in the United States is the subject of Tables 6.6 and 6.7. In the first, we see that in 1962, the top one-fifth of wealth-holders claimed over four-fifths of the nation's wealth or net worth. In fact, the inequality was even greater than those numbers suggest, since the top 1 percent held fully one-third of all wealth. By 2004, things had not changed much except to become slightly *more* unequal: the top quintile now held 84.7 percent of the nation's wealth, a bump up from its previous 81.0 percent. The noticeable drop in the share of the top 1 percent from 1998 to 2001 was largely accounted for by the bursting of Wall Street's "dotcom" bubble and subsequent bear

TABLE 6.5
U.S. Minimum Wage, 1947–2006

Year	Nominal	Inflation-adjusted	Fraction of average wage
1947	$0.40	$3.04	35%
1948	0.40	2.82	33%
1949	0.40	2.85	31%
1950	0.75	5.28	56%
1951	0.75	4.89	52%
1952	0.75	4.80	49%
1953	0.75	4.76	47%
1954	0.75	4.73	45%
1955	0.75	4.74	44%
1956*	0.96	5.99	53%
1957	1.00	6.03	53%
1958	1.00	5.86	51%
1959	1.00	5.83	50%
1960	1.00	5.72	48%
1961*	1.05	5.95	49%
1962	1.15	6.46	52%
1963*	1.18	6.54	52%
1964	1.25	6.83	49%
1965	1.25	6.73	48%
1966	1.25	6.54	46%
1967*	1.39	7.06	49%
1968*	1.58	7.71	52%
1969	1.60	7.48	50%
1970	1.60	7.14	47%
1971	1.60	6.84	44%
1972	1.60	6.63	41%
1973	1.60	6.24	39%
1974*	1.87	6.64	42%
1975	2.10	6.88	44%
1976	2.30	7.13	45%
1977	2.30	6.70	42%

continues

TABLE 6.5   Continued

Year	Nominal	Inflation-adjusted	Fraction of average wage
1978	2.65	7.40	45%
1979	2.90	7.41	46%
1980	3.10	7.13	45%
1981	3.35	7.04	45%
1982	3.35	6.65	43%
1983	3.35	6.38	41%
1984	3.35	6.14	40%
1985	3.35	5.94	38%
1986	3.35	5.83	38%
1987	3.35	5.64	37%
1988	3.35	5.44	36%
1989	3.35	5.22	34%
1990*	3.69	5.48	36%
1991*	4.14	5.93	39%
1992	4.25	5.94	39%
1993	4.25	5.80	39%
1994	4.25	5.68	38%
1995	4.25	5.54	37%
1996*	4.38	5.56	36%
1997*	4.88	6.07	39%
1998	5.15	6.31	40%
1999	5.15	6.18	38%
2000	5.15	5.98	37%
2001	5.15	5.82	35%
2002	5.15	5.73	34%
2003	5.15	5.60	34%
2004	5.15	5.46	33%
2005	5.15	5.28	32%
2006	5.15	5.15	31%

*Minimum wage changed during the course of the year; values of nominal and inflation-adjusted minimum wages reflect weighted averages for the year.

Source: Economic Policy Institute analysis based on data from the U.S. Department of Labor; accessed at http://www.epi.org/issueguides/minwage/table4.pdf.

TABLE 6.6
U.S. Wealth Distribution, 1962–2004

Wealth class*	1962	1983	1989	1998	2001	2004
Top fifth	81.0%	81.3%	83.5%	83.4%	84.4%	84.7%
Top 1%	33.4	33.8	37.4	38.1	33.4	34.3
Next 4%	21.2	22.3	21.6	21.3	25.8	24.6
Next 5%	12.4	12.1	11.6	11.5	12.3	12.3
Next 10%	14.0	13.1	13.0	12.5	12.9	13.4
Bottom four-fifths	19.1%	18.7%	16.5%	16.6%	15.6%	15.3%
Fourth	13.4	12.6	12.3	11.9	11.3	11.3
Middle	5.4	5.2	4.8	4.5	3.9	3.8
Second	1.0	1.2	0.8	0.8	0.7	0.7
Lowest	-0.7	-0.3	-1.5	-0.6	-0.4	-0.5
Total	100.0%	100.0%	100.0%	100.0%	100.0%	100.0%

*Wealth defined as net worth (household assets minus debts).

Source: Mishel, Bernstein, and Allegretto (2007), p. 254.

market that began in 2000. In any case, most of the wealth lost from the top 1 percent was balanced by a gain of wealth for households in the next 4 percent—their share rose from 21.3 to 25.8 percent. Table 6.7 breaks down the assets held by U.S. households into major categories and shows how equally or unequally they were distributed across the population in 2004. In every asset category except housing equity, the top 5 percent of households owned more than half the wealth. Their dominance is especially impressive when it comes to non-equity financial assets—items such as savings accounts, certificates of deposit (CDs), bonds, and the value of unincorporated businesses. Of these valuable assets, the top 1 percent of U.S. households own just about as much as the bottom 99 percent. When it comes to common stock, whether owned outright or indirectly in pension accounts, the top 5 percent of households own more than the bottom 95 percent.

To secure a place in middle-class America today, one needs a college education, yet access to higher education is far from equal, even when student abilities are comparable. Because of the cost factor, those from more privileged backgrounds stand a

TABLE 6.7
Household Ownership of Asset Types, 2004

Wealth class	Common stock excluding pensions*	All common stock**	Non-equity financial assets***	Housing equity	Net worth
Top 1%	39.2%	36.9%	49.1%	12.5%	34.4%
Next 4%	28.6	28.4	23.1	19.9	24.6
Next 5%	13.3	13.5	9.3	13.5	12.3
Next 10%	11.0	11.9	9.3	19.5	13.4
Bottom 80%	7.9	9.4	9.1	34.6	15.3
Total	100.0%	100.0%	100.0%	100.0%	100.0%

* Includes direct ownership of stock shares and indirect ownership through mutual funds and trusts.

** Includes direct ownership of stock shares and indirect ownership through mutual funds and trusts, IRAs, Keough plans, 401(k) plans, and other retirement accounts.

***Includes direct ownership of financial securities and indirect ownership through mutual funds, trusts, and retirement accounts, and net equity in unincorporated businesses.

Source: Mishel, Bernstein, and Allegretto (2007), p. 260.

much better chance of attending and graduating from a four-year college than do those with less privilege. This can be seen clearly in Table 6.8, which is based on a national sample of eighth-graders who were tested on their mathematical abilities in 1988 and categorized by socioeconomic status (SES). In a follow-up

TABLE 6.8
Probability of Achieving Bachelor's Degree by
Socioeconomic Status and Math Ability in 8th Grade

Math ability	Low SES	Middle SES	High SES
Low	3%	7%	30%
Middle	8%	21%	51%
High	29%	47%	74%

Socioeconomic status is determined by a combination of family income, parental education, and parental occupation.

Low math ability means bottom quartile of test-takers; middle ability means the middle two quartiles; and high ability means the top quartile of test takers.

Source: U.S. Department of Education, National Education Longitudinal Study of 1988 (NELS: 88/2000), accessed at http://nces.ed.gov/programs/youthindicators.

study in 2000, the students' eventual levels of educational attainment were noted, from "less than high school completion" to "received bachelor's degree or higher." The difference in outcomes by SES is startling. Among students testing in the lowest quartile of math ability, those from a low SES background stood only one-tenth as good a chance of graduating from college as those from a high SES background (3 percent versus 30 percent). Among students from a low SES background, those in the top quartile of ability were slightly less likely to graduate from college than high SES students who were in the *bottom* quartile of ability.

Tables 6.9, 6.10, and 6.11 present the broad picture on economic inequality by race and ethnicity. In Table 6.9, we find that among whites, there are three times as many households with incomes of $100,000 or more as there are with incomes under $10,000, based on 2005 data. Among Hispanics, the picture is quite different: more households receive under $10,000 than receive $100,000 or more. And among blacks, more than twice as many households are below $10,000 as are above $100,000. Similar inequalities can be seen as early as 1980 in the table. Racial wealth differences are highlighted in Table 6.10 and, as one would expect, they offer a much more graphic profile of inequality than income data do. Median household wealth among blacks in 2004 was $11,800; among whites, it was $118,000, or ten times as much.

TABLE 6.9
U.S. Income Extremes by Race and Hispanic Origin, 1980–2005

Year	Non-Hispanic whites		Hispanics (any race)		Blacks	
	Under $10,000	$100,000 and over	Under $10,000	$100,000 and over	Under $10,000	$100,000 and over
2005	6.4%	19.7%	10.0%	8.8%	17.1%	7.8%
2000	6.1	19.3	9.1	8.3	14.9	8.2
1995	6.5	15.1	14.6	5.4	18.5	5.3
1990	7.1	13.3	12.6	5.6	21.3	5.1
1985	7.9	11.0	13.8	4.4	21.3	3.1
1980	8.1	8.6	13.1	3.3	21.5	2.3

Source: U.S. Census Bureau (2006), Table A-1, pp. 33-34.

TABLE 6.10
U.S. Wealth in Black and White, 1983–2004
(thousands of 2004 dollars)

	1983	1989	1992	1995	1998	2001	2004
Median wealth*							
Black	$5.5	$2.5	$13.9	$9.1	$11.6	$11.4	$11.8
White	$82.9	$98.4	$82.6	$75.6	$94.6	$113.5	$118.3
Black-white ratio	0.02	0.03	0.17	0.12	0.12	0.10	0.10
Households with zero or negative net wealth							
Black	34.1%	40.7%	31.5%	31.3%	27.4%	30.9%	29.4%
White	11.3%	12.1%	13.8%	15.0%	14.8%	13.1%	13.0%
Black-white ratio	3.0	3.4	2.3	2.1	1.9	2.4	2.3
Median financial wealth**							
Black	$0.0	$0.0	$0.2	$0.2	$1.4	$1.2	$0.3
White	$23.1	$31.2	$25.4	$22.4	$43.6	$44.9	$36.1
Black-white ratio	0.00	0.00	0.01	0.01	0.03	0.03	0.01

*Wealth is net worth (household assets minus liabilities).

**Financial wealth is defined as liquid and semi-liquid assets, such as mutual funds, trusts, retirement accounts, and pensions.

Source: Mishel, Bernstein, and Allegretto (2007), Table 5.6, p. 258.

Almost 30 percent of black households had zero or negative net worth, as compared with 13 percent of white households. When it comes to financial wealth, or wealth in the form of stocks, bonds, mutual funds, retirement accounts, and so on, the gap between blacks and whites is almost unbelievably wide. The median black household has about a penny for every dollar held by the median white household. A final basis for comparison is the share of population with income below the official government poverty line. In Table 6.11, we see that the poverty rate for blacks has been between three and four times the rate for non-Hispanic whites for decades. The poverty rate for Hispanics has generally been lower than for blacks but still much higher than for non-Hispanic whites. In the past ten years, the poverty gaps between whites and the two major U.S. minorities have narrowed somewhat, but given the fluctuations often seen in those gaps, it is not clear whether there is a true equalizing trend under way.

TABLE 6.11
U.S. Poverty Rates by Race and Hispanic Origin, 1980–2005

Year	Whites	Hispanics	Blacks
2005	8.3%	21.8%	24.9%
2004	8.7	21.9	24.7
2003	8.2	22.5	24.4
2002	8.0	21.8	24.1
2001	7.8	21.4	22.7
2000	7.4	21.5	22.5
1999	7.7	22.7	23.6
1998	8.2	25.6	26.1
1997	8.6	27.1	26.5
1996	8.6	29.4	28.4
1995	8.5	30.3	29.3
1994	9.4	30.7	30.6
1993	9.9	30.6	33.1
1992	9.6	29.6	33.4
1991	9.4	28.7	32.7

continues

TABLE 6.11 Continued

Year	Whites	Hispanics	Blacks
1990	8.8	28.1	31.9
1989	8.3	26.2	30.7
1988	8.4	26.7	31.3
1987	8.7	28.0	32.4
1986	9.4	27.3	31.1
1985	9.7	29.0	31.3
1984	10.0	28.4	33.8
1983	10.8	28.0	35.7
1982	10.6	29.9	35.6
1981	9.9	26.5	34.2
1980	9.1	25.7	32.5

"Whites" are non-Hispanic whites. Hispanics can be of any race.

Source: U.S. Census Bureau (2006), Table B-1, pp. 48-51.

Inequality and the American Public: The Maxwell School Survey

How does the American public view the current degree of income inequality? Professor Jeffrey Stonecash of Syracuse University began conducting an annual national poll on American attitudes about inequality in 2004. The 2006 polling report, from which the following is excerpted, indicates a rising level of concern about U.S. income inequality. Between 2005 and 2006, for example, there was a 15 percent jump in the share of the public perceiving that income inequality had increased. Almost 55 percent of respondents thought the trend would continue. Based on this survey, it appears that seven in ten Americans believe we are becoming a society of haves and have-nots, and over half now see income inequality as a serious problem.

Perceptions of Inequality Trends

While the evidence indicates inequality is increasing, do Americans recognize this trend? Over the last several years the percentage seeing inequality as increasing has grown from 44.2 percent to 56.7 percent. The percentage that sees it as decreasing is now 16.4 percent. The sense that it will continue to increase has also risen, from 37.4 percent in 2004 to 54.7 percent in 2006. Most respondents, 70.6 percent, agree that we are becoming a society of the haves and have-nots, and only 23.4 percent disagree. The sense that inequality is increasing and will continue to increase is widespread.

Over the last 5-10 years, do you think income inequality has increased, stayed the same, or decreased?

	2004	2005	2006
Increased	44.2	41.8	56.7
Stayed the same	25.9	28.6	23.0
Decreased	23.9	24.5	16.4
No opinion	6.0	5.2	4.0

Over the next 5 years, do you think income differences will decline, stay about the same, or grow larger?

	2004	2005	2006
Increase	37.4	49.2	54.7
Stay the same	34.7	30.9	26.3
Decrease	14.1	16.9	11.4
No opinion	13.8	3.0	7.7

Do you think we are becoming a society of the haves and the have-nots?

	2004	2005	2006
Yes	67.6	75.2	70.6
No	27.8	20.5	23.4
No opinion	4.6	4.3	5.9

Those who see inequality as having increased are more likely to think it is going to increase in the future (59.4 percent will increase; 21.8 percent will stay the same; 10.8 percent will decrease), while those that think no change has occurred are more optimistic (35.9 percent will increase; 46.0 percent will stay the same; 15.9 percent will decrease). Likewise, those who see a haves and have-nots society are more likely to expect inequality to increase in the future (54.1 percent will increase; 24.8 percent stay the same) than those who do not (30.0 percent will increase; 47.3 percent stay the same).

Concerns about Inequality

When asked about the extent of opportunity and upward and downward mobility in American society, opinions are divided and can be seen in different ways. The Maxwell Poll shows that in 2006, 25.7 percent think everyone in American society has an opportunity to succeed, but 32.2 percent think only some have this opportunity. There is more optimism than pessimism about mobility, with 30.5 percent in 2006 thinking there is a lot of upward mobility and only 9.7 percent thinking there is not much mobility. In addition, only 17.3 percent see a lot of downward mobility and 27.4 percent do not see much downward mobility. Most respondents see the opportunity for upward mobility, therefore, and few see a lot of downward mobility.

Views of inequality trends are related to perceptions of opportunity. Among those that agree that we are becoming a divided society, 21.6 percent see everyone as having an opportunity and 36.2 percent think only some have opportunity. Among those who disagree, 47.2 percent see opportunity available to everyone and 9.4 percent think only some have opportunity. Among those who think inequality will increase, 22.1 percent see opportunity for everyone and 33.2 percent think only some have an opportunity. In contrast, among those who think inequality will not change, 36.3 percent think everyone has opportunity and 19.2 percent think only some have opportunity. While there are differences of opinion about opportunity in American society, those optimistic and pessimistic are not strongly polarized. If all those who see us as becoming a society of the haves and have-nots also saw little equality of opportunity *and* all those who do not see a growing divide saw widespread opportunity, conflicts over opportunity would likely become more intense.

Do you think everyone in American society has an opportunity to succeed, most do, or do only some have this opportunity?

	2004	2005	2006
Everyone	28.9	30.3	25.7
Most	45.5	39.7	40.2
Only some	24.9	29.6	32.2
No opinion	0.8	.4	1.9

How much upward mobility—children doing better than the family they come from—do you think there is in America: a lot, some, or not much?

	2004	2005	2006
A lot	33.4	34.1	30.5
Some mobility	56.4	48.9	56.1
Not much	9.1	14.8	9.7
No opinion	1.0	2.2	3.7

How about downward mobility in America—children doing worse than the family they come from—is there a lot, some, or not much?

	2004	2005	2006
A lot	19.0	16.9	17.3
Some mobility	55.0	50.2	48.2
Not much	22.9	28.3	27.4
No opinion	3.1	4.6	7.0

When asked about the seriousness of inequality, 51.6 percent of Americans now see the extent of inequality as a serious problem, an increase from 38.3 percent in 2004. Only 15.3 percent now see it as not much of a problem. The view that inequality is a serious problem is considerably greater (56.7 percent) among those who see our society as becoming one of haves and havenots. Among those who do not see us as becoming a divided society, 16.1 percent see it as a serious problem, 43.6 percent see it as somewhat of a problem, and 38.2 percent see it as not much of a problem. Among those who think all have an opportunity to succeed, 22.4 percent see inequality as a serious problem and 25.4 percent see it as not much of a problem. In contrast, among those who think only some have an opportunity to succeed, 70.6 percent see inequality as a serious problem and 5.0 percent as not much of a problem.

Do you see the current extent of income inequality in our society as a serious problem, somewhat of a problem, or not much of a problem?

	2004	2005	2006
Serious problem	38.3	46.8	51.6
Somewhat of a problem	43.1	38.5	30.6
Not much of a problem	17.1	12.6	15.3
No opinion	1.6	2.0	2.6

California Kids Investment and Development Savings (KIDS) Accounts

A good example of an asset-building proposal is the California KIDS account that was introduced into California's legislature in early 2007 by representatives Darrell Steinberg and Robert Dutton, Democrat and Republican, respectively. The state would deposit $500 into an account for each child born in California, and with modest additional deposits of $50 per month, the youngster would have a sizable nest egg by age 18. Beyond the actual accumulation of capital, the program also promises to raise the financial sophistication of families and help them form lifelong habits of saving and investing. The Q & A below was written by Olivia Calderon of the Washington, D.C. think tank New America Foundation, which strongly supports KIDS accounts and similar programs.

Questions and Answers

What does this bill do?

SB 752 creates a California Kids Investment and Development Savings (KIDS) Account for every child born in California from 2008 onward. Each account will be seeded with an initial $500 contribution by the state, and housed in the treasurer's office. Once account holders turn 18, they may withdraw the funds for college or career technical education, a first-time home purchase, or to roll over into a retirement account.

Why are these accounts important?

Success in today's economy depends not only on a job and a growing income, but increasingly on the ability to accumulate a wide range of financial assets. It is therefore troubling that the personal savings rate nationwide is negative—meaning more Americans owe more than they save—and is at its lowest since the Great Depression. Furthermore, nearly half of children in the U.S. grow up in households with zero or negative savings. Lacking savings leaves many families just a layoff or accident away from poverty. In California, 7.8 million households, or 29 percent, would last only three months at the poverty level if they lost their income and had to rely on their savings and financial assets. By creating a permanent platform for lifelong savings, KIDS Accounts have the potential to expand opportunity, broaden wealth accumulation, and fortify the American economy for the long haul by helping children and their families save. California's children may grow up knowing they own a modest pool of resources that can help them get started in life as a young adult. For some, these funds will be used to seed profitable and productive investments; for others, it may provide a sense of security that many currently lack. For all, it will provide a basis for financial literacy, and will engage them in investing in their own futures.

Who is eligible?

Every child born in California on or after January 1, 2008, will receive an account.

Why do the children of wealthy families get these accounts?

Policies that include everyone but are targeted to people with greater needs have proven to be more enduring. Including everyone in the same system will provide the strongest foundation for increased savings for all. While a KIDS Account will be universally accessible to each and every child, the majority of benefits will flow to families with low or modest incomes. Also, since a family's income level can fluctuate over the course of a career, this universal structure will ensure that children are not unfairly included in or excluded from the program because their parent's or parents' income level reached a high or low point when they were born.

Why do the children of low-income families get accounts?

The ability to move up and out of poverty often depends on one's ability to accumulate wealth. But millions of Americans live in households with few or no assets. For children in these families, which are oftentimes low-income households, KIDS Accounts would provide an easy mechanism to save. By creating the basic infrastructure for all children to build savings over time, those children of low-income families that might not otherwise have an investment account, will have the opportunity to invest in their own futures.

Is it unrealistic to expect those with low incomes to save when they already struggle to get by?

Locally administered Individual Development Accounts (IDAs), which help low-income individuals save by creating accounts and matching their savings, have proven successful throughout

California and the United States. Although the KIDS Accounts, as proposed, do not include matching funds, they do make it easier for low-income parents to begin to save by providing accounts into which they can put aside some money for their children. By simply putting the basic mechanisms in place, these accounts could make it a great deal easier for people to save.

Will funds in the accounts penalize people applying for public assistance?

No. Amounts in accounts will not be considered when determining eligibility for any state or federally funded benefit.

Who can contribute to the accounts?

Private, voluntary contributions can be made to each account. These contributions will be after-tax and can come from any source, including parents, grandparents, friends, employers, nonprofit organizations, and children themselves.

Who will control and administer the accounts?

Parents and legal guardians will serve as account custodians and make investment decisions until the account-holder reaches the age of 18. The treasurer's office will administer the account like a public pension fund, by investing it in funds and financial markets.

How much will this cost?

The Department of Finance projects that approximately 566,000 babies will be born in 2008. If the State invested $500 per child, the deposits would cost an estimated $283 million for the first year, plus administrative costs. The initial costs would undoubtedly be offset in the future, as accounts would grow from the initial deposit, and would create more investors and homebuyers in the Golden State.

How can money in a KIDS Account be used?

There are a set of withdrawal restrictions to ensure that the accounts are used for purposes that promote the building of financial assets. No withdrawals can be made from the KIDS Accounts until an account-holder turns 18. Once the child reaches the age of adulthood, he or she may withdraw the funds tax-free for college or career technical education, a first-time home purchase, or to roll over into a retirement account.

Has this been done before? How do other policies compare?

The California KIDS Account Act is innovative in many respects, but it has historic precedents both abroad and in the United States. The United Kingdom has created a national system of Child Trust Fund accounts. Every child born in the UK after September 2002 is eligible to receive a voucher of £250; children from low-income families receive an additional £250. Funds are invested until children reach the age of 18. Unlike the KIDS Accounts bill, the Child Trust Fund accounts are administered as vouchers, which parents can take to participating banks. Additionally, there are no use restrictions on withdrawals. Canada has recently proposed helping low-income families save for their children's education with Learning Bonds. This program will give low-income children a $500 endowment toward a Registered Education Savings Plan at birth, and $100 top-up deposits every year. In addition, families with low incomes will be eligible to receive a matching grant on the first $500 saved into the account. In the United States, both the Senate and House of Representatives introduced bipartisan federal KIDS Accounts proposals, known as the ASPIRE Act, in 2005. Both bills made it through their respective policy committees and on to fiscal committees.

How much would a child save in a KIDS Account?

If families saved just $50 per month, with a conservative growth rate of 5 percent, this small investment would be worth nearly $17,500 when the child turned 18. That would more than cover the cost of two years of student fees at a University of California or California State University campus. If the account-holder were to allow the funds to develop, they would grow to approximately $31,000 by age 30 and $173,000 by age 65. If the contributions or growth rate were greater, so too would be the payout.

How will this bill help promote financial literacy?

KIDS Accounts may be used as valuable teaching tools in ensuring that all children become financially literate. While parents and legal guardians will serve as account custodians and initially make investment decisions, children will have a stake in learning about an account that has their name on it. Additionally, providing every child with an account would facilitate introducing financial education into K–12 curriculum.

Ben Bernanke on U.S. Income Inequality

As chairman of the Federal Reserve Board, Ben Bernanke exercises considerable influence over U.S. financial markets. His views on any economic topic are bound to be taken seriously by investors and commentators. In the February 2007 speech excerpted below, Bernanke follows his predecessor at the Federal Reserve Board, Alan Greenspan, in publicly acknowledging the growth of income inequality in recent decades. He cites the possible reasons for this (in sections omitted because of space limitations) and then offers "policy implications," giving strong support to policies that help individuals build up their human capital.

[T]hree principles seem to be broadly accepted in our society: that economic *opportunity* should be as widely distributed and as equal as possible; that economic *outcomes* need not be equal but should be linked to the contributions each person makes to the economy; and that people should receive some *insurance* against the most adverse economic outcomes, especially those arising from events largely outside the person's control. Even when we accept these principles, however, important questions remain. For example, what is meant in practice by equality of economic opportunity? Some might limit the concept to the absence of overt discrimination against particular individuals or groups, while others might extend the term to encompass universal access to adequate housing, education, and health care. Another difficult question is how to balance the need for maintaining strong market-based incentives, which support economic growth and efficiency but may be associated with greater inequality of results, against the goal of insuring individuals against the most adverse outcomes, which may reduce inequality but also tends to diminish the strength of incentives. No objective means of answering these questions exists. One can only try to understand the various issues and trade-offs involved and then come to a normative judgment based on that understanding. . . .

Although average [U.S.] economic well-being has increased considerably over time, the degree of inequality in economic outcomes has increased as well. Importantly, rising inequality is not a recent development but has been evident for at least three decades, if not longer. The data on the real weekly earnings of full-time wage and salary workers illustrate this pattern. In real terms, the earnings at the 50th percentile of the distribution (which I will refer to as the median wage) rose about 11.5 percent between 1979 and 2006. Over the same period, the wage at the 10th percentile, near the bottom of the wage distribution, rose just 4 percent, while the wage at the 90th percentile, close to the top of the distribution, rose 34 percent. . . .

The long-term trend toward greater inequality seen in real wages is also evident in broader measures of financial well-being, such as real household income. For example, the share of income received by households in the top fifth of the income distribution, after taxes have been paid and government transfers have been received, rose from 42 percent in 1979 to 50 percent in 2004, while the share of income received by those in the bottom fifth of the distribution declined from 7 percent to 5 percent. The share of after-tax income garnered by the households in the top 1 percent of the income distribution increased from 8 percent in 1979 to 14 percent in 2004. Even within the top 1 percent, the distribution of income has widened during recent decades. . . .

What, if anything, should policymakers do about the trend of increasing economic inequality? As I noted at the beginning of my remarks, answering this question inevitably involves some difficult value judgments that are beyond the realm of objective economic analysis—judgments, for example, about the right trade-off between allowing strong market-based incentives and providing social insurance against economic risks. Such trade-offs are, of course, at the heart of decisions about tax and transfer policies that affect the distribution of income as well as countless other policy debates.

Policy approaches that would not be helpful, in my view, are those that would inhibit the dynamism and flexibility of our labor and capital markets or erect barriers to international trade and investment. To be sure, the advent of new technologies and increased international trade can lead to painful dislocations as some workers lose their jobs or see the demand for their particular skills decline. But hindering the adoption of new technologies or inhibiting trade flows would do far more harm than good, as technology and trade are critical sources of overall economic growth and of increases in the standard of living.

A better approach for policy is to allow growth-enhancing forces to work but to try to cushion the effects of any resulting dislocations. For example, policies to facilitate retraining and job search by displaced workers, if well designed, could assist the adjustment process. Policies that reduce the costs to workers of changing jobs—for example, by improving the portability of health and pension benefits between employers—would also help to maintain economic flexibility and reduce the costs that individuals and families bear as a result of economic change. Of course, devising policies that accomplish these goals in the most effective way is not straightforward, nor can such policies deal with all of the negative effects of trade and technology on affected individuals. Displaced older workers present a particularly difficult problem, as these workers have greater difficulty than others in finding new jobs and experience a greater decline in earnings than other workers if they are re-employed. Considerable debate and analysis of policy alternatives lie ahead, but these discussions will be well worth the effort.

As the larger return to education and skill is likely the single greatest source of the long-term increase in inequality, policies that boost our national investment in education and training can help reduce inequality while expanding economic opportunity. A substantial body of research demonstrates that investments in education and training pay high rates of return both to individuals and to the society at large. That research also suggests that workers with more education are better positioned to adapt to changing demands in the workplace.

In assessing the potential of education and training to moderate inequality, one should keep in mind that the economically relevant concept of education is much broader than the traditional course of schooling from kindergarten through high school and into college.

Indeed, substantial economic benefits may result from any form of training that helps individuals acquire economically and socially useful skills, including not only K–12 education, college, and graduate work but also on-the-job training, coursework at community colleges and vocational schools, extension courses, online education, and training in financial literacy. The market incentives for individuals to invest in their own skills are strong, and the expanding array of educational offerings available today allows such investment to be as occupationally focused as desired and to take place at any point in an individual's life.

Although education and the acquisition of skills is a lifelong process, starting early in life is crucial. Recent research—some sponsored by the Federal Reserve Bank of Minneapolis in collaboration with the University of Minnesota—has documented the high returns that early childhood programs can pay in terms of subsequent educational attainment and in lower rates of social problems, such as teenage pregnancy and welfare dependency. The most successful early childhood programs appear to be those that cultivate both cognitive and noncognitive skills and that engage families in stimulating learning at home.

To return to the themes I raised at the beginning, the challenge for policy is not to eliminate inequality per se but rather to spread economic opportunity as widely as possible. Policies that focus on education, job training, and skills and that facilitate job search and job mobility seem to me to be a promising means for moving toward that goal. By increasing opportunity and capability, we help individuals and families while strengthening the nation's economy as well.

Pay without Performance: The Great CEO Guarantee

The U.S. income distribution has been noticeably "stretched" at the upper end, where stratospheric salaries of chief executive officers (CEOs) are clearly a big part of the explanation. Critics, like Christian Weller and Kate Sabatini, authors of the excerpt below, assert that CEO pay is often unjustified on the basis of job performance. This compensation policy diverts valuable funds from more important corporate purposes, and ultimately may harm the economic health of the United States.

Calculated self-enrichment by America's cosseted chief executive officers has institutional shareholders up in arms and the Securities and Exchange Commission pondering new corporate disclosure rules for CEO pay. The response of corporate chieftains varies.

Some note that their boards of directors and compensation experts agree they are worth an average annual salary of between $2.5 million and $5.4 million (in 2005 dollars) including performance-based stock incentives and other perks of the famed "C Suite." Other executives simply point to their companies' share price as proof they earn every penny of their pay.

On occasion, both of these arguments may boast some basis in fact, but often the great pay guarantees that chief executives in America engineer for themselves are simply blessed by compliant boards and conflicted compensation experts without much real regard for executive performance. This is costly for shareholders, but from a public policy perspective escalating CEO pay packages are a debilitating drag on the American economy.

How costly? Every dollar of CEO compensation, which on average accounts for about 10 percent of aggregate corporate earnings, displaces a dollar that corporations could have invested in other things, such as labor, new plant and equipment, and research and development. Skyrocketing CEO pay can be detrimental to a company's longer-term performance and . . . our economy's overall competitiveness. And CEO pay that is not linked to real performance can ultimately undermine shareholders' trust in financial markets, where millions of Americans have placed their retirement savings.

Recent investigative reporting by the financial press has exposed the most egregious examples of over-compensated CEOs and the means by which they enriched themselves. Institutional investors and financial analysts also regularly crunch the numbers of individual corporations to see whether CEOs' claims of superior performance are in fact reflected in their companies' stock price. It is, however, striking to see the extent to which CEOs as a group have managed to maintain healthy pay levels even though, in some cases, their companies' stocks have performed poorly.

Our analysis of CEO pay during five years, from 2001 to 2005, shows that many companies increased the pay of their CEOs even when the company's stock price fell short of basic benchmarks, such as the S&P 500 stock price index, or even when the company's stock failed to out-perform staid U.S. Treasury bonds. Performance-based pay is meant to set the company's stock performance apart from the broader market, but if a company's stock fails to beat the S&P 500 then the basic goal of performance-based pay is not met.

Similarly, performance-based pay at the very least should encourage CEOs to lift their companies' shares above the cost of capital. This is most easily defined as the rate of interest on U.S. Treasury bonds, which serve as an anchor for other interest rates on corporate borrowing, such as commercial paper and corporate bond rates. Yet, from 2001 to 2005 many CEOs failed to meet this basic performance goal.

Our analysis of this five-year stock and bond data shows that total compensation for CEOs of well-performing companies tended to be higher than compensation for CEOs of poorly performing companies, yet the differences are small. Consider the following:

- Salaries, which account for 25 percent to 35 percent of a CEO's total compensation, are similar for CEOs of poorly performing companies and well-performing companies. The mean salary of a CEO whose company's stocks underperformed U.S. Treasury bonds during any five-year period ending between 2001 and 2005 was $982,757, compared to $943,445 for CEOs whose stocks performed better than Treasury bonds.
- The bulk of CEOs' compensation comes in forms other than salaries in order to inspire good performance, yet CEOs of companies whose stocks performed poorly still received very high compensation beyond their salaries. CEOs whose companies' stocks failed to do better than Treasury bonds during any five-year period ending between 2001 and 2005 received compensation in addition to their salary to the tune of $2.1 million.
- A substantial share of companies with underperforming stocks still chose to bump up their CEOs' compensation. For example, 16.5 percent of CEOs whose company's stocks did not rise faster than Treasury bond yields during any five-year period ending between 2001 and 2005, still received raises in their total compensation.

Such unjustified growth in CEO pay deserves serious attention. This rising share of corporate resources is diverted away from other uses, such as long-term corporate investment that is critical to the future competitiveness of our economy and job growth throughout the country. Ever-escalating CEO pay also contributes to rising income inequality in America. In the interest of a healthy and more equitable economy, it is time to rethink corporate policies and practices that can result in pay without performance for a substantial share of corporate executives.

Are CEOs Overpaid?

Nobel-Prize-winning economist Gary Becker takes a more benign view of high CEO pay levels than Weller and Sabatini (previous document). Becker argues that in the market for managerial talent, bigger companies will offer higher compensation to get the very best managers. Since the biggest American companies are now much larger than a few decades ago, it is to be expected that the pay for top management would keep pace. Likewise, since the biggest American firms tend to dwarf the biggest foreign firms, American CEO pay levels are relatively higher than in other countries.

The answer to the question of whether American CEOs are overpaid is clearly "yes" for those who earn large bonuses and generous stock options when their companies are doing badly, either absolutely or relative to competitors. *BusinessWeek* has had an annual list of the most overpaid CEOs relative to the performance of the companies they head. A number of well-known companies usually top that list.

But the concern in the media and in Congress over CEO pay is not motivated by some bad apples like these, but by the huge increase in the typical CEO pay in the U.S. during the past 25 years. The total real compensation (that is, compensation adjusted for increases in the price level) of CEOs in larger publicly traded companies during this period grew a remarkable six-fold, where compensation adds together regular pay, bonuses, stocks awarded, the value of stock options, and payouts from longer term pay programs. A big but not the only component of the increase is due to much greater use of stock options. Since median full-time real earnings during the same period only just about doubled, the gap between pay at the top and the average pay of employees widened enormously. It is hard to resist the widespread perception from these trends that CEOs and other top executives are being increasingly overpaid.

The case against the pay of American CEOs looks even more powerful by recognizing that the typical American company head receives greater total compensation than company heads in Great Britain, Canada, Japan, Spain, and in pretty much all developed countries. Clearly, American CEOs are much better paid than CEOs elsewhere, even when per capita incomes of the countries do not differ by very much.

Yet competition for top management can explain the rapid rise over time in the pay of the average American CEO. To understand how competition works in the management market, consider the strong and stable relation at any moment between the total compensation of CEOs at publicly traded companies, and the size of the companies they head. For every 10 percent increase in firm size, measured by the market value of assets, by sales, or by related variables, compensation increases by about 3 percent. This "30 percent" law held during the 1930s, and has held for every succeeding decade, including right up to the present.

Note that stock options and other forms of compensation than salaries and bonuses were unimportant until the 1970s, so this relation is not due to the rapid growth of options and compensation through shares of stock.

The usual explanation given by economists for the positive relation between compensation and firm size is that the largest companies attract the best management. Therefore, bigger companies have to pay their CEOs better in order to discourage them from going to head smaller companies. It is also socially efficient to have the best mangers run the largest companies because their greater skills then have a bigger influence, since they would manage a larger amount of labor and capital. The efficient combining of better managers with larger companies in a competitive market for top managers would imply a positive relation between firm size and the total compensation package. This analysis does not explain why the 30 percent rule holds, but it suggests that the relation between pay and size is likely to be sizable, even when top management in different sized companies do not differ greatly in skills and abilities.

We need two additional facts to explain the sharp rise in pay over time, and the much higher pay in the United States than other countries. The first is that the average size of large American companies has grown in real terms about six-fold during the past 25 years, regardless of how "large" is measured, as long as the same measure is used consistently over time. The other important fact is that the largest 50, 100, or 500 American publicly traded companies are much bigger than the largest companies in other countries.

Clearly, if large companies pay more, and if the average size of companies has grown sharply over time, average compensation would also grow, even if the value of the increasingly generous granting of stock options and equity shares were fully understood by stock markets and boards of directors. It is also possible to understand why average compensation grew about as rapidly as average company size, although the argument here is more complicated (for the details of this argument, see Xavier Gabaix [MIT] and Augustin Landier [NYU], "Why Has CEO Pay Increased So Much?" unpublished, April 17, 2006). The allocation of better managers to larger firms, and competition for these managers among companies of different sizes, means that companies in, say, 2006 would have to pay more for their CEOs than even the same-sized companies did in 1980, although much less than six times as much. The reasoning is that the 2006 companies of a given size are competing against relatively larger companies than comparable size companies did in 1980. Using this analysis, Gabaix and Landier are able to explain why total compensation of the average CEO of larger companies grew about six-fold along with the six-fold growth in average company size during the past several decades.

The same argument explains why compensation of American CEOs is much higher than that of CEOs in other countries. Since average firm size is much lower elsewhere, their pay would be more like that of pay in the U.S. in 1980 or 1990 than the pay of CEOs in today's much larger American firms. As the market for top executives becomes increasingly global, the pay of CEOs in other countries would rise, and that of CEOs in America might fall. For example, to attract Carlos Ghosn, a Brazilian working in France, to turn around Nissan, a seriously ailing company, Nissan had to pay him not at the low Japanese CEO levels, but at the much higher levels found in other countries.

I believe that the explanation based on the allocation of CEO talent largely is behind the explosion in compensation of American CEOs during the past several decades. Yet at the same time, some American CEOs are obviously grossly overpaid, since they have mismanaged their companies and still receive exorbitant compensations. But mismanagement is not new and probably has not become so much more important over time. So I am suggesting that the rapid growth of compensation of American CEOs, and its premium over compensation of CEOs in other countries, is not mainly due to a growth in the degree of excess payment of executives in the United States. Rather, on this interpretation, the main cause of the increase in pay is the greater challenges and opportunities facing executives who manage much larger combinations of resources.

The Estate Tax 'Recycles' Opportunity

Under legislation proposed by President George W. Bush and passed by Congress in 2001, the federal estate tax is slated to disappear—at least briefly—in 2010. Some have argued that abolishing the inheritance tax would worsen the current U.S. "wealth gap" and undermine the idea of American meritocracy. Chuck Collins and William Gates Sr. are among the best-known advocates for keeping the inheritance tax. In the following editorial piece, which appeared in many newspapers in late 2006, Collins and Gates warn of a major loss of revenue if the tax is eliminated. They also propose that in the future the tax be used to pay for a new program of stakeholder grants and college scholarships in order to broaden opportunity for those who were "not born wealthy." Gates is the father of Microsoft billionaire Bill Gates, and Collins is a longtime progressive activist.

In December 1906, President Theodore Roosevelt expressed alarm about the dangerous concentration of wealth and power in the United States and called on the incoming 60th Congress to pass a federal estate tax. Its primary objective, intoned T.R., "should be to put a constantly increasing burden on the inheritance of those swollen fortunes which it is certainly of no benefit to this country to perpetuate."

A century later, after a 10-year assault, the federal estate tax is here to stay. While the votes no longer exist for permanent repeal, action is still needed. Otherwise, the tax will vanish in 2010 and return in 2011, creating a one-year window for tax-free dying. Congress must act to discourage a year of mysterious accidents in affluent households, bring back predictability, and prevent further deterioration of the nation's fiscal situation.

It is likely that 2007 will be the year of estate tax reform because of these pressures and the rising cost of inaction. But before Congress simply raises exemptions or cuts rates, let's consider all our options.

Congress has been unable to have a reasoned deliberation on the topic, even after solid research and investigative journalists have dispelled most of the fallacies about the tax. The facts are clear: the estate tax raises substantial revenue from those with the greatest capacity to pay. Abolishing the estate tax would cost $1.03 trillion over the first decade. There are only three ways to fill that shortfall: cut spending, raise taxes on the non-wealthy, or, the current favorite, pile it onto the national debt.

Starting in January [2007], the amount of wealth exempted by the tax will be $2 million for an individual and $4 million for a couple and the tax rate will fall to 45 percent. At that point, less than one-third of the richest 1 percent of households will pay the tax. Ample wealth will still flow to heirs and heiresses, as the effective tax rate on a $10 million estate is only 19 percent.

Repeal advocates are still gunning for the estate tax. They have offered several reckless proposals to gut the tax under the guise of "reform." They need to explain how to pay for the billions in lost revenue.

Instead of leaving more debt for the next generation, the U.S. should retain a robust estate tax and dedicate its revenue to increasing economic opportunity for the next generation. A responsible reform would increase the amount of wealth exempted by the tax to $2.5 million for an individual and $5 million for a couple—and include provisions to assist in the transfer of closely held family businesses.

Instead of the present "flat rate" system—where a $5 million estate pays the same rate as a $5 billion estate—we should adopt a progressive rate structure. Lifting the tax off smaller estates could be paid for by higher rates on estates over $50 million.

In a November [2006] ballot initiative, Washington State voters chose by substantial margins to retain their estate tax. Revenue from the state's tax is dedicated to an Education Legacy Trust Fund that last year spent $100 million to reduce K–12 class size and provide college scholarships for working-class students. We should consider a similar design for the federal estate tax.

Such a prudent policy won't happen unless we change our attitude about taxing inheritances. No one makes a fortune alone, without the help of our society's investments. The moral justification for an estate tax is that some of us have disproportionately benefited from the fertile economic soil we have cultivated together.

How many billionaires land on the *Forbes* 400 list courtesy of our technological and scientific commons, including the Internet, airwaves, biotechnology and mechanical advances? Seeing the invisible role of the commons in individual wealth creation should foster both an attitude of gratitude and recognition of our obligation to pass on similar opportunities. Previous generations did it for us—and it is our turn to pass on the gift.

We are not fans of earmarking funds, but the estate tax should be appreciated as an "economic opportunity recycling" program. Estate tax revenue should go into an "American opportunity fund," a sort of universal GI Bill for the next generation. It could provide grants for higher education and stakeholder funds to start businesses and purchase homes.

A progressive estate tax could serve as an intergenerational pact between the wealthy at the end of their lives—and the next generation who are not born wealthy. Like the GI Bill, it could be one of the best investments our nation makes in its people's aspirations.

Being Profitable *Is* Giving Back

John Tamny, a frequent contributor to the National Review Online, *makes a strong libertarian case for abolishing the estate tax in the following piece. Those who earn great fortunes in the free market, he argues, have already "given back" to society by finding new ways to meet consumer needs and should not be penalized, upon death, by having their wealth taxed away. The von Mises referred to by Tamny is Ludwig von Mises, an Austrian economist (1881–1973) famed for his staunch defense of the market economy.*

The U.S. House of Representatives voted 272 to 162 in April [2005] to abolish the estate tax. An editorial in last Friday's *Wall Street Journal* said that President Bush needs eight Senate Democrats to cross the aisle so that total repeal becomes filibuster-proof in the upper chamber.

Regardless of the Senate outcome, a big cut in the estate tax looms. Unhappy with this inevitability, estate-tax supporters have used the media to spread the false notion that repeal will save the rich from having to "give back."

An April article in *USA Today* described the belief among estate-tax supporters that "wealthy Americans owe a special debt because their wealth would not be possible without tax-supported schools and regulatory agencies." In the same article, William Gates Sr. voiced his support for the tax as "a fair payback to society for the opportunity to do business in our marvelous economy and society." Leaving aside the questionable value of tax-supported schools and regulatory agencies, not to mention the millions of jobs created, charities funded, and taxes already paid by the wealthiest Americans, Gates and the pro–estate-tax lobby get the whole concept of giving back exactly backwards.

Von Mises once wrote that the entrepreneur who fails to use his capital to the "best possible satisfaction of consumers" is "relegated to a place in which his ineptitude no longer hurts people's well-being." Successful entrepreneurs help consumers, while failures by definition help no one, and often hurt consumers.

Successful people, by virtue of being successful, have met previously unmet market needs, saved lives, saved consumers money, and in general have removed what von Mises referred to as "uneasiness" from the marketplace. A look at the 2004 *Forbes* 400 confirms his thinking.

- Charles Schwab, the 68th richest American, made investing in the stock market easy and affordable for the middle class. In doing so he helped launch an investment boom that an increasing number of Americans are able to participate in.
- Dr. Patrick Soon-Shiong, the 234th richest American, has developed a drug (Abraxane) that is injected into cancerous tumors. The tumors feed on Abraxane, only to be wiped out by a cancer-killing "Trojan Horse" within.
- It is estimated that Wal-Mart stores save consumers $100 billion a year. In other words, Wal-Mart's customers get a raise every time they shop there. Unsurprisingly, Wal-Mart's heirs and executives take up spots four through eight on the *Forbes* 400.
- Can anyone imagine living without Google, Amazon, and travel Web sites such as Expedia? Internet trailblazers Sergey Brin and Larry Page (43), Jeff Bezos (38), and Barry Diller (215) are all *Forbes* 400 members.

That the individuals behind the products and companies that improve our lives often reside in the *Forbes* 400 should not surprise us. Indeed, the greater a person's wealth, the more likely than not that he or she did something extraordinary that benefited others. "Giving back?" High profits are the surest sign that someone has given back. Can the same be said for entrepreneurial failures?

Furthermore, it's not just morally wrong for the government to use the estate tax to redistribute wealth; it's also bad economic policy. Wealth by definition is savings. When savings are confiscated for government use, entrepreneurial opportunities in need of capital go wanting in favor of immediate consumption.

Edward Wolff, an economics professor at New York University, told *The Wall Street Journal* in May that a poll showing a majority of the "rich" back estate-tax reform is a sign that "any notion of noblesse oblige is disappearing." Wolff gets it wrong, too. As the late Warren Brookes once said, "We are blessed by the genius of the few."

When the brilliant few innovate and improve our existence, we are receiving their very best and being given to in spades. The estate tax penalizes society's greatest benefactors, and for doing so should be repealed.

Andrew Carnegie on What to Do with a Fortune [1889]

The 19th-century steel magnate Andrew Carnegie is considered the foremost American philanthropist of his time. His essay "Wealth," later re-titled "The Gospel of Wealth," placed a heavy responsibility on those who accumulated great fortunes to do right by their fellow citizens, not through bequests at death but through active administration of charitable giving during their lifetimes. Carnegie, whom history remembers in part for the violence with which his hired security men put down the Homestead Strike in 1892, believed he had found a key to achieving "harmony" between rich and poor. In the excerpts below, he also states his approval for highly progressive wealth taxation. Carnegie's mention of Shylock refers to a money lender in William Shakespeare's The Merchant of Venice.

We start, then, with a condition of affairs [laissez-faire capitalism] under which the best interests of the race are promoted, but which inevitably gives wealth to the few. Thus far, accepting conditions as they exist, the situation can be surveyed and pronounced good. The question then arises—and, if the foregoing be correct, it is the only question with which we have to deal—What is the proper mode of administering wealth after the laws upon which civilization is founded have thrown it into the hands of the few? And it is of this great question that I believe I offer the true solution. . . .

The growing disposition to tax more and more heavily large estates left at death is a cheering indication of the growth of a salutary change in public opinion. The State of Pennsylvania now takes—subject to some exceptions—one-tenth of the property left by its citizens. The budget presented in the British Parliament the other day proposes to increase the death-duties; and, most significant of all, the new tax is to be a graduated one. Of all forms of taxation, this seems the wisest. Men who continue hoarding great sums all their lives, the proper use of which for public ends would work good to the community, should be made to feel that the community, in the form of the state, cannot thus be deprived of its proper share. By taxing estates heavily at death the state marks its condemnation of the selfish millionaire's unworthy life.

It is desirable that nations should go much further in this direction. Indeed, it is difficult to set bounds to the share of a rich man's estate which should go at his death to the public through the agency of the state, and by all means such taxes should be graduated, beginning at nothing upon moderate sums to dependents, and increasing rapidly as the amounts swell, until of the millionaire's hoard, as of Shylock's, at least

> " . . . The other half
> Comes to the privy coffer of the state."

This policy would work powerfully to induce the rich man to attend to the administration of wealth during his life, which is the end that society should always have in view, as being that by far most fruitful for the people. Nor need it be feared that this policy would sap the root of enterprise and render men less anxious to accumulate, for to the class whose ambition it is to leave great fortunes and be talked about after their death, it will attract even more attention, and, indeed, be a somewhat nobler ambition to have enormous sums paid over to the state from their fortunes.

There remains, then, only one mode of using great fortunes; but in this we have the true antidote for the temporary unequal distribution of wealth, the reconciliation of the rich and the poor—a reign of harmony—another ideal, differing, indeed, from that of the Communist in requiring only the further evolution of existing conditions, not the total overthrow of our civilization. It is founded upon the present most intense individualism, and the race is prepared to put it in practice by degrees whenever it pleases. Under its sway we shall have an ideal state, in which the surplus wealth of the few will become, in the best sense, the property of the many, because administered for the common good, and this wealth, passing through the hands of the few, can be made a much more potent force for the elevation of our race than if it had been distributed in small sums to the people themselves. Even the poorest can be made to see this, and to agree that great sums gathered by some of their fellow-citizens and spent for public purposes, from which the masses reap the principal benefit, are more valuable to them than if scattered among them through the course of many years in trifling amounts. . . .

This, then, is held to be the duty of the man of Wealth: First, to set an example of modest, unostentatious living, shunning display or extravagance; to provide moderately for the legitimate wants of those dependent upon him; and after doing so to consider all surplus revenues which come to him simply as trust funds, which he is called upon to administer, and strictly bound as a matter of duty to administer in the manner which, in his judgment, is best calculated to produce the most beneficial results for the community—the man of wealth thus becoming the mere agent and trustee for his poorer brethren, bringing to their service his superior wisdom, experience, and ability to administer, doing for them better than they would or could do for themselves. . . .

Thus is the problem of Rich and Poor to be solved. The laws of accumulation will be left free; the laws of distribution free. Individualism will continue, but the millionaire will be but a trustee for the poor; intrusted for a season with a great part of the increased wealth of the community, but administering it for the community far better than it could or would have done for itself. The best minds will thus have reached a stage in the development of the race in which it is clearly seen that there is no mode of disposing of surplus wealth creditable to thoughtful and earnest men into whose hands it flows save by using it year by year for the general good. This day already dawns. . . . Men may die sharers in great business enterprises from which their capital cannot be or has not been withdrawn, and is left chiefly at death for public uses, yet the man who dies leaving behind him millions of available wealth, which was his to administer during life, will pass away "unwept, unhonored, and unsung," no matter to what uses he leaves the dross which he cannot take with him. Of such as these the public verdict will then be: "The man who dies thus rich dies disgraced."

Giving Back, Big Time:
The Carnegie-Buffett Connection

In June 2006, Warren Buffett, the world's second-richest man, announced that he would be giving the bulk of his fortune to the foundation already established by the world's richest man, Bill Gates, to be used for charitable endeavors. David Nasaw, a historian at City Uni-

*versity of New York and biographer of Andrew Carnegie, offers some re-
flections on similarities between Buffett and Carnegie in the following
op-ed that appeared in* The Los Angeles Times.

It has taken almost 120 years, but millionaires are finally beginning to follow Andrew Carnegie's advice. Hundreds of articles have appeared in the last six months comparing Bill Gates
and a variety of 21st century philanthropists to Carnegie. In June,
Warren Buffett explicitly referred to Carnegie and his writings in
explaining why he had decided to leave $31 billion in Berkshire
Hathaway stock to the Bill & Melinda Gates Foundation.

In his 1889 "Gospel of Wealth" essays, Carnegie demanded
that the wealthy give away their fortunes in their lifetimes. Those
who did not would "pass away 'unwept, unhonored, and unsung' . . . . Of such as these the public verdict will then be: 'The
man who dies thus rich dies disgraced.'"

By his own measure, Andrew Carnegie did not die disgraced.

He sold his steel company to J. P. Morgan in 1901 (Carnegie
got $226 million), and Morgan proclaimed him "the richest man in
the world." Carnegie was an unapologetic capitalist. He defended
the right of businessmen to make the largest profit possible, and he
wasn't ashamed of cutting his workers' wages, increasing their
hours, crushing their unions or violently breaking strikes, as at his
Homestead mill in 1892.

But Carnegie also heeded his own "gospel," developing a
moral philosophy of capitalism that resonates today. He handed
out more than $350 million (tens of billions in 2006 dollars) to
small colleges, technical schools, and libraries. He established a
scientific research institution in Washington; provided trusts to
pay students' tuition and professors' pensions; built a library/
museum/concert hall complex in Pittsburgh; and gave millions
of dollars to campaigns for world peace and to establish the
Carnegie Corp., dedicated to the "advancement and diffusion of
knowledge."

Even smart and hardworking millionaires did not, Carnegie
argued, earn their fortunes by themselves. "Wealth," he declared,
"is not chiefly the product of the individual, but largely the joint
product of the community."

Buffet, in a *Fortune* interview in June, recalled Carnegie's
words. He had, he explained, told his first wife in 1952 that he expected to get rich mostly "because I was born with the right skills

in the right place at the right time. . . . We agreed with Andrew Carnegie, who said that huge fortunes that flow in large part from society should in large part be returned to society."

Buffett's understanding of the ways in which wealth falls into the hands of the lucky few accords entirely with Carnegie's. Buffett credited his wealth to being "wired at birth" with investment acumen, the help of parents and others, and the fact that he lived in "a rich, populous country in which enormous quantities of marketable securities were traded and were sometimes ridiculously mispriced." Carnegie similarly made his fortune because his Scottish immigrant parents settled in Pittsburgh, a city blessed with abundant coke and iron ore and located at the center of a westward-reaching rail network.

The two men also see eye to eye on at least one way that society ought to collect its due from the rich: the much attacked and debated estate tax.

"I would hate to see the estate tax gutted," Buffett said as he announced his gift to the Gates Foundation. "It's a very equitable tax. It's in keeping with the idea of equality of opportunity in this country, not giving incredible head starts to certain people."

Carnegie, who was opposed to income taxes and property taxes, nevertheless supported near 100 percent inheritance taxes on large estates. Those who held on to their money, he said, instead of distributing it for the good of society, had no moral right to decide what happened to it after their deaths: "By taxing estates heavily at death, the state marks its condemnation of the selfish millionaire's unworthy life."

Carnegie did not support estate taxes because he believed the state needed more money. (As a good Republican, he was in favor of smaller, not larger, government.) An inheritance tax was necessary because it preserved the ability of men like him to rise to the top through their wits. The hereditary transmission of wealth from generation to generation would create dynastic power over business and politics. This was bad for capitalism, bad for democracy, bad for the children of the rich who were handed leadership positions they had not earned and worse for the poor and middle classes that had to struggle against unreasonable odds to achieve leadership positions.

Carnegie's demand that the wealthy give away their riches—or lose them to inheritance taxes—remains an extreme idea. The fact that the Republican-led Congress has severely cut what it calls the "death tax" is evidence of that. So is the commotion that greeted Buffett's largesse—the gift of about 85 percent of his fortune.

But Buffett's acknowledgment of Carnegie's vision also is evidence that a good idea—however extreme—will survive. Carnegie's gospel is alive, and spreading.

Being Poor

When Hurricane Katrina struck New Orleans on August 29, 2005, the impact was catastrophic. The storm left well over a thousand dead—even now there is no exact count. Media coverage of the disaster centered on the city's Ninth Ward, where a level of poverty was revealed beyond what most Americans could comprehend. John Scalzi wrote "Being Poor" in reaction to the many who asked why the residents had not heeded warnings to evacuate the city. (Short answer: they couldn't afford to.) "Being Poor" struck a chord. It was widely circulated and discussed. Many alternative "being poor" lists were subsequently posted to the Internet.

Being poor is knowing exactly how much everything costs.

Being poor is getting angry at your kids for asking for all the crap they see on TV.

Being poor is having to keep buying $800 cars because they're what you can afford, and then having the cars break down on you, because there's not an $800 car in America that's worth a damn.

Being poor is hoping the toothache goes away.

Being poor is knowing your kid goes to friends' houses but never has friends over to yours.

Being poor is going to the restroom before you get in the school lunch line so your friends will be ahead of you and won't hear you say "I get free lunch" when you get to the cashier.

Being poor is living next to the freeway.

Being poor is coming back to the car with your children in the back seat, clutching that box of Raisin Bran you just bought and trying to think of a way to make the kids understand that the box has to last.

Being poor is wondering if your well-off sibling is lying when he says he doesn't mind when you ask for help.

Being poor is off-brand toys.

Being poor is a heater in only one room of the house.

Being poor is knowing you can't leave $5 on the coffee table when your friends are around.

Being poor is hoping your kids don't have a growth spurt.

Being poor is stealing meat from the store, frying it up before your mom gets home and then telling her she doesn't have to make dinner tonight because you're not hungry anyway.

Being poor is Goodwill underwear.

Being poor is not enough space for everyone who lives with you.

Being poor is feeling the glued soles tear off your supermarket shoes when you run around the playground.

Being poor is your kid's school being the one with the 15-year-old textbooks and no air conditioning.

Being poor is thinking $8 an hour is a really good deal.

Being poor is relying on people who don't give a damn about you.

Being poor is an overnight shift under fluorescent lights.

Being poor is finding the letter your mom wrote to your dad, begging him for the child support.

Being poor is a bathtub you have to empty into the toilet.

Being poor is stopping the car to take a lamp from a stranger's trash.

Being poor is making lunch for your kid when a cockroach skitters over the bread, and you looking over to see if your kid saw.

Being poor is believing a GED actually makes a goddamned difference.

Being poor is people angry at you just for walking around in the mall.

Being poor is not taking the job because you can't find someone you trust to watch your kids.

Being poor is the police busting into the apartment right next to yours.

Being poor is not talking to that girl because she'll probably just laugh at your clothes.

Being poor is hoping you'll be invited for dinner.

Being poor is a sidewalk with lots of brown glass on it.

Being poor is people thinking they know something about you by the way you talk.

Being poor is needing that 35-cent raise.

Being poor is your kid's teacher assuming you don't have any books in your home.

Being poor is six dollars short on the utility bill and no way to close the gap.

Being poor is crying when you drop the mac and cheese on the floor.

Being poor is knowing you work as hard as anyone, anywhere.

Being poor is people surprised to discover you're not actually stupid.

Being poor is people surprised to discover you're not actually lazy.

Being poor is a six-hour wait in an emergency room with a sick child asleep on your lap.

Being poor is never buying anything someone else hasn't bought first.

Being poor is picking the 10-cent ramen instead of the 12-cent ramen because that's two extra packages for every dollar.

Being poor is having to live with choices you didn't know you made when you were 14 years old.

Being poor is getting tired of people wanting you to be grateful.

Being poor is knowing you're being judged.

Being poor is a box of crayons and a $1 coloring book from a community center Santa.

Being poor is checking the coin return slot of every soda machine you go by.

Being poor is deciding that it's all right to base a relationship on shelter.

Being poor is knowing you really shouldn't spend that buck on a Lotto ticket.

Being poor is hoping the register lady will spot you the dime.

Being poor is feeling helpless when your child makes the same mistakes you did, and won't listen to you beg them against doing so.

Being poor is a cough that doesn't go away.

Being poor is making sure you don't spill on the couch, just in case you have to give it back before the lease is up.

Being poor is a $200 paycheck advance from a company that takes $250 when the paycheck comes in.

Being poor is four years of night classes for an Associate of Arts degree.

Being poor is a lumpy futon bed.

Being poor is knowing where the shelter is.

Being poor is people who have never been poor wondering why you choose to be so.

Being poor is knowing how hard it is to stop being poor.

Being poor is seeing how few options you have.

Being poor is running in place.

References

Becker, Gary. "Are CEOs Overpaid?" The Becker-Posner Blog, May 14, 2006.

Bernanke, Ben S. "The Level and Distribution of Economic Well-Being." Remarks before the Greater Omaha Chamber of Commerce, Omaha, Nebraska (2007). Accessed at http://www.federalreserve.gov.

Calderon, Olivia. "Q & A on California Kids Investment and Development Savings (KIDS) Accounts," Senate Bill 752 (2007). Accessed at http://www.newamerica.net.

Carnegie, Andrew. "Wealth." *North American Review* 148, no. 391 (June 1889): 653–664.

Collins, Chuck, and William Gates, Sr. "The Estate Tax 'Recycles' Opportunity." *Roanoke Times* (December 24, 2006).

Nasaw, David. "Giving Back, Big Time." *The Los Angeles Times* (November 2, 2006): A19.

Scalzi, John. "Being Poor." *The Chicago Tribune* (September 15, 2005): A27.

Stonecash, Jeffrey M. *Inequality and the American Public—Results of the Third Annual Maxwell School Survey Conducted September – October 2006.* Syracuse, NY: Maxwell School of Citizenship & Public Affairs, Syracuse University, 2007.

Tamny, John. "Being Profitable *Is* Giving Back." *National Review Online* (July 14, 2005). Accessed at http://www.nationalreview.com.

Weller, Christian, and Kate Sabatini. "The Great CEO Guarantee: Get Really Well-Paid Regardless of Your Performance." Washington, DC: Center for American Progress, 2006. Accessed at http://www.american progress.org.

7

Directory of Organizations

A wide range of U.S. organizations have shown an interest in the growing gap between rich and poor, whether focused on investigating the causes and consequences of the gap or on policies to reverse it. For some, the interest is not in inequality per se but rather in the condition of those on the bottom rungs of the ladder—those in poverty. A couple of examples are the National Coalition for the Homeless and America's Second Harvest. For such groups, a reduction of poverty and insecurity is the main goal to be sought, and a lessening of inequality would be merely a secondary benefit. For other organizations, the perceived injustice of the current level of economic inequality is the primary issue. This would be a reasonable way to characterize United for a Fair Economy or the Legal Aid Society of New York, to name two examples. With both the poverty-oriented and injustice-oriented organizations, there is, not surprisingly, a straightforward willingness to advocate for steps that would benefit those in the lower ranks of the income distribution.

Policy institutes—known to most of us as "think tanks"—are well represented in the list below. Those with a liberal perspective outnumber those of a conservative bent for the simple reason that liberals tend to be more engaged with, indeed disturbed by, the widening gap between America's haves and have-nots. Conservatives, as noted in chapter 2, are more likely to view rising inequality as a cyclical phenomenon that should not concern us unduly nor be used as an excuse for government interventions into the economy. They do not ignore the issue entirely, and thus three of the highest-profile think tanks on the right are included in the directory. Several institutes with a special, scholarly commitment to

201

matters of inequality and poverty also make the list, such as the Institute for Research on Poverty and Stanford's Center for the Study of Poverty and Inequality. Overall, the list is selective and could easily be extended. Those who have a reason to do so can make use of the "links" feature found on almost every Web site.

American Enterprise Institute for Public Policy Research (AEI)
1150 17th St. NW, Washington, DC 20036
(202) 862-5800 Fax: (202) 862-7177
E-mail: vrodman@aei.org
http://www.aei.org

Oldest of the big three conservative think tanks (the others being Cato and Heritage), AEI was founded in 1943 as a nonprofit, nonpartisan institution aiming to advance the values of "limited government, private enterprise, and individual liberty." Its resident and adjunct scholars pursue studies across the full range of public policy issues, both foreign and domestic, and disseminate their findings in monographs, research papers, videos, and conference presentations. In recent years, AEI has taken a relatively slight interest in U.S. poverty, the major exception being the "Welfare Reform Academy" project administered by AEI scholar Douglas J. Besharov through the University of Maryland. The Academy helps officials and others understand how best to implement and evaluate new programs under the 1996 welfare reform law. AEI also has two scholars on staff with expertise in income inequality, Marvin Kosters and Richard Vedder, although they do not write on this issue regularly.

Publications: AEI posts large numbers of newsletters, op-eds, papers, and speeches on its Web site; in addition, some longer papers (monographs) may be purchased from AEI Press. A shorter paper of interest is "Fair Taxes? Depends on What You Mean by 'Fair'" (7/16/07), by Gregory Mankiw, a Yale economist who served as chairman of President George W. Bush's Council of Economic Advisors. This essay addresses the question of whether the rich are taxed enough. More in-depth on the same topic is "The Trouble with Taxing Those at the Top," a June 2007 article in the AEI *Tax Policy Outlook*.

America's Second Harvest (ASH)
35 E. Wacker Dr., Ste. 2000, Chicago, IL 60601

(312) 263-2303 or (800) 771-2303
http://www.secondharvest.org

The mission of America's Second Harvest is two-fold: to feed the nation's hungry through a network of member food banks and to advocate for policies that would end hunger. From its beginnings in Phoenix in the 1960s, ASH has become the largest private hunger-relief agency in the country. It established its headquarters in Chicago in 1984, although it also maintains an office in the nation's capital. Through its network of food banks serving all 50 states, the District of Columbia, and Puerto Rico, ASH supports about 94,000 local food assistance programs, from soup kitchens to after-school feeding programs—some 25 million (mainly low-income) people. Among other initiatives, ASH operates a Back-Pack Program and a Kids Café. The former provides backpacks of nonperishable, nutritious food to low-income children over weekends, school vacations, and, in some cases, the summer. (Exact program details vary among local food providers.) The latter is a program set up in 1993 under which ASH provides hot meals and snacks to low-income kids in places where they get together, such as Boys and Girls Clubs, church halls, and public schools. ASH has received the top, four-star rating from Charity Navigator for the efficiency with which it uses donated resources to provide services to those in need.

Publications: In addition to a variety of fact sheets on hunger, ASH also issues two key documents: *Hunger in America* and *The Almanac of Hunger and Poverty in America.* The first builds on extensive client and agency surveys to render a detailed profile of those receiving emergency food assistance; the *Hunger Almanac* is a compilation of hunger statistics and information about hunger programs in all 50 states.

Association of Community Organizations for Reform Now (ACORN)
739 8th St. SE, Washington, DC 20003
(877) 55-ACORN Fax: (202) 546-2483
E-mail: natacorndc@acorn.org
http://acorn.org

The Association of Community Organizations for Reform Now, ACORN, was formed in 1970 as the *Arkansas* Community Organizations for Reform Now—an offshoot of the National Welfare Rights Organization. From its roots in Little Rock, ACORN grew to become a national quasi-political force advocating for the rights of low- and moderate-income people across the country. Some of the things ACORN has successfully pushed for are: community reinvestment by banks; urban homesteading programs for low-income residents; physical, curricular, and staffing improvements in urban public schools; no-shut-off agreements with utility companies; and the passage of living wage ordinances. ACORN is perhaps best known for the last-named activity. It has been a leader in getting living wages passed in Boston, Chicago, Detroit, and Oakland, California, and has established a Living Wage Resource Center (online) to assist those trying to pass similar ordinances in additional jurisdictions. A major current campaign by ACORN is to ensure paid sick leave for workers in both the public and private sectors.

Publications: ACORN has prepared reports on such issues as the living wage, the minimum wage, home foreclosures, unclaimed EITC benefits, lending costs to minority urban homeowners, and the impact of Hurricane Katrina on black homeowners in New Orleans, all of which can be downloaded.

Boston College Center on Wealth and Philanthropy (CWP)
McGuinn Hall 515, 140 Commonwealth Ave., Chestnut Hill, MA 02467
(617) 552-4070 Fax: (617) 552-3903
E-mail: cwp508@bc.edu
http://www.bc.edu/cwp

Established at Boston College in 1970, the Center on Wealth and Philanthropy meets a need that could only emerge in a society with considerable wealth: to help affluent individuals find meaningful ways to help others, and in the process develop their own spirituality through charitable giving. The CWP aims to assist people in self-reflection about what they want to accomplish with their philanthropy. Its director, Paul Schervish, is an authority on what is called donor behavior. Research at the CWP explores both the everyday acts of charity that are barely recognized as such and the more dramatic acts by which wealth is bequeathed from the older generations to the younger. Schervish and his Center have been in the media with forecasts of the volume of wealth that is set to be transferred as the baby boomers pass from the scene—estimated at a minimum of $41 trillion. Schervish has professional credentials in both divinity and sociology, and he takes a particular interest in the spiritual dimensions of philanthropy.

Publications: A variety of papers authored or co-authored by Mr. Schervish are available for download or purchase at the CWP Web site; they deal with economic, social, geographic, psychological, and spiritual aspects of philanthropy.

The Brookings Institution

1775 Massachusetts Ave. NW, Washington, DC 20036
(202) 797-6000 Fax: (202) 797-6004
E-mail: communications@brookings.edu
http://www.brookings.edu

The Brookings Institution can fairly claim to be the oldest think tank in the country: its forerunner, the Institute for Government Research, was founded in 1916. Centrist in its political outlook, Brookings is an "institution" in more than the technical sense. It is at the heart of the policymaking establishment in Washington, D.C., where its experts conduct research on just about everything policy-related, from science and technology to politics and the economy. It is not a gross exaggeration to say that from the 200-plus scholars and visiting scholars currently at Brookings, a newly elected president could recruit an entire cabinet and many of the needed deputies and support staff. Its work on the rich-poor divide extends from the global context to various aspects of U.S. society. Brookings is home to some of the nation's top poverty and welfare scholars—Isabel Sawhill, Gary Burtless, and Ron Haskins—and their names are on most of its research concerning income inequality and poverty. Brookings hosts briefings, speeches, and panel discussions on a weekly, sometimes daily, basis.

Publications: Brookings offers the full panoply of policy publications: articles, op-eds, testimony, policy briefs, all accessible at their Web site. They also publish about 50 books each year along with several journals, of which two are particularly relevant: *The Future of Children* (jointly with Princeton's Woodrow Wilson School of Public and International Affairs) and *Brookings Papers on Education Policy.*

Cato Institute

1000 Massachusetts Ave. NW, Washington, DC 20001-5403
(202) 842-0200 Fax: (202) 842-3490
http://www.cato.org

Founded in 1977, Cato is a nonprofit, right-oriented think tank in Washington, D.C. It prefers the labels "libertarian" and "market liberal" to "conservative" as descriptions of its ideological stance in favor of small government and free markets. Its roughly 40 policy scholars and 70 policy adjuncts include some very high-powered economists and other academics. Cato takes an interest in a wide range of issues—political, legal, philosophical, economic, and scientific. Income inequality is not a major focus, but from time-to-time, Cato issues interesting research or opinion pieces on income inequality and taxation. Scholars associated with the institute frown on the types of policies discussed in chapter 2 that would lessen—or aim to lessen—the current degree of income inequality in the United States. They tend to favor flat taxes, not progressive taxes, and consistently seek reductions in taxation and government spending.

Publications: The Cato Institute publishes vast quantities of libertarian analysis and opinion in the form of books, policy studies, journals, briefs, and white papers. Cato also puts out a lot of free online material, including the *Daily Dispatch,* the monthly *Cato Unbound* magazine, and the quarterly *Cato's Letter.* Of special interest was the February 2007 edition of the online forum "Cato Unbound," which was devoted to the topic "Interrogating Inequality" and included follow-up entries in blog style. Participants were persuasive and well-informed.

Center for American Progress (CAP)
1333 H St. NW, 10th Fl., Washington, DC 20005
(202) 682-1611
E-mail: progress@americanprogress.org
http://www.americanprogress.org

Established in 2003, the Center for American Progress is a liberal response to the conservatively oriented think tanks like Cato and Heritage (see p. 214), although CAP consistently substitutes the term "progressive" for "liberal." It promotes the value of open, effective government in helping to solve social and economic problems. Its guiding philosophy might best be described as Clintonian pragmatism. President Clinton, whose one-time chief of staff, John Podesta, presides over CAP, was known for favoring centrist, non-ideological social policies during his 1993–2001 term of office. On the professional staff at CAP are about 70 experts on all the major public policy issues. CAP develops new ideas and policy initiatives in a number of areas. Two thematic fields that relate to income inequality are "Economic Mobility" and "Task Force on Poverty." Speeches and panel discussions with invited guests occur on a regular basis at the center, and videos of the proceedings are posted to the CAP Web site. In 2006, for example, CAP hosted a session on "Ending Child Poverty: The United Kingdom's Commitment, the United States' Challenge," featuring presentations by the UK Secretary of State for Work and Pensions and a former top official in the Clinton administration. Their remarks are available on the Web site.

Publications: CAP issues reports and recommendations on various policy initiatives, such as the 72-page "From Poverty to Prosperity" (April 2007), which outlined a CAP program designed to halve the U.S. poverty rate in 10 years. The center also puts out newsletters that alert subscribers to upcoming CAP events and to columns, backgrounders, and talking points its staff have written. Anyone can register to receive the newsletters.

Center on Budget and Policy Priorities (CBPP)
820 1st St. NE, Ste. 510, Washington, DC 20002
(202) 408-1080 Fax: (202) 408-1056
E-mail: communications@cbpp.org
http://www.cbpp.org

Since its establishment in 1981, the Center on Budget and Policy Priorities has built a reputation for timely, accurate analysis of fiscal issues at both the federal and state level. Its particular emphasis is on the way government policies affect low- and moderate-income individuals and families. While this suggests a liberal slant, the CBPP is actually known to be fiscally conservative: it keeps a close eye on spending and tax levels out of a concern that scarce resources remain available to meet pressing social needs. Its analyses of the tax cuts of President George W. Bush have focused as much on lost tax revenues as on their supposed tilt toward the wealthy. The devolution of many federal programs to the states in recent years has brought a corresponding shift in CBPP research and consulting activity, so that about half of its work is now state-oriented, in part through its State Fiscal Analysis Initiative. Because it is so nimble and accurate in its analyses, the CBPP is often cited on Capitol Hill and in the media.

Publications: The CBPP offers a unique online resource: slideshows on several issues of public interest. Two that relate to the rich-poor gap are "Putting Tax Cuts into Context" and "Issues Surrounding the Federal Estate Tax." Policy reports and fact sheets on poverty, low-income immigrants, taxes, the EITC, and low-income housing may be accessed at the Web site.

Center for Law and Social Policy (CLASP)
1015 15th St. NW, Ste. 400, Washington, DC 20005
(202) 906-8000 Fax: (202) 842-2885
http://www.clasp.org

The Center for Law and Social Policy was founded in 1968 as a public interest law firm, with high-powered backing from former Supreme Court Justice Arthur Goldberg. In 1981, the firm reconceived itself as a nonprofit research and advocacy center dedicated to low-income family issues. CLASP lawyers and policy analysts work in several areas to improve the stability and financial security of poor families. They have been heavily involved, for example, in efforts at the federal and state levels to strengthen child support programs and find ways for children to be supported even when the absent parent is not making payments. (Child support is a far more serious problem for low-income families than for those on higher rungs of the income ladder.) CLASP takes a strong interest in work supports for single parents leaving welfare, such as child care, transitional jobs, and training programs. Reflecting its own institutional roots, CLASP advocates for legal services to be available to those of limited means. It is a vigorous defender of the Legal Services Corporation (see p. 217), which tends to experience fluctuating support from Congress depending on election results.

Publications: In each of the fields in which it works, CLASP offers fact sheets, reports, policy briefs, legislative analyses, and transcripts of testimony, all of which can be downloaded. Their materials on child support are particularly informative.

Center for Social Development (CSD)
One Brookings Dr., St. Louis, MO 63130-4899
(314) 935-7433 Fax: (314) 935-8661
E-mail: csd@gwbmail.wustl.edu
http://gwbweb.wustl.edu/csd

Founded in 1994 and located within the George Warren Brown School of Social Work at Washington University, the Center for Social Development is a research and policy center with two main interests: civic engagement and asset building. Under the direction of Michael Sherraden, CSD has been an intellectual and institutional driver of the asset-building movement that many see as an essential part of any overall strategy for narrowing the rich-poor divide in the United States. It has been a pioneer in researching individual development accounts (IDAs) and has conducted pilot programs to see how effective such accounts can be. (An IDA is a savings plan under which dollars saved by individuals are matched by either government or private sources, with the accumulated savings available for the purchase of a home, retirement, or other good purposes.) Participating in an IDA can raise financial literacy, promote entry into the economic mainstream, stabilize families, and bolster communities. CSD has major foundation support for a State Assets Policy Project, under which the center advises and works with states to develop state-level assets policies. Almost half the states now have IDA programs in place.

Publications: A variety of reports, working papers, and speech transcripts dating back to 1995 are available for downloading from the CSD Web site. The website has a useful feature for researchers—an extensive list of keywords that can assist them in performing a successful search of CSD publications.

The Century Foundation (TCF)

41 E. 70th St., New York, NY 10021
(212) 535-4441 Fax: (212) 535-7534
E-mail: info@tcf.org
http://www.tcf.org

Established in 1919 by Edward Filene, of Boston department store fame, the Century Foundation is one of the oldest public policy research institutes in the country. Centrist in outlook, its bywords are "effective government," "open democracy," and "free markets." One of its continuing policy interests is inequality, both economic and educational. Its education expert, Richard D. Kahlenberg, has written extensively on the benefits of economically integrated classrooms. Kahlenberg and about a dozen other fellows at TCF write and speak on a broad range of issues. They also convene forums with policy makers, academics, and the public, which explains why TCF maintains offices in both New York City and Washington, D.C.

Publications: Aside from the shorter commentary and opinion items that occasionally deal with rich-poor issues, the TCF

Web site also features reports and issue briefs that can be down-loaded, and lists books by TCF authors that can be purchased from online booksellers.

Children's Defense Fund (CDF)
25 E St. NW, Washington, DC 20001
(202) 628-8787 or (800) 233-1200
E-mail: cdfinfo@childrensdefense.org
http://www.childrensdefense.org

Because children have the highest poverty rate of any age group in the United States, an organization dedicated to helping children is implicitly concerned with the issue of inequality. To put it another way, if all the goals of the Children's Defense Fund were achieved tomorrow, the nation's measured levels of inequality—and poverty—would be lowered instantly. A private, nonprofit organization, the CDF was founded in 1973 as an outgrowth of the civil rights movement. Its founder, Marian Wright Edelman, widely considered the nation's most effective advocate for children, remains its president. CDF works for children's health, readiness for school, safe care when parents are at work, and moral upbringing. It has established a number of signature programs with catchy names and solid policy rationales. An example is SHOUT (Student Health Outreach Project), which connects high school and college students with local agencies to get uninsured children enrolled in the health coverage they are entitled to, either through Medicaid or the Children's Health Insurance Program (CHIP). CDF keeps track of congressional votes on issues critical to children and issues an annual "scorecard" on individual members of Congress. Beyond advocacy and activism, CDF also engages in policy analysis of issues related to children's well-being.

Publications: The CDF puts out a variety of child-related guides and reports, some of which are highly practical, for example, "Fact Sheets for Grandparents and Other Relatives Raising Children" (one for every state). Ms. Edelman's weekly "Child Watch" column and the monthly CDF newsletter can be read online.

Citizens for Tax Justice (CTJ)
1616 P St. NW, Ste. 200, Washington, DC 20036
(202) 299-1066 Fax: (202) 299-1065
E-mail: mattg@ctj.org
http://www.ctj.org

Citizens for Tax Justice is a nonprofit research and advocacy organization that has pushed, since 1979, for federal, state, and local tax policies that place a fair burden on the rich and the poor. It tends to see the rich as undertaxed, the poor as overtaxed. CTJ has a stated interest in curbing corporate tax avoidance; holding down federal deficits and debt; ensuring an adequate level of tax revenues to fund essential services; and promoting a tax structure that does not distort the economy. It was given major credit for putting tax reform on the political agenda in the mid-1980s, and it has played a key role in illustrating the consequences of the tax cuts of President George W. Bush since 2001. Its analysts have shown that those tax cuts tend to bloat the federal deficit while conferring quite large benefits on the wealthy. For example, CTJ calculated that the cuts reduced President Bush's own 2005 tax bill by some $26,000 and Vice-President Cheney's bill by over $1 million. CTJ staff members research tax issues, place op-ed pieces in major newspapers, and testify before congressional and state legislative committees. The director, Bob McIntyre, is the omnipresent public face of CTJ.

Publications: CTJ puts out short, data-filled, accessible analyses of various tax issues, usually those involved in ongoing controversy. Many are variations on a central theme—that the tax code favors the rich. These briefs can be downloaded at no cost from the CTJ Web site.

Corporation for Enterprise Development (CFED)
777 N. Capitol St. NE, Ste. 800, Washington DC 20002
(202) 408-9788 Fax: (202) 408-9793
E-mail: info-dc@cfed.org
http://www.cfed.org

The Corporation for Enterprise Development was established in 1979 as a nonpartisan, nonprofit organization dedicated to bringing low-income, low-wealth people into the nation's financial mainstream. Broadly stated, the mission of CFED is to identify and test, and then help implement, ideas for expanding economic opportunity. It has been a big supporter of individual development accounts (IDAs) or matched savings accounts, but has moved in some new directions, too, such as microenterprise, Native American entrepreneurship, and a program to assist self-employed business owners with tax preparation. CFED partners with policy makers, community groups, and financial institutions to promote the goal of a wider sharing of economic opportunity. It works at the federal, state, and local levels with both public and private agencies.

Publications: CFED issues an annual *Development Report Card for the States* that ranks each state's economic health and prospects based on a wide range of criteria. It also puts out fact sheets and brochures on IDAs and other asset-building ideas.

Demos
220 5th Ave., 5th Fl., New York, NY 10001
(212) 633-1405 Fax: (212) 633-2015
E-mail: info@demos.org
http://www.demos.org

Demos calls itself a "network for ideas and action." It is also a nonpartisan research and advocacy organization that believes democracy is undermined by the growth of inequality and insecurity among Americans. One of its three major themes of research and advocacy is "Economic Opportunity"; under that rubric it looks at issues related to debt buildup, the vulnerability of the middle class, inequality and its consequences, the financial challenges facing young adults, and asset building programs. Demos sponsors speakers and conferences occasionally. It arranged a notable conference on inequality in 2004, which led to publication of the book *Inequality Matters: The Growing Economic Divide in America and Its Poisonous Consequences.* Like some other think tanks, Demos has both a team of staff experts and administrators and a stable of fellows who are scholars and writers working out and debating new ideas.

Publications: A variety of Demos papers, available online or in hard copy, document the economic challenges facing the middle class and those who aspire to it. How well (or badly) people are handling credit and debt is a topic featured prominently in these reports. "Around the Kitchen Table," a monthly e-journal, explores economic problems facing America's poor.

Economic Mobility Project (EMP)
1025 F St. NW, Ste. 900, Washington, DC 20004
(202) 552-2000 Fax: (202) 552-2299
http://www.economicmobility.org

Still in its early stages as an initiative sponsored by the Pew Charitable Trusts, the Economic Mobility Project tackles the question of whether the American dream of economic mobility remains alive. The EMP represents a unique partnership among four Washington think tanks—two on the conservative side (Heritage, AEI) and two on the liberal side (Brookings, Urban Institute). Some of the leading American scholars on poverty and inequality sit on its advisory board. The project hopes to establish "nonpartisan agreement on the facts, figures and trends related to mobility" and to spark a national debate on ways to keep opportunity alive for generations to come.

Publications: The EMP will produce reports and white papers and hold events to publicize issues related to mobility. It has already produced a short introductory report, "Economic Mobility: Is the American Dream Alive and Well?" (2007), by Isabel Sawhill and John Morton, which can be downloaded from the Web site.

Economic Policy Institute (EPI)

1333 H St. NW, Ste. 300, East Tower, Washington, DC
20005-4707
(202) 775-8810 Fax: (202) 775-0819
E-mail: epi@epi.org
http://www.epinet.org

The Economic Policy Institute calls itself "the first organization to focus on the economic condition of low- and middle-income Americans and their families." It has been an important liberal think tank in Washington, D.C. since it was founded in 1986 by a half-dozen innovative thinkers on the left: Jeff Faux, Barry Bluestone, Robert Reich, Robert Kuttner, Ray Marshall, and Lester Thurow. EPI works in a number of fields that relate to the rich-poor gap in the United States, from the living wage and welfare reform to tax policy and union organizing. The basic thrust of EPI policy advocacy is toward the notion of "broadly shared prosperity and opportunity." EPI supports a fair reward for labor, including higher minimum wages. It defends the usefulness of social safety-net programs, and favors a more robust program of educational investment in American youth. It is mistrustful of current trade levels with China and concerned about the "offshoring" of U.S. jobs.

Publications: Half of the EPI "Issue Guides" are on topics germane to the rich-poor divide in the United States: minimum wage, living wage, poverty and family budgets, and welfare. All of the guides, as well as a host of other reports, op-ed pieces, and speeches by EPI staff and associates, can be downloaded from the Web site. The institute's signature publication, *The State of Working America,* is issued biennially and can be purchased online or at bookstores. It contains a wealth of information on the U.S. economy and the developing record of inequality.

Food Research and Action Center (FRAC)
1875 Connecticut Ave. NW, Ste. 540, Washington, DC 20009
(202) 986-2200 Fax: (202) 986-2525
http://www.frac.org

The Food Research and Action Center was started in New York City in 1970. FRAC made a name for itself as a strong anti-hunger organization during the 1970s, with lobbying and lawsuits to create or strengthen nutrition programs for school children, seniors, and pregnant and nursing mothers. The goal of FRAC remains the eradication of hunger and undernutrition in the United States. To achieve that goal, FRAC conducts research on hunger issues and their solution; advocates for policies to end hunger; acts as a watchdog over current regulations and policies; offers training to and coordinates actions among program administrators, policymakers, and advocates; and works to keep the public informed about the hunger issue. Two of its current programs are notable: the Campaign to End Childhood Hunger, which is coordinated by FRAC but involves citizen groups in every state, and D.C. Hunger Solutions, which is aimed at improving nutrition and ending hunger in the nation's capital.

Publications: A number of carefully prepared reports are available at the Web site, such as "Food Stamp Access in Urban America: A City-by-City Snapshot" (2006) and "Hunger Doesn't Take a Vacation: Summer Nutrition Status Report" (2007). Although all are downloadable, some of the reports may be purchased in hard copy as well. Many outreach brochures are also available, in English and Spanish.

Heritage Foundation
214 Massachusetts Ave. NE, Washington, DC 20002-4999
(202) 546-4400 Fax (202) 546-8328
E-mail: info@heritage.org
http://www.heritage.org

Founded in 1973 and based in Washington, D.C., the Heritage Foundation is regarded as the nation's premier conservative think tank, devoted, as it notes on its Web site, to "building an America where freedom, opportunity, prosperity and civil society flourish." With an operating budget in excess of $40 million in 2006, Heritage outranks its peer institutions, AEI and Cato, in financial resources. Its dozens of experts write and speak on a wide range of policy issues, with an influence in Washington much enhanced by the fact that Republicans have had control of the executive branch for all but eight years since the election of 1980. The basic Heritage position on income inequality is that it does not pose a serious problem. Measured inequality has increased, but much of that is due to an increase in performance-based compensation (especially for CEOs) that raises productivity and efficiency. Heritage opposes minimum wage laws and efforts to make union organizing easier. Its position on poverty is that it is a less serious problem in the United States than many believe.

Publications: The Heritage Foundation issues copious special reports, Web memos, backgrounders, and weekly, monthly, and bimonthly newsletters on all sorts of topics. Many touch upon income inequality and what should—or should not—be done about it.

High/Scope Educational Research Foundation
600 N. River St., Ypsilanti, MI 48198-2898
(734) 485-2000 Fax: (734) 485-0704
E-mail: info@highscope.org
http://www.highscope.org

Proponents of early childhood education hail it as a potential means of boosting the life chances of those born and raised at a socioeconomic disadvantage. Among the studies that have furnished statistical support for preschool interventions, none has been more influential than the Perry Preschool Project carried out in the 1960s and monitored later by the High/Scope Educational Research Foundation, a private, independent foundation established in 1970. Three-to-four-year-old children from disadvantaged minority backgrounds in Ypsilanti, Michigan, were given a quality preschool experience and then tracked for decades to see how they compared, on a host of economic and social indicators, with similar children who had not gotten the preschool experience. Results were decidedly positive, and the High/Scope methods and curriculum became the gold standard for preschool educators. High/Scope has continued to be a leader in the field of pre-K and elementary school research and curriculum development. Its educational materials are used in roughly one-fifth of all Head Start classrooms, and its demonstration preschool, still in Ypsilanti, is visited by educators regularly. Centers for the distribution of High/Scope active-learning materials have been established in, among other places, the United Kingdom, Mexico, and Indonesia.

Publications: A wide range of educational products—classroom resources, group activities, lesson-planning and assessment tools—can be ordered from the online store. High/Scope publishes a magazine, *ReSource,* with articles about early childhood education; print subscriptions are free, and articles can also be downloaded.

Institute for Research on Poverty (IRP)
University of Wisconsin-Madison, 1180 Observatory Dr.,
3412 Social Science Bldg., Madison, WI 53706-1393
(608) 262-6358 Fax: (608) 265-3119
E-mail: djohnson@ssc.wisc.edu
http://www.irp.wisc.edu

The Institute for Research on Poverty was established in 1966 as a nonprofit, nonpartisan center for research into the causes and consequences of poverty and inequality. IRP scholars, whether affiliated with the University of Wisconsin or with other academic institutions, develop and assess social policy alternatives and train future poverty scholars. Their work on poverty deals with fundamental questions about low-wage labor markets, the intergenerational transmission of poverty, race and poverty, and how best to measure the extent of poverty. The IRP also coordinates meetings of the Midwest Welfare Peer Assistance Network (WELPLAN), a group of upper-Midwest welfare officials trying to make welfare reform work in their states. Inequality has been a concern of IRP through its association with two major foundations on a wide-ranging social inequality project, which resulted in a 2004 conference and a book, *Social Inequality* (see chapter 8).

Publications: IRP publishes its house journal, *Focus,* three times a year; it is quite accessible to the nonspecialist, often features articles on inequality, and is downloadable. More in-depth discussion papers and special reports are also posted on its Web site.

Legal Aid Society of New York (LASNY)
199 Water St., New York, NY 10038
(212) 577-3300 Fax: (212) 509-8761
http://www.legal-aid.org

Not only is there a health gap, an education gap, and a shelter gap between America's rich and poor; there is also a "justice gap." Americans with ample income and wealth are able to afford the best legal assistance when they need it. Those of modest means must settle for much less, or nothing. The Legal Aid Society of New York is probably the oldest of more than 100 similar groups around the country that help to level the legal playing field for the poor. Founded in 1876, LASNY began as an organization helping German immigrants cope with legal difficulties. By 1899, it was setting up offices in the boroughs outside Manhattan, and a few years later it expanded its original mandate to include not only civil but also criminal cases. Another significant expansion, into juvenile practice, took place in 1962. Large numbers of New York law firms, including the most prestigious "white shoe" firms, support LASNY with pro bono work and monetary contributions. (A standard donation level for participating firms is $600 per lawyer in the firm.) Beyond the usual caseload of domestic violence and housing eviction threats, LASNY also gets involved with prisoner rights, homeless rights, predatory lending cases, immigrant issues, and HIV/AIDS cases.

Publications: LASNY offers little in the way of standard publications, but its Web site has an interesting history of the organization, FAQs, and self-help information and hotlines for those facing legal emergencies.

Legal Services Corporation (LSC)
3333 K St. NW, Washington, DC 20007
(202) 295-1500 Fax: (202) 337-6797
E-mail: info@lsc.gov
http://www.lsc.gov

Established by Congress in 1974, the Legal Services Corporation applies federal funds to the support of local agencies that help the poor with legal problems. Examples of such local agencies are: Legal Aid of Western Missouri, Texas RioGrande Legal Aid, and the Legal Aid Foundation of Los Angeles. LSC grants are made through a competitive application process. In 2007, some

138 programs or agencies received LSC funding at more than 900 offices across the country. The majority of the legal problems on which clients are helped fall into one of two categories: family issues, such as child custody or domestic violence, and housing issues, such as tenant-landlord disputes. Other problems arise in connection with employment, government benefits, health, or consumer complaints. The population eligible to receive LSC-funded legal assistance is normally those with incomes at or below 125 percent of the poverty line—roughly 50 million people. Surveys indicate that half or more (perhaps *many* more) of the individuals who apply for such assistance are turned away for one reason or another. Case resolutions exceed 1 million each year, however. Most are not high-profile court cases but rather settlements achieved with a letter, a phone call, or a referral. Three out of four clients are women, a majority of whom have children.

Publications: The reports and studies at the LSC Web site tend to be bureaucratic in nature, and the online "LSC Resource Library" is probably of more use to lawyers than the general public. Highly informative, however, is the 2005 report, "Documenting the Justice Gap in America," which can be downloaded.

Levy Economics Institute of Bard College
Blithewood, Bard College, Annandale-on-Hudson, NY
12504-5000
(845) 758-7700 Fax: (845) 758-1149
E-mail: info@levy.org
http://www.levy.org

The generosity of Leon Levy, a Wall Street financier-turned-philanthropist, made possible the establishment in 1986 of a nonprofit, nonpartisan economic research institute at Bard College. The Levy Institute maintains an active schedule of conferences, workshops, and seminars at Blithewood, on the Bard campus. Of its seven sponsored research programs, one in particular, "The Distribution of Income and Wealth," concerns the topic of rich and poor directly, and several others are linked to it indirectly (gender, immigration, 21st century economic policy). The scholars associated with the Levy program on income distribution are some of the top researchers in the field, including Edward Wolff, Susan Mayer, James K. Galbraith, and Branko Milanovic. Scholars at Levy have developed a comprehensive measure of economic welfare, the LIMEW (Levy Institute Measure of Economic Well-Being), which gives a more reliable picture of average well-being than the government's official measures, such as per capita income. This, in turn, makes possible a more accurate calculation of the overall extent of economic inequality in the United States and a better sense of disparities among racial and age groups.

Publications: The Levy Institute puts out policy briefs, policy notes, working papers, books, and *LIMEW Reports.* Most of its publications relate to macroeconomic problems, but a significant number deal with issues of poverty and income distribution.

National Center for Children in Poverty (NCCP)
215 W. 125th St., 3rd Fl., New York, NY 10027
(646) 284-9600 Fax: (646) 284-9623
E-mail: info@nccp.org
http://www.nccp.org

Any long-term remedy for the widening disparities between rich and poor will almost certainly involve the issue of child poverty, which is more extensive in the United States than in all other industrialized nations. The National Center for Children in Poverty, part of the Mailman School of Public Health at Columbia University, has been focused on this issue since 1989. The NCCP envisions a society in which all children are nurtured by healthy, economically stable families; it helps translate that vision into reality through research, data-gathering, networking with practitioners, policy development, and advocacy. Much of its work is done in collaboration with state partners—not surprisingly, given how many policies affecting child well-being are set at the state level. NCCP renders a valuable service to the entire field of child care and early education with its Web resource, "Research Connections." This online resource provides access to some 11,000 items and 132 datasets that relate to the support of children and working families. Another useful feature of the NCCP Web site is a "policy wizard" that makes it possible to create a customized table for any state detailing which programs and benefits it offers, levels of benefits, etc.

Publications: The NCCP posts many up-to-date fact sheets, briefs, and reports on its Web site, and they can be searched efficiently by title, date, or topic.

National Coalition for the Homeless (NCH)
2201 P St. NW, Washington, DC 20037
(202) 462-4822 Fax: (202) 462-4823
E-mail: info@nationalhomeless.org
http://www.nationalhomeless.org

The mission of the National Coalition for the Homeless, founded in 1982, is basic: to end homelessness in the United States. The NCH engages in public education and advocacy on this issue, organizing its efforts into four main areas. The first is housing justice: the NCH believes "safe, decent, accessible, affordable, and permanent" housing is the right of every person, regardless of his or her life circumstances. People experiencing homelessness should be provided with shelter that meets these standards. In the area of economic justice, the NCH campaigns for what is called a "universal living wage." Health care is a major concern for the homeless; disease and disability can be both a cause and an effect of homelessness. The NCH has supported periodic renewal and added funding for the Health Care for the Homeless program that Congress created 20 years ago. And finally, the NCH seeks to have the civil rights of the homeless recognized and enforced.

    Publications: A number of reports and fact sheets are available at the NCH Web site, including an annually updated (and disturbing) report on violence against the homeless. A number of items are for sale as well, such as a voting rights manual, an organizing manual for National Hunger and Homelessness Awareness Week, and a directory of housing and homeless advocacy groups across the country.

National Low Income Housing Coalition (NLIHC)
727 15th St. NW, 6th Fl., Washington, DC 20005
(202) 662-1530 Fax: (202) 393-1973
E-mail: info@nlihc.org
http://www.nlihc.org

The National Low Income Housing Coalition works to end what it calls "America's affordable housing crisis." The NLIHC coalesced in the late 1970s from a loose grouping of labor unions, civil rights activists, public interest advocates, church groups, and the National Organization for Women. Long led by Cushing Dolbeare, and since 1998 by Sheila Crowley, the NLIHC tries to ensure that the public, policy makers, and advocates for the poor are well informed about the housing needs of the lowest-income households; it also lobbies to retain and expand federal housing and housing-assistance resources for those with low incomes. One of the NLIHC's top legislative priorities is passage of the National Affordable Housing Trust Fund Act, which would provide funds to build, preserve, and rehabilitate 1.5 million affordable homes during a 10-year period. Aside from how much housing is available to low-income Americans, the conditions under which they buy, rent, and live in that housing concerns NLIHC. It takes an interest, for example, in discrimination, eviction practices, flat rent versus tiered rent, lead safety, and similar housing issues.

Publications: At the NLIHC Web site there is an *Advocate's Guide* that defines and explains dozens of terms used in discussions of housing and community development policy; an archive of the weekly *Memo to Members,* summarizing current housing issues on Capitol Hill and elsewhere; and reports produced by the organization's small research staff.

National Student Campaign against Hunger and Homelessness (NSCHH)
407 S. Dearborn, Ste. 701, Chicago, IL 60605
(312) 291-0349 x301 Fax: (312) 275-7150
E-mail: info@studentsagainsthunger.org
http://www.studentsagainsthunger.org

The National Student Campaign against Hunger and Homelessness has its roots in the national (and global) outpouring of concern about African hunger in the 1980s, joined to a growing awareness of U.S. hunger and homelessness at about the same time. Organizationally, the new entity got its start in 1985 with major support from an existing national network of student activists, the state-level Public Interest Research Groups (PIRGs). Over time, the Campaign has evolved to become a clearinghouse of information, an opportunity for students to develop activist and leadership skills—almost 500 high schools and colleges are part of NSCHH—and, most importantly, a means for young adults to put their beliefs into action through community service. The Campaign engages in fundraising, "sleep-outs," community action, planning/holding national conferences, and advocacy for systemic solutions.

Publications: A variety of reports on hunger, homelessness, and affordable housing are available on the Web site; authorship usually is by an organization other than NSCHH. Manuals and fact sheets are also downloadable.

New America Foundation (NAF)
1630 Connecticut Ave. NW, 7th Fl., Washington, DC 20009
(202) 986-2700 Fax: (202) 986-3696
http://www.newamerica.net

The New America Foundation, founded in 1999, is a nonprofit, "post-partisan" research institution in Washington, D.C., best characterized as centrist rather than liberal or conservative. It strives to offer fresh thinking on "both sides of the political divide"—new ideas from new voices. Already it has achieved a reputation for producing smart domestic policy proposals. The administration of California Governor Arnold Schwarzenegger, for example, turned to NAF in 2005 and 2006 for ideas on how to reform the health care system in California; the final result was widely considered an important step forward. (NAF is probably the only East Coast think tank that maintains a second office in Sacramento, the capital of California.) In addition to advocating universal health care, a policy change that would clearly benefit America's poor, NAF addresses the rich-and-poor issue through work on "Ownership and Assets," one of its key research areas. Its staff has put forward various initiatives designed to increase the U.S. savings rate, broaden U.S. home ownership, eliminate asset limits in public assistance programs, and link tax refunds to savings options. All of these proposals are aimed at helping low- and middle-income families achieve greater economic security.

Publications: The fellows and staff at NAF promote new ideas through issue briefs, articles published in mainstream outlets like *The New York Times* and *The American Prospect Online,* and trade books. The first two can be downloaded from the NAF Web site; the books must be purchased from book dealers.

Physicians for Human Rights (PHR)
2 Arrow St., Ste. 301, Cambridge, MA 02138
(617) 301-4200 Fax: (617) 301-4250
E-mail: web@phrusa.org
http://physiciansforhumanrights.org

Physicians for Human Rights was founded in 1986 by a half-dozen doctors in the Boston area, several of whom had gained first-hand knowledge of human rights abuses by governments in

Latin America and wanted to do something in response. Over the years, PHR's membership has expanded to some 5,000 medical professionals, including doctors, nurses, scientists, and public health specialists. Its mission remains the same—to use the skills and dedication of health professionals to advance global health and protect human rights. While most of PHR's work is done overseas, its Health and Justice for Youth campaign addresses problems connected with the U.S. juvenile justice system. That system impacts and criminalizes low-income (and minority) youths disproportionately, often treating them as adults. PHR believes this is wrong and brings expertise in adolescent brain development to bear as it campaigns for more rehabilitative and community-based alternatives to incarceration. As part of its Health and Justice for Youth initiative, PHR also advocates the abolition of capital punishment for minors. (It has the support of three former surgeons general on this.) On an issue involving both juvenile and adult interactions with the justice system, PHR opposes mandatory minimum prison sentences for low-level drug crimes.

Publications: PHR issues fact sheets on different dimensions of the juvenile justice issue. It released a lengthier report, *The Consequences Aren't Minor: The Impact of Trying Youth as Adults and Strategies for Reform,* in the spring of 2007. That report can be read online. PHR has a strong interest in recruiting medical students and puts out an advocacy toolkit and other start-up materials for them.

Russell Sage Foundation (RSF)
112 E. 64th St., New York, NY 10065
(212) 750-6000 Fax: (212) 371-4761
E-mail: info@rsage.org
http://www.russellsage.org

For the past century, the Russell Sage Foundation has sponsored social science research aimed at "the improvement of social and living conditions" in the United States. In the first years after its founding in 1907, the RSF was chiefly known for a venture in direct assistance to working families: Forest Hills Gardens. This was an early example of a planned residential community in Queens, New York. Ironically, the homes ended up being too expensive for lower-class families and are today among the priciest in the borough. RSF had more success with an effort in the 1920s and 1930s to give a solid academic grounding to the emerging profession of social work. It even permitted the New York School of Social Work to share its (first) building near Gramercy Park. In the late 1940s, RSF consciously reoriented its funding away from direct support of charitable activities and toward a new role as facilitator and disseminator of social science research, a role it continues to play. In 1999, RSF partnered with the Carnegie Corporation to sponsor a project on social inequality that has as its main purpose to determine whether families that lag economically are also put at other kinds of long-term disadvantage.

Publications: Over many decades, RSF has published or co-published, in book form, much of the best research that it sponsored. The RSF list is stellar; since 1990 it includes *Uneven Tides: Rising Inequality in America* (1993), *Social Programs That Work* (1998), *Understanding Poverty* (2001), *Poor Kids in a Rich Country: America's Children in Comparative Perspective* (2003), and *Social Inequality* (2004). RSF also posts working papers to its Web site, many on aspects of social inequality.

Stanford Center for the Study of Poverty and Inequality (SCSPI)
McClatchy Hall Bldg. 120, 2nd Fl., 450 Serra Mall, Stanford, CA 94301-2047
(650) 724-6912 Fax: (650) 736-9883
E-mail: inequality@stanford.edu
http://www.stanford.edu/group/scspi

The recently established (2006) Stanford Center for the Study of Poverty and Inequality commits one of the nation's great universities to a leadership role in addressing what has become, in its view, "one of the most pressing problems of our time." The SCSPI monitors trends, develops policy, and trains new professionals to enter careers related to inequality matters. Stanford's programmatic commitment to the study of poverty and inequality is broad-gauged: it is putting resources into undergraduate work, master's degree work, faculty seminars, visiting scholars, internships for its undergraduates, and more. So far, only two other major American universities seem as invested as Stanford in the idea that students should have a formal option of in-depth study of inequality—Cornell has an inequality concentration for undergraduates, and Harvard offers a multidisciplinary program for PhD students at the Kennedy School of Government. If the inequality trend continues in the economy, and if journalists and scholars continue to document its repercussions, one would be surprised *not* to see other academic institutions following in Stanford's footsteps.

Publications: The SCSPI publishes *Poverty, Inequality, and Policy Magazine* as well as two book series: *Studies in Inequality* and *Controversies in Inequality.* Working papers and trend data are also available through its Web site.

United for a Fair Economy (UFE)
29 Winter St., Boston, MA 02108
(617) 423-2148 Fax: (617) 423-0191
E-mail: info@faireconomy.org
http://www.faireconomy.org

Since its founding in 1995, the nonpartisan, nonprofit, left-oriented United for a Fair Economy has worked to "raise awareness that concentrated wealth and power undermine the economy, corrupt democracy, deepen the racial divide, and tear communities apart." UFE puts an almost unique organizational emphasis on the issue of economic inequality in the United States. It works to educate the public on the advantages of, and ways to better achieve, a society without "dramatic disparities of income, wages, wealth, health, safety, respect, and opportunities for recreation and personal growth." As part of its educational outreach, UFE has given its signature workshop, "The Growing Divide: Economic Inequality and the Roots of Insecurity," to some 70,000 people, and has trained more than 400 to lead those workshops and other sponsored events. It multiplies its influence through media outreach and measures the success of those efforts in terms of "media hits" (more than 2,000 in the past two years). UFE takes a particular interest in tax fairness and racial economic justice. Its Responsible Wealth Project brings together affluent Americans who share a concern about growing wealth inequality, and its Tax Fairness Organizing Collaborative has built an 18-state grassroots network since 2004 to push for fair and adequate taxation, while combating widespread anti-tax, anti-government attitudes. UFE's Racial Wealth Divide Project was begun in 2001 to organize minority communities to adopt wealth-building strategies, with a long-range goal of ending racial wealth disparities.

Publications: UFE puts out fact sheets and backgrounders on inequality issues, as well as a monthly e-newsletter. Workshop materials can be downloaded from the Web site. UFE's annual *State of the Dream* report features themes relevant to the economic challenges faced by black and/or Hispanic communities. The bi-annual *Tax Fairness Action News* had its inaugural issue in the spring of 2007. Some of the most cogent UFE documents relate to the estate tax, the future of which remains unsettled.

8

Selected Print and Nonprint Resources

As the gap between America's rich and poor grows wider and deeper over time, so too does the literature on this critical issue. The resources one may consult for a fuller understanding of how, and why, the U.S. income distribution has been changing in recent decades come in several formats. On the print side, there are important articles in academic journals and newspapers of national stature, and there are books that delve into specific aspects of the rich-poor divide in all the depth one could want. On the nonprint side, there are Internet resources offering detailed statistics and other relevant information with the advantage, often, of being more up-to-date than comparable print materials. With the Internet, however, one does have to exercise some caution in one's reliance on the "facts" presented, always weighing the credibility of the source. And finally, there are a number of videos that would be of interest to anyone who wants to grasp the implications of the trend toward an economically more polarized U.S. population.

Print Resources

Articles

Borjas, George J. "The Labor Demand Curve Is Downward-Sloping: Reexamining the Impact of Immigration on the Labor

Market." *Quarterly Journal of Economics* 118, no. 4 (November 2003): 1335–1374.

Borjas argues that recent immigrants to the United States have been lower-skilled than their predecessors and therefore have put downward pressure on wages at the low end of the labor market. If true, this worsens the income gap.

Cowen, Tyler. "A Contrarian Look at Whether U.S. Chief Executives Are Overpaid." *The New York Times* (May 18, 2006): C4.

An economics professor at George Mason University gives a concise version of the argument that rising CEO pay, which contributes to the widening rich-poor gap, is accounted for by the growing stock-market value of U.S. corporations. If the CEO performs well, he or she is worth every penny paid.

Gertner, Jon. "What Is a Living Wage?" *The New York Times Magazine* (January 15, 2006): 38–45, 68, 72.

Its title is slightly misleading, because this article deals not only with the living wage but also the minimum wage—in depth and with great clarity. It puts a human face on the issues, focusing on the hard-fought and ultimately successful battle for a citywide living wage in Santa Fe, New Mexico.

Heckman, James J. "Catch 'em Young." *The Wall Street Journal* (January 10, 2006): A14.

Nobel laureate Heckman makes the case, with op-ed brevity, for publicly funded early childhood interventions to help low-income children.

Hertz, Tom. "Understanding Mobility in America." Center for American Progress (April 26, 2006). Accessed at http://www.americanprogress.org.

Hertz shows that the odds of a low-income child, or even a middle-class child, eventually becoming rich in the United States are actually quite low—lower than many people probably want to believe.

Johnston, David Cay. "Corporate Wealth Share Rises for Top-Income Americans." *The New York Times* (January 29, 2006): A22.

Johnston won a Pulitzer Prize in 2001 for his reporting on the U.S. tax system. He is the author of *Perfectly Legal: The Covert Campaign to Rig Our Tax System to Benefit the Super-Rich—and Cheat Everybody Else* (2005). In this article, he reports that the top 1 percent of U.S. households increased their ownership share of corporate wealth to 57.5 percent in 2003 (in 1991, that share was only 37.8 percent).

Kennickell, Arthur B. "Currents and Undercurrents in the Distribution of Wealth, 1989–2004." Federal Reserve Board (January 30, 2006). Accessed at http://www.federalreserve.gov.

Kennickell, a senior economist at the Federal Reserve, summarizes the findings of the board's most recent triennial survey of household wealth in the United States. This survey has been the chief basis for estimates of U.S. personal wealth since the 1980s.

Kuznets, Simon. "Economic Growth and Income Inequality." *American Economic Review* **45, no. 1 (March 1955): 1–28.**

This is the classic article in which Nobel laureate Kuznets sets forth his theory relating income inequality to the stage of economic development. The trend of rising U.S. inequality, however, does not fit his theory.

Piketty, Thomas, and Emmanuel Saez. "Income Inequality in the United States, 1913–1998." *Quarterly Journal of Economics* **118, no. 1 (February 2003): 1–39.**

Piketty and Saez are considered the top experts on U.S. income inequality, and this article is referred to frequently. Saez updates the key statistics at his personal Web page: http://elsa.berkeley.edu/~saez/

Porter, Eduardo. "More Than Ever, It Pays to Be the Top Executive." *The New York Times* **(May 25, 2007): A1.**

This article reports on the little-noticed fact that compensation for top U.S. executives has not only outdistanced their companies' ordinary employees but also the executives just below the top.

Sala-i-Martin, Xavier. "The World Distribution of Income: Falling Poverty and . . . Convergence, Period." *Quarterly Journal of Economics* **121, no. 2 (May 2006): 351–397.**

A Columbia University professor argues that on a global scale the gap between rich and poor has actually been narrowing. A major factor in the global picture is the improvement in per capita incomes in India and China. This global finding is, of course, not inconsistent with a widening rich-poor gap within the United States.

Smeeding, Timothy. "Poor People in Rich Nations: The United States in Comparative Perspective." *Journal of Economic Perspectives* **20, no. 1 (Winter 2006): 69–90.**

A leading scholar in the measurement of poverty internationally finds that in the first years of the 21st century, the United States has the highest per capita gross domestic product (GDP) among a group of 11 industrialized nations—and also the highest (or second-highest) poverty rate for every demographic except single adults.

Tritch, Teresa. "The Rise of the Super-Rich." *The New York Times* **(July 19, 2006). Accessible at http://select.nytimes.com/ 2006/07/19/opinion/19talkingpoints.html.**

This article provides a nice overview of the so-called "super-rich" and, in the online version, many helpful links to other sources.

Wessel, David. "As Rich-Poor Gap Widens in U.S., Class Mobility Stalls." *The Wall Street Journal* **(May 13, 2005): A1.**

Wessel summarizes the new research findings that indicate, at best, no overall change in class mobility in the United States during the past 35 years, and less mobility than is found in a number of European nations and Canada.

Books
The Rich-Poor Divide
Bowles, Samuel, Herbert Gintis, and Melissa Osborne Groves, eds. *Unequal Chances: Family Background and Economic Success.* **New York: Russell Sage Foundation; Princeton, NJ: Princeton University Press, 2005. 304 pages. ISBN 0-691-11930-9.**

We have long known that, statistically speaking, parents who are poor tend to have children who grow up to be poor, and the same holds true for the rich. But recent research has revealed an even stronger tendency for the status of parents to be passed on to their children, or, to put it the other way, an even lower degree of intergenerational mobility than we thought existed. *Unequal Chances* examines this issue from various vantage points—economic, racial, and psychological. Especially useful are Chapter 2, "The Apple Falls Even Closer to the Tree Than We Thought," which summarizes the new findings on lower intergenerational mobility, and Chapter 5, "Rags, Riches, and Race," which reports that upward mobility for blacks is much lower than for whites in the United States. Somewhat technical in places, this book may convince many readers that family background really matters.

Collins, Chuck, and Felice Yeskel. *Economic Apartheid in America: A Primer on Economic Inequality & Insecurity*, rev. ed. New York: The New Press, 2005. 254 pages. ISBN 1-59558-015-8.

Its hyperbolic title aside, this book provides a useful guide to how the left views wealth and income inequality in the United States. It covers a lot of ground: the causes and consequences of inequality, the actions that are needed to reduce it, and the steps that will be required to build a movement toward a "fair" economy. As a radical critique of U.S. (and global) corporatist capitalism, this volume, even with its determinedly reader-friendly approach (plenty of boxed features, tables, and cartoons) may not win legions of converts. It gets weighed down by its own ideological baggage, especially in Chapter 4, with its explications of dominance, subordination, class continuum, etc. But the rest of the book is much livelier and should be of interest to many outside the radical fold. The key message seems to be that as the gap widens between those at the top of the economic heap and everyone else, the winners are trying to change the rules in ways that protect and enhance their advantages. With evidence and argument, the authors give this notion real plausibility.

Jacobs, Lawrence R., and Theda Skocpol, eds. *Inequality and American Democracy: What We Know and What We Need to Learn*. New York: Russell Sage Foundation, 2005. 246 pages. ISBN 0-87154-413-X.

In 2003, a task force of the American Political Science Association (APSA) took up the issue of rising economic inequality in the United States and its effects on our democratic system. Some of the biggest names in political science were recruited to join the project. They met, they pondered, they deliberated, and this book is the result. Broadly, the experts find that a growing concentration of economic power at the top has been accompanied by an amplification of the political "voice" of the privileged. They can make their voices heard partly at the ballot box—high-income individuals vote at higher rates than low-income individuals—and partly with campaign contributions. The result is a government more responsive to the wishes of the privileged than to the needs of the underprivileged. Government policy did not cause the inequality trend, but given the heightened influence of those who have been raised to the top rungs of the ladder, U.S. public policy now does very little to reverse or even moderate that trend. (Other governments do more.)

Lardner, James, and David A. Smith, eds. *Inequality Matters: The Growing Economic Divide in America and Its Poisonous Consequences.* **New York: The New Press, 2005. 328 pages. ISBN 1-56584-995-7.**

This volume offers a progressive take on the growing inequality between America's haves and have-nots. The 23 short chapters were originally presented at the "Inequality Matters" conference at New York University in 2004; most have been revised for this book. In addition to the income gap, authors address the education gap, health gap, ethnic gap (differential opportunities for advancement), and the gap between what America's democratic process should look like and what big money has done to it. These consistently interesting essays present as wide a range of perspectives on inequality as the overall framework of liberal-to-radical discontent with current trends would allow. A particularly good chapter, "What the Numbers Tell Us," by Heather Boushey and Christian Weller, concludes with the remark that if many of us are downplaying the magnitude of the inequality trend, it is because "the evidence is telling us something about America that we are not eager to hear" (p. 40).

McCarty, Nolan, Keith T. Poole, and Howard Rosenthal. *Polarized America: The Dance of Ideology and Unequal Riches.* **Cambridge, MA: MIT Press, 2006. 240 pages. ISBN 0-262-13464-0.**

Of all the consequences of growing economic inequality in the United States, perhaps none is more troubling than the effect it is having on our politics. The authors of this study begin with a simple fact captured in a graph on page 6: from the 1970s onward, both the Gini index of economic inequality and a political polarization index moved sharply higher, with the two curves essentially overlapping. "Polarization" in this context refers to House Republicans moving rightward from the center and House Democrats moving (somewhat) leftward. It can also be shown that high-income voters increasingly identify with the Republican Party, and low-income voters with the Democrats. These trends do not bode well for a moderation of the inequality trend since they have "moved the political system away from public policy that might alleviate income inequality" (p. 165). The final two chapters will be of greatest interest to general readers. Here, the authors' polarization theories are applied to such policy issues as the minimum wage, estate taxes, income taxes, Social Security, and welfare—issues on which our polarized politics have shifted us away from redistributive policies. Is there any hope of pulling back from polarization? The authors do not give much reason to think so.

Mishel, Lawrence, Jared Bernstein, and Sylvia Allegretto. *The State of Working America 2006/2007.* **Ithaca, NY: Cornell University Press, 2007. 426 pages. ISBN 978-0-8014-7355-5.**

Issued biennially by the Economic Policy Institute, a liberal think tank in Washington, D.C., *The State of Working America* has become a trusted *vade mecum* for those, particularly on the liberal side of the aisle, who want to understand how the economy is impacting workers and families in the United States. The book is chock-full of tables and graphs that help one make sense of economic developments across sectors and over time. One of the most startling graphs is Figure 1I (p. 57), which shows how family incomes have fared by quintile since 1947: the lowest quintile did quite well for a generation (1947–73) but has badly lagged the other four quintiles ever since 1973. Topics receiving full-chapter treatment include lifetime income and wealth mobility, the divergence between wage growth and productivity growth, the performance of the U.S. job market, wealth disparities, poverty in all its dimensions, regional economic differences, and international comparisons.

Neckerman, Kathryn M., ed. *Social Inequality.* **New York: Russell Sage, 2004. 1,017 pages. ISBN 0-87154-621-3.**

This monumental work is the product of a unique research effort begun in 2000 with funding from the Russell Sage Foundation and the Carnegie Corporation of New York. The basic question posed to almost 50 of the nation's foremost social scientists (organized into teams) was this: has the growing income gap in recent decades produced a comparable widening between rich and poor on other social indicators, such as health, education, family structure, and political participation? If it has, then a self-reinforcing trend of social disadvantage may have begun that will make reversing the inequality trend that much more difficult. The research results reported by the experts are, as one would expect, complex and nuanced—and not very encouraging. Take political participation (part V) as an example. If the poor were becoming more politically active, their voting and other forms of political activism could lead to legislation that would work to their advantage. Alas, that has not been the case: voter turnout is higher for those with more income and education, and while turnout has declined at all income levels, it has declined most for the poorest. *Social Inequality* has already become a standard reference work in the study of inequality.

The New York Times. *Class Matters.* New York: Times Books, 2005. 288 pages. ISBN 978-0805080551.

In May and June of 2005, *The New York Times* ran a series of articles on class divisions in the United States. The growing rich-poor divide was treated as one aspect of the overall topic. Various reporters contributed to the series, and *Class Matters* presents all 11 articles in one volume. Several chapters stand out: "Shadowy Lines That Still Divide," the series opener, provides a broad overview of class in the United States and of the topics to be addressed in subsequent articles. The online version of this chapter— the entire series remains available at http://www.nytimes.com/ pages/national/class—offers some remarkable interactive graphics. "Life at the Top in America Isn't Just Better, It's Longer" looks at the life expectancy advantage, and the survival advantage after a medical emergency, enjoyed by those with better educations and income levels compared with those with worse. "The Richest Are Leaving Even the Rich Far Behind" is perhaps the most valuable chapter for gaining an understanding of the growing gap between rich and poor.

Sacks, Peter. *Tearing Down the Gates: Confronting the Class Divide in American Education.* Berkeley, CA: University of California Press, 2007. 376 pages. ISBN 978-0-520-24588-4.

Economic inequality in the United States is bound up inextrica-
bly with educational inequality, according to Peter Sacks. Each
begets the other. This is a familiar vicious-circle refrain among
those studying the American classroom and the American class
system. What sets Sacks's book apart from other work dealing
with the dual inequality question is its emphasis, not made clear
in the title, on the issue of unequal access to higher education.
Through numerous case studies, he demonstrates how different
are the prospects of getting a good college education for those
growing up poor and those brought up in more fortunate circumstances. The gap has much to do with the leg up that privileged children enjoy from intellectual stimulation in the home,
superior instruction in their public and private schools, private
tutoring on "gatekeeping tests" like the SAT and ACT, and, obviously, their parents' deeper pockets when the time arrives to consider college. But that is only part of the story. The other part
concerns state and federal budgetary decisions, and changes in
financial aid policy by universities themselves, that have system-
atically undermined the ability of working-class students to go to
college. Sacks supports his arguments with helpful graphs and
lively prose.

Shapiro, Thomas M. *The Hidden Cost of Being African American: How Wealth Perpetuates Inequality.* **New York: Oxford
University Press, 2004. 238 pages. ISBN 0-19-518138-7.**

Thomas Shapiro, a sociologist at Brandeis University, has written
extensively on racial wealth differences in the United States. In
Black Wealth/White Wealth (1995), Shapiro and coauthor Melvin
Oliver described with data and documents the large, enduring
wealth differences that separate the two races. Here, the topic is
the same but the approach more personal and anecdotal. Shapiro
interviewed almost 200 families in Boston, Los Angeles, and St.
Louis to see how important family wealth (or its lack) was for
their economic advancement. The answer turned out to be: very
important. It matters particularly when young couples go to buy
their first home. Whites tend to get help on a down payment
from their parents; blacks tend not to, since their parents are
much less likely to have wealth to pass along. Larger down payments help whites secure lower interest rates and better houses
in better neighborhoods, with better schools for their children to
attend. In this and other ways, Shapiro contends, the unequal

wealth holdings of the past are reproduced in the present. Asset-based policies could break the pattern.

Wolff, Edward N. *Top Heavy: The Increasing Inequality of Wealth in America and What Can Be Done about It,* **rev. ed. New York: The New Press, 2002. 116 pages. ISBN 1-56584-665-6.**

Edward Wolff, an economics professor at New York University, has been called the nation's foremost authority on wealth distribution. This short book, originally issued as a Century Foundation report, makes his knowledge available to a general audience. Wolff explains in lay terms what wealth is; why it is at least as important a metric as income; what the historical trends have been; how the structure of household wealth holdings has been changing; how U.S. wealth patterns compare to other countries; how wealth is currently taxed; and how it might be taxed more directly and progressively. Wolff finds the current level of wealth inequality "pronounced" and argues that policy remedies are urgently needed.

The Rich and Their Circumstances
Conniff, Richard. *The Natural History of the Rich: A Field Guide.* **New York: W.W. Norton, 2002. 344 pages. ISBN 0-393-01965-9.**

If the famous American economist Thorstein Veblen had been more interested in natural history, his groundbreaking 1899 classic, *The Theory of the Leisure Class,* might have borne a strong resemblance to this book. Richard Conniff is a naturalist and prolific journalist who writes frequently for *National Geographic* and *Smithsonian Magazine.* In this quirky, entertaining book, he views the rich—especially the super-rich—as a kind of subspecies of humankind, finding many parallels between their behavior and that of other members of the animal kingdom, whether chimps, apes, or hummingbirds. The rich display their wealth in the same way that males of many species display their feathers or other finery. They build palaces and McMansions, acquire yachts and Impressionist paintings, and even arrange to be shot into space (for $20 million). Veblen called it conspicuous consumption, and Conniff does not improve on that term. He does, however, use well-chosen anecdotes and examples from the most unexpected quarters to freshen up some of Veblen's most basic points.

Frank, Robert. *Richistan: A Journey through the American Wealth Boom and the Lives of the New Rich.* New York: Crowne, 2007. 277 pages. ISBN 978-0-307-33926-3.

Robert Frank, not to be confused with the Cornell economics professor of the same name (author of *The Winner-Take-All Society*), is a journalist with expertise in wealth. Indeed, he is the "wealth reporter" for *The Wall Street Journal,* and much of the material in *Richistan* has already appeared there. The premise of this book is that America's rich today are a different breed from earlier decades, in the sources of their money, the diversity of their demographic, and the unpredictability of their politics. We learn, for example, that a good portion of the most recently minted millionaires and billionaires are liberal Democrats ("Learjet liberals"); that a billion-dollar fortune can originate just as readily in the invention of a new brand of vodka (Grey Goose) as in the monopolization of a basic industry; and that significant numbers of the new rich are *not* white males in their 60s or older. Much of the book falls somewhere between casual empiricism and anecdote; it could never be mistaken for social science. But that does not make it any less enjoyable—or appalling—to read.

Frank, Robert H., and Philip J. Cook. *The Winner-Take-All Society: Why the Few at the Top Get So Much More Than the Rest of Us.* New York: Penguin, 1996. 272 pages. ISBN 978-0140259957.

This book, first published in 1995, was an early attempt to make sense of the widening U.S. income gap that was starting to cause concern in the late 1980s. Frank and Cook focused their attention on the upper end of the scale, offering an analytical framework for understanding why peak earners seemed to be leaving everyone else—even in the top quintile—far behind. The winner-take-all earnings pattern was particularly noticeable in certain markets, such as entertainment, sports, and the arts. The authors ventured several reasons why winners were "taking all," one being the growth of national and international media markets, which made it essential to have a bankable "star" in one's movie in order to ensure box office success. With such an imperative, $15 million paydays for Michael Douglas, Arnold Schwarzenegger, and Eddie Murphy were almost to be expected. Frank and Cook found the winner-take-all phenomenon understandable, but in some important ways unfortunate. The main problem is that too many young people are drawn into these kinds of industries, full of confidence that they will be winners, and the result is a distorted allocation of resources, both human and nonhuman.

Hacker, Andrew. *Money: Who Has How Much and Why.* **New York: Scribner, 1997. 254 pages. ISBN 0-684-19646-8.**

Andrew Hacker, a professor emeritus in political science at Queens College (New York City), has been lauded for his ability to bring political numbers to life, as he did most notably in his 1992 *Two Nations: Black and White, Separate, Hostile, Unequal.* In his more recent *Money,* the topic is economic inequality, which lends itself even more naturally than racial inequality to elucidation by numbers. More a collection of chapter-length essays than a monographic development of one overriding concept, this book has many fascinating things to say about the distribution of American incomes, particularly those at the top. Three chapters illuminate the heights of the U.S. income range: "1 Million a Year," "At the Very Top," and "Hail to the Chief!" The last refers to chief executive officers (CEOs) and their compensation levels in the mid-1990s. Not only is Hacker very perceptive and skillful in the handling of data, but he also writes exceedingly well.

Keister, Lisa A. *Getting Rich: America's New Rich and How They Got That Way.* **New York: Cambridge University Press, 2005. 310 pages. ISBN 978-0-521-53667-7.**

Lisa Keister, a sociologist at Duke University with a solid background in economics, presents a primer on wealth in the United States: who has it, how they got it, and how they pass it along to the next generation. Her dual disciplinary training serves her well as she navigates the statistical and conceptual issues surrounding this topic. In a systematic fashion, she explores the components of wealth as ordinarily defined; reviews the long-term trends in wealth mobility (how far people rise or fall in the wealth rankings over time); and looks at the ethnic, family-size, educational, geographic, and religious factors that appear to influence one's chances of accumulating wealth. Interesting insights abound. The wealthy tend to come from families in which there are few siblings. Their parents tend to be more highly educated than average. In terms of religious upbringing, they are much likelier to be Jewish or Episcopalian than Baptist or any other conservative Protestant sect. And they tend to be self-employed, that is, entrepreneurial. Keister is currently working on a book that will explore more fully the relationship between religious belief and wealth and poverty.

Phillips, Kevin. *Wealth and Democracy: A Political History of the American Rich*. New York: Broadway Books, 2002. 474 pages. ISBN 0-7679-0533-4.

In what might be seen as a sequel to his 1990 *The Politics of Rich and Poor*, Kevin Phillips offers here a political and economic history of the United States as viewed through the lens of wealth. Phillips is clearly disillusioned by the current state of American democracy, which he sees as weakened and tainted by the power of moneyed elites. In his telling, U.S. history presents a mixed spectacle of democratic advancement, boosted by technological progress and expanding trade, encountering setback after setback at the hands of a corrupted political system. Phillips is an admirer of the Progressive Era muckrakers, and perhaps sees himself following in their footsteps. (He enjoys using terms like "plutocracy" and "plutography.") The logic of Phillips's arguments can be hard to pin down, his tone can be overheated at times, and his nonlinear chronology can befuddle. But his knack for well-chosen graphs, tables, and examples, his undisguised enthusiasm for combative populist politicians like Teddy Roosevelt, and above all his high-minded take on a very serious subject make this required reading for anyone concerned about the current state of U.S. economic polarization.

The Poor and Their Circumstances

DeParle, Jason. *American Dream: Three Women, Ten Kids, and a Nation's Drive to End Welfare*. New York: Viking, 2004. 422 pages. ISBN 0-670-89275-0.

In 1991, Bill Clinton, running for president as a new Democrat, pledged to "end welfare as we know it." At the close of his first term he did so—or rather, he and a Republican Congress did so. The welfare reform law of 1996 was a landmark in the history of American social policy. Policy wonks on the right and left energetically supported or opposed the measure prior to its passage; in later years, both sides agreed that it had been good for some welfare families, bad for others. This important book by a seasoned *New York Times* journalist takes the reader behind the scenes of the legislative battles that eventually produced the new welfare law. At the same time, it chronicles the family history and ongoing struggles of three black women and their children in and out of the welfare system. DeParle is a knowledgeable student of social policy who nearly won not one but two Pulitzer Prizes for his reporting on welfare. The candor and empathy with which he presents the stories of Angie, Jewell, and Opal help make this book the best possible solvent for stereotypes about poverty and welfare.

Ehrenreich, Barbara. *Nickel and Dimed: On (Not) Getting By in America.* **New York: Henry Holt, 2002. 230 pages. ISBN 978-0-80506-389-9.**

Nickel and Dimed is a classic first-person account of the low-wage labor market in the United States at the turn of the 21st century. Although it no longer appears on the bestseller lists, it continues to sell briskly—aided no doubt by college adoptions for courses in sociology, economics, public policy, and women's studies. (There are 17 discussion questions at the end of the book.) The premise is appealingly simple: a highly educated, well-published author leaves her comfortable daily routines behind and applies for a series of low-paying jobs: waitress, nursing home aide, house cleaner, and Wal-Mart associate. Can she make ends meet on what she is paid? Time and again, she finds that she cannot. She also discovers that low-wage labor involves endless indignities, from lunch breaks that amount to five-minute "pit stops" at convenience stores, to drug tests as a condition of employment, to wage rates that do not rise to overtime levels when, by law, they should. Ehrenreich writes with a unique blend of humor, indignation, and irony. She has profoundly altered the way many people think about low-paying jobs.

Harrington, Michael. *The Other America: Poverty in the United States.* **New York: Macmillan, 1962. ISBN 0-684-82678-X.**

This classic work, still available in various paperback editions, opened the nation's eyes to the glaring social problem of poverty. Its chapters shed light on rural poverty, black poverty, the poverty of urban slums and skid rows, and poverty among the elderly. (Harrington observed that the elderly experienced more poverty than any other age group—the opposite of what is seen today.) In 1962, the Census Bureau did not yet calculate and publish a national poverty rate; there was no Medicare or Medicaid; and the "War on Poverty" had not yet been launched. Hence, *The Other America* acted as a sort of wakeup call to the nation, and, incidentally, to the administration in office at the time. President John F. Kennedy is said to have read the book, or at least a review of it in *The New Yorker*, and been impressed sufficiently to set in motion the anti-poverty initiative that eventually (under President Lyndon B. Johnson) took shape in the so-called War on Poverty. Harrington (1928–1989) was a lifelong socialist, a fact that, in the United States, put distinct limits on his influence. Although he wrote extensively after *The Other America*, that remains the work for which he is most remembered.

Iceland, John. *Poverty in America: A Handbook*, 2nd ed. Berkeley, CA: University of California Press, 2006. 223 pages. ISBN 978-0520248410.

John Iceland knows poverty statistics intimately from having spent five years working in, and eventually heading, the Poverty and Health Statistics Branch of the U.S. Census Bureau. He knows the significance of the data from his professional training as a sociologist. (He currently teaches at the University of Maryland.) Iceland's handbook offers a good basic introduction to U.S. poverty, with chapters covering such topics as how the government measures poverty, how the public views it, what are the characteristics of the "poor" population, what are the causes of poverty, why poverty remains at high levels, and what policies are available to combat it. "Social stratification" aside, *Poverty in America* is refreshingly free of jargon and far more readable than one might expect of a "handbook." The six-page concluding chapter is a model of compression and synthesis.

Kozol, Jonathan. *Savage Inequalities: Children in America's Schools*. New York: Harper Perennial, 1992. 262 pages. ISBN 978-0060974992.

Jonathan Kozol has been studying America's public schools for four decades, and he isn't much happier with what he sees today than he was in 1968, when he published his first book, *Death at an Early Age*. All of his books are worth reading for the insights that a keen and sensitive observer of American inequality brings to this difficult national issue. In *Savage Inequalities*, Kozol details the immense differences to be found in the educational experiences of inner-city minority kids and suburban white kids. Some of the most telling comments come from the disadvantaged children themselves as they struggle to understand why they are treated so much worse, in terms of academic programs and physical facilities, than their peers in more affluent neighborhoods. A special strength of Kozol's book is that he allows his subjects—students, teachers, and administrators—to speak for themselves, without authorial filter. The clear overlap of the racial with the economic divide in American schools, already noted in this book, is explicitly dealt with in Kozol's more recent book, *The Shame of the Nation: The Restoration of Apartheid Schooling in America* (2005).

Rainwater, Lee, and Timothy M. Smeeding. *Poor Kids in a Rich Country: America's Children in Comparative Perspective.* **New York: Russell Sage, 2003. 263 pages. ISBN 0-87154-705-8.**

For social-policy reasons, and probably for sentimental ones as well, we seem to care more about *children* in poverty than any other age group. The policy reasons are related to the fact that children who grow up in poverty go through the rest of their lives altered by the experience; thus, policies that lift children out of poverty could yield lifelong benefits to them and to society. Because we care about poor children, it behooves us to understand their situation from a variety of angles, including the international perspective. That is what *Poor Kids in a Rich Country* helps us do. The authors, both authorities in the field of international poverty research, compare child poverty in the United States to that in 14 other developed nations. What they report is disheartening. In the United States, for example, one child in five lived in a family with income below one-half the median national income in 1997, thus qualifying as "poor" by the European poverty yardstick. Their families were "not able to participate enough in community activities to be perceived, by both themselves and others, as regular members of society" (p. 22). The second part of the book and its appendices are more for specialists than for general readers, but the bulk of the volume is accessible and informative.

Shipler, David K. *The Working Poor: Invisible in America.* **New York: Vintage, 2005. 352 pages. ISBN 978-0375708213.**

To understand in a direct, personal way how people can fall into poverty and stay there, an excellent place to begin is Shipler's *The Working Poor.* A Pulitzer-Prize-winning journalist and an observer who combines balance and empathy, Shipler describes the lives of a dozen or so individuals (some in couples) who struggle every day to stay afloat in the world's richest country. Some have experienced sexual and emotional abuse as children and never quite recovered. Some have been poorly parented. Some are held back by early pregnancy and childbearing. Shipler amply demonstrates how long-lasting the cost of personal mistakes made early in life can be, but he also makes it clear that events entirely beyond a person's control can be just as damaging. An escape from poverty can never be as easy as finding a good job, a government program, or an affordable child care provider. Many things must come into alignment and stay that way to ensure a successful exit from poverty. To that end, Shipler advocates the creation of "gateways" at such key institutions as schools, hospitals, and welfare offices through which a range of services can be delivered to those requiring them. He is also a supporter of high-quality job-training programs, as described in the chapter "Work Works."

Public Policy
Balkin, Karen, ed. *Poverty: Opposing Viewpoints.* San Diego: Greenhaven Press, 2004. 222 pages. ISBN 0-7377-1697-5.

As a subject of policy discussion and public debate, poverty has a matchless ability to highlight the fault lines between liberalism and conservatism. This volume, in Greenhaven's useful *Opposing Viewpoints* series, takes up four thematic questions: "Is Poverty a Serious Problem?" "What Are the Causes of Poverty in America?" "How Can Poor People in the United States Be Helped?" and "Is Worldwide Poverty a Serious Problem?" To each question, experts offer their answers, most of which hew either to the liberal or conservative approach. Various subtopics are addressed, such as housing discrimination, hunger, the minimum wage, and marriage promotion. The worldwide poverty section is not strictly relevant to the U.S. rich-poor gap but can be seen as a good contextualizing aid.

Bebchuk, Lucian, and Jesse Fried. *Pay without Performance: The Unfulfilled Promise of Executive Compensation.* Cambridge, MA: Harvard University Press, 2004. 278 pages. ISBN 0-674-01665-3.

To an unknown and probably unknowable extent, the explosive growth at the top of the U.S. income distribution has come in the form of fattened CEO compensation packages. For some years now, Lucian Bebchuk and Jesse Fried, professors at Harvard University and the University of California, Berkeley, respectively, have been working on issues of corporate governance. In this important book, they take readers through chapter and verse on how the executive compensation game is played, and why the current "pay for performance" practices are not delivering, consistently, the kind of increased shareholder value that was expected of them when they were introduced in the early 1990s. High on the list of reasons, according to Bebchuk and Fried, is the fact that "arms-length" bargaining between CEOs and their boards of directors (or compensation committees) has been the exception rather than the rule. Far too often, directors fail to stand up for the interests of shareholders when striking a pay bargain with the top executive. They may feel sympathetic toward, or beholden to, that individual; they also may feel insulated from any outrage that might result from an overly generous bargain. The authors suggest several changes in corporate governance that might bring a closer alignment of pay and performance.

Gates, William H., Sr., and Chuck Collins. *Wealth and Our Commonwealth: Why America Should Tax Accumulated Fortunes.* **Boston: Beacon Press, 2003. 166 pages. ISBN 0-8070-4719-8.**

In 2001, when President George W. Bush and the Republican leadership in Congress proposed that the U.S. estate tax be eliminated, many millionaires and even a few billionaires publicly protested. They were led in this surprising "man bites dog" development by the authors of *Wealth and Our Commonwealth.* Collins and Gates (father of Microsoft founder Bill Gates) lay out, in this short book, a multi-pronged argument for continuing to tax large wealth accumulations at least once per generation. They warn that growing inequality threatens to undermine American democracy as well as the health of the economy. They also review the history of the estate tax; examine the arguments and political maneuvering against the estate tax; and lend support to the notion that estate-tax repeal would take a heavy toll on charitable contributions by the wealthy.

Heckman, James J., and Alan B. Krueger. *Inequality in America: What Role for Human Capital Policies?* **Cambridge, MA: MIT Press, 2003. 370 pages. ISBN 0-262-58260-0.**

The papers and discussion collected in this volume were originally presented at a 2002 symposium at Harvard. In revised form
they are uniformly first-rate. Princeton economist Alan Krueger
leads off with a summary of the inequality trend that has made
the United States so much more unequal than it was in 1973, and
the philosophical, religious, political, and economic reasons why
we care. He then proposes a variety of targeted human capital
policies, ranging from preschool interventions and class size reductions to job-training programs, that might lift the trajectory of
those headed for a low-income future. James Heckman, a Nobel
laureate who teaches at the University of Chicago, takes what
might be called a more conservative approach: he (and coauthor
Pedro Carneiro) downplay the promise of the GED, college
tuition-assistance, and Job Corps-type programs as ways to lift
up the lower end of the workforce. Rather, they see early childhood interventions, like the Perry Preschool Project, as smarter
investments of public funds. Comments by discussants and re-
joinders by the original authors clarify many points but leave a
distinct impression that economists are not yet in agreement on
what should be done about the growing rich-poor gap.

Pollin, Robert, and Stephanie Luce. *The Living Wage: Fighting
for a Fair Economy.* **New York: The New Press, 1998. 250 pages.
ISBN 1-56584-588-9.**

Even the most optimistic supporters of the living wage do not
see it as a cure-all for the widening chasm between the top and
bottom of the U.S. wage distribution, but many believe it has a
place in any progressive strategy for boosting the position of
low-paid workers around the country. This book, by two economists at the University of Massachusetts, Amherst, lays out the
case for and against the living wage, with a strong conclusion in
favor of it. Events have overtaken this study to some extent (it
was completed in late 1997); for example, Santa Fe, New Mexico,
received national attention in 2004 when it adopted a citywide
living wage after a fierce political fight. But the arguments and
cost-benefit calculations set out in *The Living Wage* are the kind
that have been, and will be, rehearsed time and again as the living wage movement expands. The scope and features of Los Angeles's living wage, adopted in 1997, are covered extensively
here.

Sherraden, Michael. *Assets and the Poor: A New American Welfare Policy.* **Armonk, NY: M.E. Sharpe, 1991. 325 pages. ISBN 978-1563240669.**

Michael Sherraden's book was not written in response to growing wealth and income inequality in the United States; at the beginning of the 1990s, that trend was less well recognized—and less prolonged—than it has become today. Rather, the book grew out of Sherraden's concern that welfare policy had "gone off track" and was badly in need of revision. Specifically, he argued that welfare needed to be something more than income maintenance; it needed also to be about assets. In part II of this book, Sherraden gave his now-classic exposition of why assets matter, and it is as worthy of study today as it was in 1991. Assets improve the stability of the household, give people more of a future orientation, promote the acquisition of human capital, help people focus and specialize, give them a foundation for risk-taking (in its positive sense), increase social influence, and more. For all of these reasons, policy makers need to devise and implement asset-building programs, such as individual development accounts (a term that made its first appearance in Chapter 10 of Sherraden's book). Today, asset-based programs are an integral part of every broad plan or policy to improve the circumstances of those on the lower rungs of the economic ladder.

Wilkinson, Richard G. *The Impact of Inequality: How to Make Sick Societies Healthier.* **New York: The New Press, 2006. 368 pages. ISBN 978-1595581211.**

Richard Wilkinson has made a name for himself on the issue of health and inequality. In this book and other writings, he argues that societies with large disparities in income tend to be less healthy, with higher rates of coronary disease and shorter lives, than societies that are more equal. This holds true even if the more unequal nation is much wealthier on average than the more equal one; thus, life expectancy in the United States is lower than in Greece, a country with only half its per capita GDP. Inequality breeds stress, social hostility, insecurity, and violence at the societal level, and, at the individual level, a range of physiological effects that can, and do, shorten lives. To put it bluntly, inequality kills. The key to improving social health is as easy to state as it is difficult to carry out: reduce inequality.

Nonprint Resources

Web Sites

Cato Institute
http://www.cato.org

Cato and Heritage are the two conservative (Cato prefers the term "libertarian") think tanks in Washington, D.C., that can be counted on for analyses and opinions downplaying the importance of the rich-poor gap and opposing nearly all policy proposals aimed at narrowing it. Both have stables of experts, issue a variety of publications, and maintain group blogs. (Cato's blog is fresher and more readable.)

Center on Budget and Policy Priorities (CBPP)
http://www.cbpp.org/pubs/povinc.htm

The CBPP Web site features a research section on "poverty and income" with good coverage of many issues related to the U.S. distribution of income. In most cases there is a two- or three-page summary of the issue with a link to the lengthier underlying report. The perspective is moderately liberal, and the online archive extends back to 2001.

FedStats
http://www.fedstats.gov

FedStats serves as a diving board into the sea of federally generated data on a vast range of topics, including aspects of the widening gap between rich and poor. An alphabetical list of topic links includes such items as Food Stamps, Head Start, minimum wage, personal wealth, poverty, union membership, and wages. Obviously some of the links are to agencies listed below, such as the U.S. Census Bureau.

Heritage Foundation
http://www.heritage.org/Research/welfare/povertyinequality.cfm

This is a good starting place for anyone who wants to see how conservatives think about income inequality in the United States. With the trend toward greater inequality showing little sign of slackening, Heritage is issuing more memos and "backgrounders" on the subject.

Inequality.org
http://www.demos.org/inequality

Maintained by two decidedly liberal organizations (Demos and the Institute for Policy Studies), this site is organized in two sections: "By the Numbers" offers illuminating graphics on the rich-poor gap in the United States, and "In the News" reports recent developments relating to economic inequality, with an emphasis on political and racial aspects of inequality.

Moving Ideas: The Electronic Policy Network
http://www.movingideas.org

This Web site pools content from about 185 progressive, nonprofit organizations involved in policy research and advocacy. Click an issue on the issue list—"poverty and wealth," for example—and view a page of items organized into research reports, action alerts, articles, press releases, commentary, and a listing of organizations that take an interest in the issue.

NewsBatch
http://www.newsbatch.com

NewsBatch calls itself "your Internet guide to an understanding of policy issues," and economic inequality is one of the roughly 30 issues it follows. At this site, you can access recent news stories from print media, view relevant charts (for example, the Gini coefficient), and track congressional votes on bills relating to income inequality.

Opportunity 08
http://www.opportunity08.org

The Brookings Institution and ABC News jointly sponsor this menu of "independent ideas for our next president." A key policy area is labeled "our society," and three of its subfields are relevant to the rich-poor gap in the United States: poverty, social insurance, and upward mobility. The recommendations offered are progressive but not radical.

Robb Report
http://www.robbreport.com

The Robb Report offers a "luxury portal" to a wide range of high-end products and services for the well-heeled. Here one may have a look at personal aircraft, yachts, vacation trips—a chance to play elephant polo is featured in one African tour—and, of course, luxury residences, complete with home theaters, home gyms, and many other amenities. This Web site makes crystal clear how advantageous U.S. economic growth has been for those in the top 1 percent of the income distribution.

Too Much: A Commentary on Excess and Inequality
http://www.cipa-apex.org/toomuch

Edited since 1985 by author and labor journalist Sam Pizzigati, this site documents what some might call the wretched excess of the wealthy. The flavor of Too Much is indicated by a section called "Lifestyles of the Rich and Shameless." One may sign up to receive weekly installments of the commentary by e-mail.

United for a Fair Economy (UFE)
http://www.faireconomy.org

The UFE Web site gives a progressive take on issues tied to economic inequality, with news updates in several categories: tax fairness, the Responsible Wealth Project (a UFE offshoot), racial wealth divide, estate tax, and global action. A Research Library link brings up information on the wealth gap, low-wage work, CEO pay, etc. "Executive Excess 2007," an annual report co-produced by UFE and the Institute for Policy Studies and now in its fourteenth year, can be downloaded from the site.

United Nations Development Programme (UNDP)
http://www.undp.org

An interest in economic inequality often springs from a concern about poverty. To see U.S. poverty with some perspective, one should try to place it in a global context. That suggests a visit to the UNDP Web site, since the UNDP has a mandate to measure global poverty and assess the various policy approaches to its alleviation and elimination. This Web site has links to the annual *Human Development Report* issued by the UNDP, which includes several poverty measures for all countries.

U.S. Bureau of Labor Statistics (BLS)
http://www.bls.gov

A good understanding of the rich-poor gap in the United States requires a clear sense of the distribution of earnings as well as of the legal and institutional aspects of U.S. labor markets. For these kinds of information, one should turn, at least initially, to the BLS Web site. It is where the government posts data on wages, benefits, collective bargaining, unemployment, demographic characteristics of the labor force, and much more.

U.S. Census Bureau
http://www.census.gov/hhes/www/income/income.html

This is the key stepping-off point for any study of U.S. income trends. The Census Bureau issues authoritative income data each year, with detailed coverage extending back to 1967. On the main Web page are links to reports and research papers, definitions of terms, guidance on how the income data are collected, and an entry point for access to microdata files that allow the user to create his or her own statistical tables. (Several of the tables in chapter 6 are based on data from this Web site.) Through this site one can also get to the federal government's annual poverty report, issued each August under the title "Income, Poverty, and Health Insurance Coverage in the United States" and reported in all major news media. (There is no comparable wealth report.)

U.S. Conference of Mayors
http://www.usmayors.org

Since 1983, the U.S. Conference of Mayors has been the most prominent government entity in the nation taking a serious interest in the problem of homelessness. At its Web site, under Reports & Publications, one can download the latest annual *Hunger and Homelessness Survey*, along with a press release in both print and video versions.

U.S. Federal Reserve Board
http://www.federalreserve.gov/pubs/oss/oss2/scfindex.html

The Federal Reserve Board's Survey of Consumer Finances is rightly regarded as the primary source of reliable information on the all-around financial condition of U.S. families. These surveys have been conducted on a triennial basis since 1983, and all the summary data are available, as well as a couple of precursor surveys done in 1962 and 1963.

U.S. Internal Revenue Service
http://www.irs.gov/taxstats

Much of what we know about the personal distribution of wealth and income in the United States comes from federal tax data, and many of the contentious policy proposals for closing the gap between rich and poor involve taxation. For these reasons, the IRS's Tax Statistics Web site can be a useful source of information. Much of the material will only make sense to a tax expert, but some—like the categorization of different types of assets held by the wealthy—is of general interest.

The Wealth Report
http://blogs.wsj.com/wealth

The Wall Street Journal's official "wealth reporter," Robert Frank, posts observations about the rich, including examples of egregious conspicuous consumption, on this blog almost every day. Apparently the subject is inexhaustible. Frank is the author of *Richistan* (see book list above).

The World Bank
http://www.worldbank.org

Along with the UNDP, the World Bank is the other international agency issuing key statistics that might help one put U.S. poverty (and wealth) into a global perspective. Its *World Development Indicators* is a compendium of economic data for all countries with a population of 1 million or more, and includes per capita income data.

Videos

America Today: Looking for the Union Label
Date: 2001
Length: 29 minutes
Price: $129.95 (VHS or DVD)
Source: Films for the Humanities & Sciences

Nearly every attempt to explain the growing gap between rich and poor makes reference to the decline of organized labor in the

United States. This video provides a basic historical and institutional background to the development of the labor movement, examines what has changed in recent decades, and features interviews with various experts, including labor leaders, on why union membership has declined so precipitously.

Combating Childhood Poverty
Date: 1995
Length: 26 minutes
Price: $129 (VHS)
Source: Insight Media

With children continuing to have the highest poverty rate of any age group in the United States—more than one in six for the year 2006—there is good reason to focus on the youth demographic when considering antipoverty efforts. This short video looks at two federally funded programs in one of New York City's poorest neighborhoods to see what difference the government can make.

A Day's Work, A Day's Pay
Date: 2002
Length: 57 minutes
Price: $240 (VHS or DVD; lower cost for libraries, public schools, or rental)
Source: New Day Films

The ultimate safety net for low-income Americans is cash welfare, a joint federal-state system that was stringently reformed in 1996. Many welfare recipients were forced to accept public employment ("workfare") in exchange for continued payments. This video looks at the experience of three individuals who participated in the workfare program established by New York City under Mayor Giuliani. It follows their growing frustration with the program and their efforts—ultimately successful—to resist it.

Eyes on the Fries: Young Workers in the Service Economy
Date: 2004
Length: 21 minutes
Price: $25 individual, $65 institutional (VHS or DVD)
Source: UC Berkeley Labor Center

A widening spread between the wages of the highest-paid and lowest-paid Americans is mainly due to massive gains at the top, but the proliferation of low-skill, entry-level service jobs at the bottom is part of the story, too. Many of those jobs are taken by the young, who tend to receive few benefits, little job security, and almost never a union card. This video highlights the growth of service-sector jobs in the United States and the disproportionate share of them taken by young adults. In documentary style, real workers are allowed to voice their frustrations about the "McJobs" they hold and, on the other hand, the encouragement they have received from San Francisco's action in raising its minimum wage. The video comes with a curriculum kit that could be of use in a post-viewing discussion.

For Richer, For Poorer
Date: 2005
Length: 25 minutes
Price: $195 (VHS or DVD); $45 (rental)
Source: Bullfrog Films

This video is about the disturbingly wide gap between rich and poor in Brazil, a country often cited for the extent of its inequality. Brazil is not the United States, but those who express concern about current inequality trends in the U.S. point to Brazil as a cautionary case. President Lula da Silva has pledged to make Brazilian society more equal in terms of education, health care, and land distribution, and although extreme inequality remains, the country has cut its rate of "extreme" poverty in half, meeting a UN Millennial Development goal years ahead of schedule.

Homeless: A Contextual Case Study
Date: 2004
Length: 25 minutes
Price: $149 (DVD)
Source: Insight Media

It is important to avoid stereotypes about the homeless. Most of the poor are not homeless, but most of the homeless almost certainly are poor. This video humanizes the homeless issue by focusing on a 40-year-old man who has been homeless for over two decades. It does not sidestep the correlations between homelessness and alcoholism and drug abuse.

Is Wal-Mart Good for America?
Date: 2005

Length: 60 minutes
Price: $29.99 (VHS or DVD)
Source: Shop PBS

Although it does not address the rich-poor issue directly, this video has much to say about the loss of well-paying jobs in the United States as a result of globalization and the importance of one corporation, Wal-Mart, in transforming the U.S. economic landscape. Most consumer goods can now be manufactured more cheaply abroad; hence, about 80 percent of Wal-Mart's suppliers are now located in China. American workers who exchange their old factory jobs for "associate" positions at Wal-Mart stores experience a distinct step downward in economic security. At the same time, four of the fifteen wealthiest individuals in America share the same last name: Walton.

Michael Harrington and Today's Other America: Corporate Power and Inequality
Date: 2001
Length: 84 minutes
Price: $75 (Video rental)
Source: Filmakers Library

Michael Harrington's *The Other America*, published in 1962, shined a bright light on U.S. poverty and led, by some accounts, to the mobilization of political will that produced President Lyndon B. Johnson's War on Poverty. Harrington (1928–1989) made a life's work of unmasking American poverty and corporate exploitation of labor, as this engaging video makes clear. Some of the topics the video explores are unions, migrant labor, the health care system, and inner-city poverty. There are interviews with notable contemporaries of Harrington, like John Kenneth Galbraith, William F. Buckley, and Charles Murray.

On the Edge: America's Working Poor
Date: 2004
Length: 22 minutes
Price: $69.95 (VHS or DVD)
Source: Films for the Humanities & Sciences

This video represents an interesting collaboration between ABC's *Nightline* program and journalist David Shipler, author of *The Working Poor* (see books section above). It profiles three individuals who struggle to get by on below-poverty-level wages and face financial meltdown if even one minor mishap occurs. In one case, that mishap takes the form of an unexpected automobile repair. In the other two, loans at sky-high interest rates take their toll. Ted Koppel interviews Shipler on the general issue of poverty among working Americans.

Payday for CEOs
Date: 2007
Length: 60 minutes
Price: $29.95 (DVD)
Source: Shop PBS

The first segment of the *Bill Moyers Journal* (PBS) broadcast on June 8, 2007 (roughly 20 minutes) deals with a specific instance of CEO overcompensation. At least that is the view Moyers takes of the pay awarded to the top executives of Northwest Airlines, one of several domestic U.S. carriers that fell into bankruptcy after 9/11 and gradually worked their way out. Northwest employees made wage concessions of 20–40 percent, had their pensions frozen, and lost some of their health benefits. Meanwhile, their CEO was given an annual pay package in excess of $25 million. The segment can be viewed online, and a full transcript is also available at the PBS Web site.

A Question of Fairness
Date: 2003
Length: 58 minutes
Price: $29.98
Source: Shop PBS

In this November 21, 2003, broadcast of the PBS program *NOW*, hosted by Bill Moyers, the issue of economic inequality is confronted head-on. Because Moyers has a well-earned reputation as a liberal journalist, it comes as no surprise that he sees the United States evolving into a two-class society, or that he locates the source of this trend in an unfair tilting of public policy toward corporations and against workers. Three specific cases of such policy imbalance are explored. Especially intriguing is the saga of a Republican governor (Alabama) who tried to revamp the most regressive state tax system in the nation; his effort to shift the tax burden toward those better able to bear it was roundly defeated by voters.

Take It from Me: Life after Welfare
Date: 2001
Length: 78 minutes
Price: $295 (VHS or DVD), $75 (rental)
Source: Filmakers Library

This is one of the better videos that take a sympathetic look at the tough transitions many thousands of mothers had to make from welfare to work after passage of the 1996 welfare reform law. Many of the difficulties faced by the four women featured in the video were shared by millions of the nation's poor who were *not* on welfare before or after 1996, and those difficulties have not disappeared.

Waging a Living
Date: 2005
Length: 85 minutes
Price: $99 (VHS or DVD; video rental, $85)
Source: Filmakers Library

This well-made, powerful film has been likened to a video version of Barbara Ehrenreich's *Nickel and Dimed* account of the extreme difficulty so many working Americans have in making ends meet. It is a crisp documentary account, shot over a three-year period, of four ethnically diverse individuals who struggle to keep their families afloat on wages that don't stretch far enough. (When one mother achieves a $450 monthly pay raise after earning an associate's degree, she loses $600 in public assistance.) There is no heavy editorializing; the subjects speak for themselves, bluntly and at times despairingly.

Contact Information for Video Distributors and Vendors

Bullfrog Films
P.O. Box 149, Oley, PA 19547
(610) 779-8226 Fax: (610) 370-1978
E-mail: info@bullfrogfilms.com
http://www.bullfrogfilms.com

Filmakers Library
124 E. 40th St., New York, NY 10016
(212) 808-4980 Fax: (212) 808-4983
E-mail: info@filmakers.com
http://www.filmakers.com

Films for the Humanities and Sciences
P.O. Box 2053, Princeton, NJ 08543-2053
(800) 257-5126 Fax: (609) 671-0266
E-mail: custserv@films.com
http://www.films.com

Insight Media
2162 Broadway, New York, NY 10024
(800) 233-9910 Fax: (212) 799-5309
E-mail: custserv@insight-media.com
http://www.insight-media.com

New Day Films
P.O. Box 1084, Harriman, NY 10926
(888) 367-9154 Fax: (845) 774-2945
E-mail: orders@newday.com
http://www.newday.com

PBS Home Video
P.O. Box 609, Melbourne, FL 32902-0609
(800) 531-4727 Fax: (866) 274-9043
http://shoppbs.org

UC Berkeley Labor Center
2521 Channing Way, Ste. 5555, Berkeley, CA 94720-5555
(510) 642-0323 Fax: (510) 643-4673
E-mail: laborcenter@berkeley.edu
http://laborcenter.berkeley.edu/publications

Glossary

asset-building A policy area that focuses on strategies for helping low-income families and individuals build up their financial assets.

assortative mating A social pattern in which individuals marry others who are similar in significant ways. Some believe the tendency of well-educated, upwardly mobile men to marry women with the same characteristics is contributing to growing economic inequality.

capital gain A form of income rarely received by low-income individuals but often contributing to the income of the wealthy. Such a gain occurs when an asset, for example, a share of stock or a piece of land, is sold at a higher price than was originally paid for it, the rise in value constituting a capital gain. If tax rates on capital gains are lowered, as happened in 2003, it is considered a favorable change for the rich.

conservative A political-philosophical position according to which the wide and growing gap between incomes of the rich and poor is a normal, cyclical expression of the capitalist economy. The conservative policy position on the rich-poor gap would be to let it play itself out, without government intervention.

conspicuous consumption A term coined by American economist Thorstein Veblen (1857–1929) to describe showy displays of one's wealth in order to impress others. Such displays are often cited by those critical of the current gap between rich and poor.

decile One-tenth of the whole; the share of income going to the top decile is sometimes contrasted with the share going to the bottom decile.

estate tax A tax levied on the accumulated assets of an individual at the time of his/her death and payable by the individual's heirs or beneficiaries. The first $2 million of the estate is exempt from the federal estate tax in 2008; on amounts in excess of $2 million, the tax rate ranges from 18 percent at the low end to 55 percent at the high end, making this one of the most progressive taxes in the country.

Gini coefficient, Gini index The most common yardstick of overall income (or wealth) inequality for a country. A Gini of zero indicates total equality; a Gini of 100—or 1 in an alternative calibration—indicates total inequality.

household income ratio by percentile   A measure of income dispersion formed by dividing one income percentile by another, for example, the 95th by the 20th. The U.S. Census Bureau computes and publishes several such ratios annually, and they allow one to see whether there is a trend in income dispersion (inequality).

income   The flow of money to an individual or family that sustains it economically. Income takes various forms, including wages, salaries, interest, rents, dividends, and disability payments.

income mobility   Movement upward or downward on the income scale, usually measured as a movement from one income quintile to another during a period of time that could range from one year to one generation. High income mobility is thought by some to be a reasonable counterweight to a high degree of income inequality.

individual development account (IDA)   A strategy pioneered by sociologist Michael Sherraden under which low-income individuals can put small sums into savings accounts and have their contributions matched by community organizations. This becomes a way to build assets and economic security.

Kuznets's law   The idea, presented in 1955 by economist Simon Kuznets, that the degree of income inequality is linked to the stage of a nation's economic development: in the transition from a pre-industrial, rural economy to a more urbanized, industrial economy, income inequality may rise, but as time goes on, it will tend to decrease. Confidence in the validity of the "law" has fallen off in recent decades.

liberal   A political-philosophical position that finds the widening gap between rich and poor disturbing, problematic, and unacceptable. A liberal policy approach would favor higher taxes on the rich, lower taxes on the poor, asset-building efforts, and more public investment in programs benefiting low-income families.

median   The middle observation in a set of data, with as many values above as below that value. A historical series of median income values cannot, in itself, establish a trend toward greater income inequality, but a ratio, such as the 95th percentile to the median income, can do so.

merit scholarship   A form of financial aid used by colleges to attract the most "meritorious" applicants (as determined by SAT scores, typically). As an alternative to the more traditional *need*-based forms of assistance, such scholarships tend to drain dollars away from possible support of low-income students.

net worth   The value of one's assets minus one's liabilities; hence, a measure of one's overall personal wealth.

percentile   A value on a scale that runs from zero to 100 that indicates the percentage of observations that are lower. For example, the government says that in 2005, the 80th percentile for household incomes was $91,705, meaning that 80 percent of U.S. households had incomes below that amount.

plutocracy   Rule by the wealthy, not (as in democracy) by the majority of the people; a term used by those who fear that concentrated economic power can be translated into political power.

poverty threshold   The income level below which an individual or family is officially categorized as poor. In many countries, the threshold is drawn at one-half the median national income; the United States uses a different, more complex (and outdated) threshold.

progressive tax   A tax that puts a heavier relative burden on the rich than on the poor; for example, the U.S. income tax for single persons is 10 percent at the low end but 35 percent on annual income amounts over $337,000.

quintile   One-fifth of the whole; in studies of income distribution, the share of income going to the top quintile is often contrasted with the share going to the bottom quintile.

regressive tax   A tax that puts a heavier relative burden on the poor than on the rich; for example, the FICA (Social Security) tax takes a larger percentage out of a minimum-wage worker's income than it takes from a corporate CEO's income.

relative poverty standard   A poverty line that defines poverty as having an income below some standard, typical measure of income. In much of Europe, the poverty line is drawn at one-half the median income; those below the line are considered poor. (The United States has a more complicated "absolute" standard of poverty.)

socioeconomic status (SES)   The overall social condition of a family or individual as determined by a formula that takes into account income level, parents' education, parents' occupation, and sometimes other variables. SES is considered a strong predictor of one's life chances; hence, a child with high SES has a better-than-average prospect of growing up to be rich, etc.

super-rich   A term used by journalists, commentators, and others that lacks any concrete meaning but is intended to designate the very wealthiest people in society, for example, the top one-tenth of 1 percent in a ranking by income or wealth.

trickle-down effect   The notion that boosting the incomes of the wealthy will end up benefiting those lower down the income scale through a "trickling down" of spending. This idea is sometimes brought forward in support of tax cuts that provide big gains to the richest individuals.

union premium The difference between what a union worker earns and what a non-union worker doing the same type of job earns. The steady erosion of union membership and thus of union premiums may be one cause of rising wage inequality in the United States.

wealth The monetary value of possessions, whether tangible or financial, that individuals accumulate over time. By contrast with income, which is an annual measure of monetary flow, wealth is a "point-in-time" measure of accumulated value. Persons of great wealth do not necessarily have substantial incomes, and vice versa. The most publicized listing of the richest Americans (*Forbes*) is based on wealth.

wealth mobility Movement upward or downward on the wealth scale. As with income mobility, a high degree of wealth mobility is considered by some to be a reasonable compensation or trade-off for a high actual extent of inequality.

Index

Labor unions
and deunionization trend, 39–40, 59–60
and immigration, 64
and income inequality, 40–41
and membership rate, 40
and union premium, 40
and wage distribution, 39–41
and wage inequality, 59–60
LASNY. *See* Legal Aid Society of New York
Latin America, 5, 37, 82, 83–84, 87, 89, 95
Latvia, 94
Lee, Spike, 14
Legal Aid Society of New York (LASNY), 201, 217
Legal Services Corporation (LSC), 217–218
Lesotho, 81, 82, 159
"The Level and Distribution of Economic Well-Being" (Bernanke)
excerpt from, 179–182
Levy, Frank, 35
Levy Economics Institute of Bard College, 218–219
Liberals
and asset-building programs, 72
and CEO compensation, 62
and Earned Income Tax Credit, 60–61
and income distribution, xiii, 47
and income inequality, 25–26
and policy institutes, 201
and taxes, 26–27
Lieberman, Joe, 134
LIS. *See* Luxembourg Income Study
Living standards, 11
Living wage ordinances, 58–59
opponents of, 59
See also Minimum wage
Los Angeles, California, 23, 58
LSC. *See* Legal Services Corporation
Luxembourg Income Study (LIS), 85–86

Manchester, Connecticut, 58
Market income, and poverty, 86
Market system, 43

Marshall, Alfred, 43
Marx, Karl, 131
Math ability, and educational attainment, 166–168, 167 table 6.8
Mathtech, Inc., 20
Mayer, Oscar, 131
Mazumder, Bhashkar
biographical information on, 142–143
McLanahan, Sara, 127
biographical information on, 143–144
MDGs. *See* Millennium Development Goals
Mean logarithmic deviation (MLD), 89. *See also* Gini index; Theil index
Median income, 13, 15, 23, 85–86
Medicaid, 86
Medicare, 66, 67, 86, 103
Mellon, Andrew, 3
Mental health, and income inequality, 16–17
Merit scholarships, 21, 56. *See also* Scholarships
Mexico, 36, 104, 159
Middle class, 3
and college education, 55–57
definition of, 21–22
and income distribution, 22–23
and neighborhoods and suburbs, erosion of, 23
shrinkage of, 21–23
See also Social class
Middle East, 95
Milanovic, Branko, 91
Mill, John Stuart, 34
Millennium Development Goals (MDGs), 81, 95–96
Milwaukee, Wisconsin, 58
Minimum wage, 27
and federal *vs.* state rates, 41
rates, in U.S., 1947–2006, 58, 163, 164–165 table 6.5
and Republican Party, 42
and unemployment, 41
and wage inequality, 41–42, 57–58
and women, 42
See also Living wage ordinances

About the Author

Geoffrey Gilbert is a professor of economics at Hobart and William Smith colleges in Geneva, New York. He did his undergraduate work at Dartmouth College and holds a Ph.D. in economics from Johns Hopkins University. The author of two previous handbooks in the Contemporary World Issues series, on world population and world poverty, Gilbert has written extensively on the history of economic thought.